TEJO

KEY TO ENDPAPER MAP

1. Praça do Comércio
2. Rossio
3. Luis de Camões
4. Chiado
5. Largo de Barão do Quintela (statue of Eça de Quieroz)
6. Bairro Alto
7. Estação do Rossio
8. Santa Catarina
9. Largo de S. Roque
10. Largo do Carmo
11. Castelo de S. Jorge
12. Alfama
13. Campo de Santa Clara
14. S. Vicente
15. Museu de Artilharia
16. Madre de Deus
17. Av. da Liberdade
18. Praça Marquês de Pombal
19. Parque Eduardo VII— Estufa Fria
20. Praça Duque de Sadlanha
21. Campo Pequeno
22. Av. da República
23. Gulbenkian Fundação
24. Praça de Espanha
25. Estrêla
26. Jardim Botanico
27. Largo do Rato
28. Rua do Seculo
29. Largo do Conde Barão
30. Museu de Arte Antiga
31. Largo de Santos
32. Cais do Sodré
33. Mouraria
34. Praça de Londres
35. Praça Pasteur
36. Sé Catedral
37. Martinho (café restaurant)
38. Brasileira (café)
39. Gondola (restaurant)
40. Irmãos Unidos (café)
41. Leão Douro (restaurant)
42. Mesquita (casa do Fado)
43. Ascensor de Santa Justa
44. Cortador (restaurant)
45. Tavares (restaurant)
46. Porta do Abrigo
47. Promater (nursing home)
48. Parreirinha (restaurant)
49. Borges Hotel
50. York House
51. Fenix
52. Tivoli
53. Ritz
54. A Quinta (restaurant)

LISBON

DAVID WRIGHT
and
PATRICK SWIFT

LISBON
a portrait and a guide

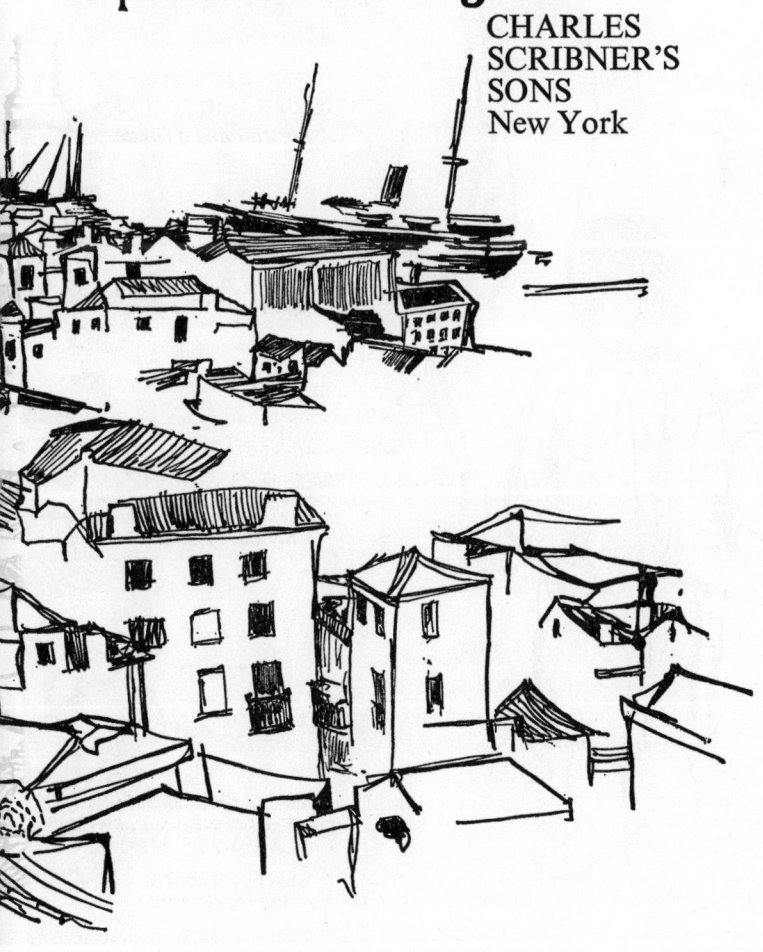

CHARLES
SCRIBNER'S
SONS
New York

BY THE SAME AUTHORS
ALGARVE
A Portrait and a Guide

**MINHO AND
NORTH PORTUGAL**
A Portrait and a Guide

© *1971 by David Wright
and Patrick Swift*

*All Rights Reserved.
No part of this book may be
reproduced in any form without
the permission of Charles
Scribner's Sons*

A–3.72 (I)

*Printed in Great Britain
Library of Congress Catalog
Card Number 75–39155*

SBN 684–12896–9
(Trade cloth)

Contents

A Lisbon Diary	DAVID WRIGHT	9
Coming to Lisbon: Santa Catarina and District	PATRICK SWIFT	65
Visit to a Hidden Lisbon	PATRICK SWIFT	78

Notes and Observations
    Rossio
    Chiado
    Eça de Quieroz
    Fernando Pessoa
	PATRICK SWIFT	87

O Fadista!	PATRICK SWIFT	102

Bullfight	PATRICK SWIFT	115
Eating in Lisbon	PATRICK SWIFT	131
A Little History	PATRICK SWIFT	148

    Museum of Ancient Art
    Sé Catedral
    The Church of São Roque
    Madre de Deus
    Moistero de Jerónimos
    Ethnological Museum, Belém
    Torre de Belém
    Feira de Art Popular, Belém
    Museu dos Coches
    Museu da Cidade
    Gulbenkian Foundation

Preface to a Journey	PATRICK SWIFT	190
A Journey by the Tagus	DAVID WRIGHT	195

    Abrantes
    Castelo Branco
    Nisa
    Castelo de Vide
    Marvão
    Portalegre
    Elvas
    Estremoz

Postscript to a Journey	PATRICK SWIFT	235
An End and a Beginning	PATRICK SWIFT	241
The Portuguese Enigma	PATRICK SWIFT	245
Advice to Travellers	PATRICK SWIFT	255
Index		267

THE DECORATIONS THROUGHOUT
ARE BY PATRICK SWIFT

List of Illustrations
Between pages 158 and 159

    Alfama

    Street lift to Largo do Carmo

    Cinema, Rossio

    Rua da Bica

    In the flea market

    The fishmarket

    In the Mouraria

    General view of Lisbon

The bullfight

Statue of Eça da Quieroz

Fountain in Rossio

Castelo Branco, Bishop's Garden

Fountain in the Bishop's Garden

Steps in the Bishop's Garden

The flea market

The fishmarket

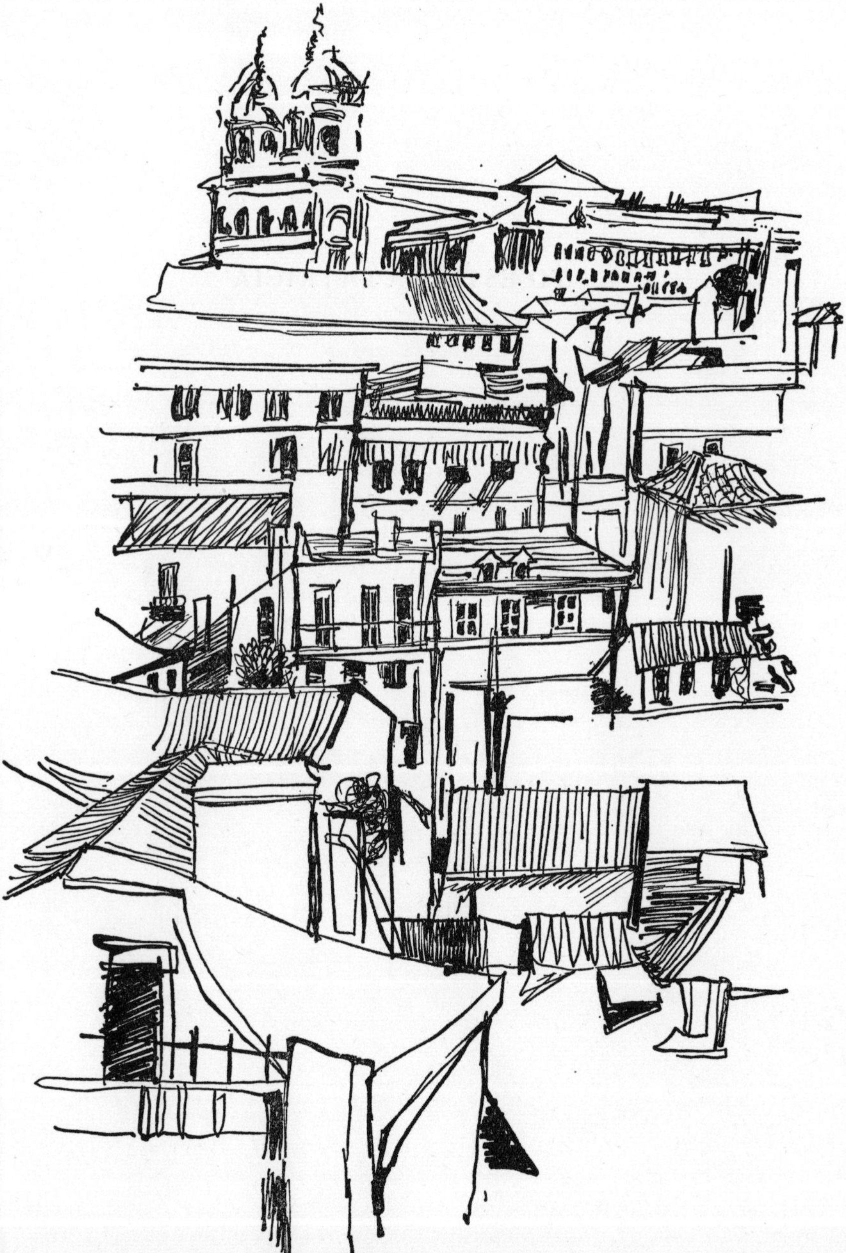

TO ESTELLA PATRICIA

A Lisbon Diary

DAVID WRIGHT

What I look for, when I go abroad, is not a change of locality and climate. I want a change of environment, customs, language, cuisine, habits of living—in a word a change of culture. It's becoming harder to find; an ineluctable result of the gearing of civilisation to mass-production and the mass-media. Thus one comes across the same pattern of wallpaper. the same formica-topped tables in the class of café—anonymous hygienic, and interchangeable—that infests New York, Wolverhampton, Lyons, Tarragona, Athens, Accra and Padua. The same food from the same tins and packets and tubes. In almost all cities the only public resorts that preserve the uniqueness of local individuality ('atmosphere', but that's already a packaged, travel-agent's word) seem to be the cheaper and scruffier kind of pub, café, bistro, taberna, trattoria, kafeion, shebeen, caff or diner. Bourgeois resorts are always first to be standardised.

If one travels, as I do, for change, to revisit the living past rather than look at its corpse earnestly embalmed in museums and galleries, or in scrubbed-down and cellophane-wrapped ruins and excavated sites, there are not many places left to go. Perhaps one should be more interested in the future than the past. Yet it is the past that has scarcity-value. It is disappearing every day while the future is coming at us like a jumbo-jet.

As I write I reflect that it is seven years, almost to the day, since first I visited Portugal. Until then I had wandered, one way or another, over a good bit of Europe. Yet I went to Portugal by accident—my imagination had not been fired beforehand, as in the case of France, Italy, Spain and Greece. I expected nothing and found everything.

Particularly in Lisbon. It was completely foreign, in other words itself and not yet another segment of the western world's *ville tentaculaire*. Not only was it foreign in geography and culture, architecture, people and customs, but in time. For Lisbon, when I came there in 1962, still belonged, materially as well as spiritually, to the nineteenth century. Already there were the supermodern hotels, born of glass, concrete, and standard fittings, at the top end of the Avenida da Liberdade; skyscraper flats in the suburbs and contemporary housing projects round the periphery. But in the heart of Lisbon, between Rossio and the waterfront with the old pre-earthquake quarters of Alfama climbing up to the castle of St. George on one hand, and the Bairro Alto on the other, the clock seemed to have stopped around the year 1900, or at a pinch 1910. Though Alfama is medieval, the Bairro Alto seventeenth century, while the grid pattern of Baixa (built after the 1755 earthquake) reflects the Age of Reason, in Lisbon the nineteenth century is paramount. Its tramcars grumble through the streets, its breakneck funiculars grind up cobbled lanes. As much as the Eiffel Tower, the baroque ironwork of the street-lift to Largo do Carmo expresses the imaginative energy of nineteenth-century engineers, ornament coruscating through the functional.* And there are the interiors; for example my first and favourite hotel, the Francfort in Rossio, with its art-nouveau elevator emphasising the mahogany solidity of the foyer; the overpowering rococo of cafés like the Brasileira in the Rua Garrett; the dingy brass and marble splendours of pub-restaurants like the Leão d'Ouro in the Rua 1° de Dezembro.

As Paris becomes more Anglo-americanised and expensive, I turn to Lisbon as a substitute or refuge. Yet it would be fatuous to compare two cities so different; each has its peculiar splendours and miseries. The Seine does not compete with the Tagus, nor for that matter the Tagus with the Seine. Lisbon may be a provincial city, but it is its very provincialism that, at this moment of time, defends and preserves its individuality. Parisian wines and cuisine remain of course supreme, but are rapidly retreating from the range of this particular pocket. At first I did not think much of Lisbon as a place to eat, but that was at the beginning of my acquaintance, when I did not know where to go or what to pass by. As a place to drink, with its 6000 individualistic pubs and tabernas, not all of which I have as yet managed to visit, Lisbon bears away the bell. Particularly as each little taberna is unique in furniture, accoutrements, decorations, appendages, bric-à-brac; surrealistic mélanges, yet as homogeneous and appropriate to patrão and clients as an old and favourite hat.

One of the pleasures of cities is—or was, before the surrender to the internal combusion engine—simply walking the streets to take in their variety and delight one's eye with vistas, façades, windows, doorways, lamp-posts, shop-fronts, street-markets, or the occasional set-piece provided by some fountain, church, park or palazzo. Here Lisbon scores heavily. Perhaps no other city besides Venice is so consistently pleasurable for the pedestrian wanderer. It is not a question of aesthetics, of solemn architectural appraisement: what Lisbon has is a notably Portuguese characteristic—the ability to surprise as well as charm. Thus I once came across, near the Sé Catedral at the foot of the Alfama, a little public garden enclosed by walls

---

* This street lift was in fact built by Eiffel, who was also responsible for the magnificent bridge over the Douro at Oporto.

illustrated with robust blue azulejos depicting the conquest of Lisbon by Dom Afonso Henriques in 1147, and also—an attractive touch—a miniature public lending library in the shape of a small wooden bookcase in a corner of its terrace. The stone balconies of this garden overlook the glittering spread of the Tagus, its warehouses, boats, and feluccas below. Now for the surprise. Silhouetted against this eighteenth-century background of ships and water, you see the straight, angular, spidery interlacing of a little forest of television antennae—

> Pure abstract design
> By some master of pattern and line

as Auden has it—a composition like one of Kenneth Armitage's sculptural doodles.

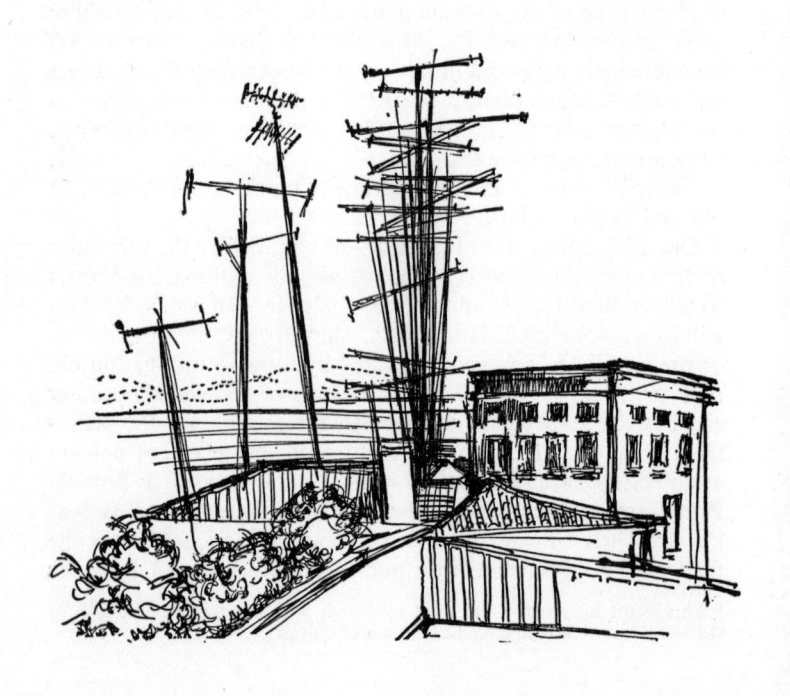

Yet most of my many visits to Lisbon have been flying ones, a week or a few days at most, before going south to Algarve or north to the Minho. For this reason I was reluctant to come in with Swift when he proposed that we should write a book about the city. I could not pretend to know it as he does. I have lived the best part of my life in London, and long enough in Rome, Athens, Paris, Venice, and even Liverpool and Johannesburg, to realise that there is a sense in which cities are harder to know than countries. The history and geography of a city can be seen at too many levels and from too many angles, none of them affording more than a small part of the truth or reality of the whole. And there are so many interlocking strata and ways of living, often pursued by the same individual, as anyone who has lived in Holborn, worked in W.1., pubbed in Soho, and dined or drabbed in Chelsea, can testify...

In the role of a fly-by-night tourist I write of Lisbon: what follows in this chapter is his diary.

October 1969: THURSDAY

On the whole, the best time to go to Portugal is latish September or October. Summer is not quite over, the greatest heat has gone, the rainy season has not quite arrived. Hotels and resorts are neither crowded nor abandoned; it is still warm enough to swim. The autumnal fruit is ripening; by September the grape harvest is under way, while towards the end of October comes the season for game, when the little country restaurants include hare and partridge on the menu. On the other hand, my wife thinks it a pity to miss the English autumn...

The morning warm and clear, the day like a pearl. Pip and I arrive in good time at the West London Air Terminal. We did not hang around waiting for our flight bus to take us to the airport but boarded the first to leave. Humming along the flyovers and elevated motorway above the roofs of gutted Chiswick seems a more futuristic form of travel than flying itself (if you want to see the shape of things to come, try having a cup of tea at 3 a.m. in one of the neon and formica M1 roadhouses). At Heathrow we have time in hand to subside over a pre-flight whisky in the great glass departures lounge overlooking the airfield. Time to watch abstract planes slip in and out like puppet models on the telly, time to reflect how extraordinary people look in airports, as if invented for the occasion. Outlandish hats, prodigious cameras, stupendous handbags, weird impedimenta (why is that man carrying four pairs of rubber galoshes in a polythene bag?).

The four hours' flight to Lisbon is nearly always interesting, unless cloud blocks the view. There is the island of Jersey, like a pebble in a basin, and, after the long amble over the Bay of Biscay, that moment of drama when the ochre bastions of Iberia appear on the horizon. The plane flies about 30,000 feet over the peninsula, its Atlantic littoral fringed with a thin yellow paring—endless sandy beaches—and split every now and then by one of the four great rivers that disembogue in the west: the first is the Minho, the northern frontier of Portugal, and the last is the Tagus, on whose broad estuary Lisbon rides. As we come down over Lisbon, still 10,000 feet up, the air hostess remarks over the intercom: 'Fasten seat belts. Goodbye, and thank you.'

Nevertheless we touch down in one piece. There is no special bus service from Lisbon airport to the city centre. However, the taxi ride costs only about twenty escudos, a bit less than the airbus fare from the West London Air Terminal to Heathrow. I hail one of the familiar green taxis and in a moment we are spinning towards Rossio through the outlying housing estates, and down broad green-bordered avenues punctuated by magniloquent public statuary. As we pass the odd and imposing nineteenth-century redbrick bullring (which for some reason keeps reminding me of Leicester Gaol), we find ourselves falling for Portugal all over again. Of all the cities of Europe, Lisbon probably offers the most attractive approach from its airport. Within twenty minutes the taxi draws up outside our old hang-out, the Francfort Hotel in Rossio; its traffic scudding by like autumnal leaves, its black and white mosaic pavements obliterated under the scurrying feet of clerks and typists. It was three years since we were last in Portugal.

As, during that period, half our bit of London had been bulldozed flat and its Regency terraces replaced by vertical glass cubes like filing cabinets, we were prepared for changes. But time goes slowly in Portugal. The old Francfort was exactly as we had left it. Even the bell-boy, who in 1966 had been no older than nine or ten, seemed nine or ten still; he hadn't grown an inch. Nothing had changed, except that they had at last completed the new tube station at the north end of the square, and traffic appeared to be heavier . . .

The Francfort was once a haunt of the cigar-puffing astrakhan-coated bourgeoisie in the nineteenth century, or so it is presented in the novels of Eça de Quieroz. But time has moved on, leaving it stranded. A long, formal façade is presented to the neon-littered Rossio (Lisbon's Piccadilly) and a plain backside to the Praça da Figueira: the latter is a wide, placid open space behind which rises one of the seven hills of Lisbon, capped by the yellow battlements of the Castelo de S. Jorge.

Whenever I return to Lisbon, almost the first thing I do is to walk up the hill to this castle. So we dumped our bags at the Francfort, and climbed up the cobbled lanes and alleys of the Alfama, the old Arab quarter, past cliff-hanging miniature squares, stone staircases, and merchants' houses faced with gleaming azulejo tiles; balconies hung with potted plants and trailing creepers, airing bedspreads and lines of washing; every corner punctuated by one of those grotty little tabernas bursting with gigantic oak winebarrels, ebony with dirt and the patina of generations of drinkers. Prices had gone up. A glass of wine now cost one and a half or two escudos—about double what it used to. At one of the little cafés outside the castle gate we had a glass of vinho verde.

In this café hung a painting—a home-made but elaborate watercolour portrait of a group of men dressed in slightly absurd finery—set against an elaborate tinsel collage background. It was entitled, in Portuguese, 'The Pilgrimage of the Well-Dressed'. The picture caught my attention, not only

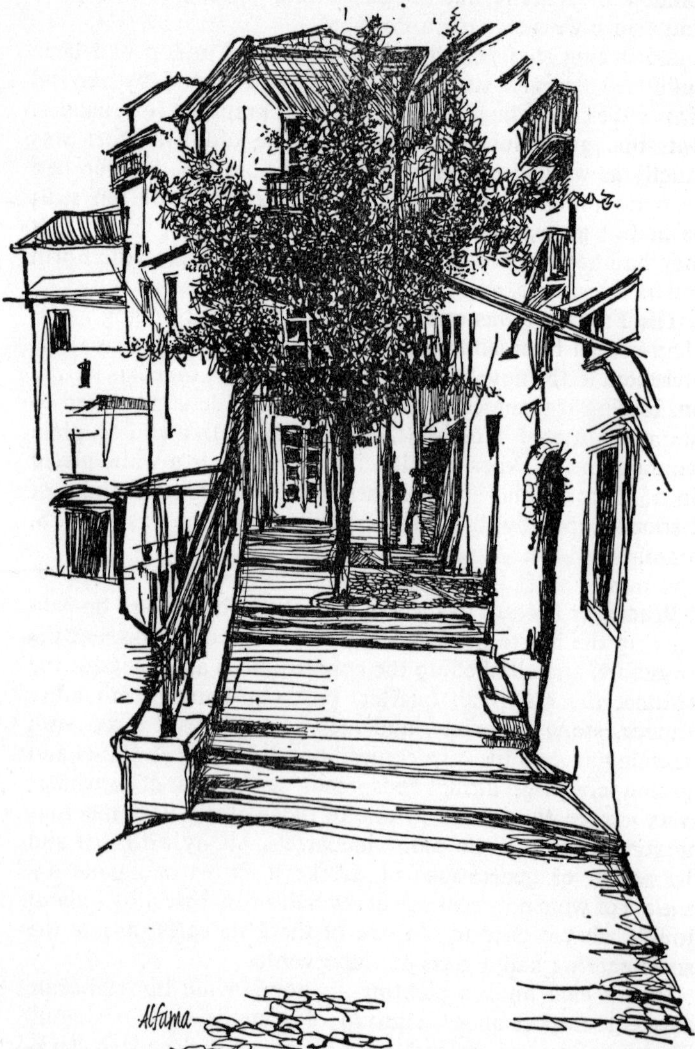
Alfama

A LISBON DIARY

because of its oddity and the fact it was a rather good 'primitive' but also because we had seen a fellow to it in one of the pubs on the way up to the castle—a portrait-group of ragged beggars with the complementary title, 'The Pilgrimage of the Badly-Dressed'. I determined to find out about them, but decided to wait till we had joined forces with the Swifts as our Portuguese might be too rudimentary to follow the patrão's explanation.*

The outer gate of the castle stood outside our café. Having paid for the drinks and said goodbye to the patrão, we walked up the carriageway to the parade ground. Populated with heroic statuary, white peacocks, and ancient olive trees, it extends between the battlements and the remains of the keep. The Castelo is as old as Julius Caesar, though with numberless deletions and additions since his day. The Visigoths built its walls; the Moors made it their citadel; the Master of Avis turned it into a royal palace. This Portuguese champion freed his country from Spanish domination at the Battle of Aljubarrota, in 1385 with the help of John of Gaunt's longbowmen. He became Dom João I, married John of Gaunt's daughter Phillipa, and dedicated the castle, by way of compliment, to the patron saint of England. English crusaders, in fact, had helped to storm the citadel and take it from the Moors in 1147. Their Portuguese allies seem glad to have seen the backs of them, though one Englishman, Gilbert of Hastings, stayed on to become Bishop of Portugal and a builder of Lisbon's Sé Catedral. The storming of the citadel is commemorated by a seventeenth-century bust placed over the archway of the old gate—placed there by a descendant of the hero whose likeness it perpetuates. This was Martim Moniz, the soldier who, when the Moors retired through the gateway after a vigorous sortie against the besiegers, ran after them to place himself in the entrance to prevent the closing of the gate. His crushed body preserved the opening through which the crusaders were able to burst their way into the stronghold.

The parade ground commands one of the most magnificent views of Lisbon, even of that city of panoramas and vistas. Heavy and elaborate bronze cannon poke their snouts over

* See p. 144 for further information about these pictures.

the limestone walls, their vague aim directed at a great sheet of water like an inland sea bounded by the river's further shore. This consists of a low reach of hills whose fluid line is broken by an angular and gigantic granite cross. Thence the eye is led towards an immense new suspension bridge near the mouth of the river, where the distant Torre de Belém glints like a pearl on the waterfront. Directly below the castle is Rossio, with the straight parallel streets of Baixa leading to Black Horse Square and the Tagus. On the other side of Rossio ascend the hills on which stand the earthquake-wrecked Convent do Carmo, the clustered houses of Bairro Alto, and the far-off dome of the Estrêla basilica dominating the towers and cupolas of lesser churches and palaces. A panoramic guide map in coloured azulejo tiles has recently been placed on the battlements with all the landmarks and principal buildings written in. It is a good place for the newcomer to get a grasp of the geography of the city.

We wandered through the outer and inner keeps of the old citadel. These have been turned into gardens even more enchanting than those of the Palatine in Rome; but then the Portuguese have a genius for this sort of thing. Great masses of flowering creepers, bougainvillaea, morning glory, and others I could not name but remembered from my South African childhood, spread over the ruined walls. White doves roosted in ivy-covered niches, white peacocks and peahens preened themselves on the baroque stone mouldings; white guinea-fowl pecked the lawns; white ducks, white swans and white geese swam in the still waters of the moat. There were standing pools browsed by more exotic tenants: flamingoes, cassowaries, and herons—one of whom we saw helping himself to live goldfish from a pond. Gnarled olive trees seemingly as old as the castle provided shade. The inmost keep contained a large aviary housing falcons rigidly perching on the branches of a tree; another confined three or four heavy-bodied ravens with purplish-black plumage. As we returned to the esplanade overlooking the walls of the citadel, we encountered a flushed bevy of stripe-trousered wedding-guests; a formal reception was in progress at the little café on the ramparts.

At the hotel that evening we found a note from the Swifts. They had arrived that day from Algarve, and proposed to look for us in the Irmãos Unidos, the café next door to the Hotel Francfort. So our reunion took place under the café's famous cubist oil painting of Fernando Pessoa, with his pince-nez, coffee-cup, and copy of the magazine *Orpheu*. The Irmãos Unidos had been one of his ports of call in the days when it was a dingy little wine-barrelled taberna-restaurante—one doubts if the poet would much frequent the chromium-glittering cocktail-cabinet it has since become.*

The Swifts arrived accompanied by the Portuguese painter Lima de Freitas and Helle, his beautiful blonde Danish wife. Lima was an electric little man with black beard and glasses. He had just been appointed principal of the new Lisbon Art School, which was to be officially opened in a couple of days. The six of us adjourned to a little chicken-on-the-spit charcoal-grill restaurant in the Rua Portas de S. António—the street running parallel to the Avenida da Liberdade—where Lima invited us to see the still-unfinished premises of his art school. It was in one of the old palaces near the river, he explained. Swift offered to take us to it. We arranged to meet next morning at the Brasileira.

---

* As I write, I hear that the Irmãos Unidos ('United Brothers') has ceased to exist. It used to be a haunt of nineteenth-century liberals, of the novelist Eça de Quieroz, and later of Fernando Pessoa (commemorated by a wall-tablet set under his portrait). Later still, the South African poet Roy Campbell used to drink there when in Lisbon. I quote from a recent letter of Swift's: 'The Irmãos Unidos has closed down. Bankrupt. It turned out that that picture of Pessoa was their most valuable asset. They bought it for 30,000 escudos about a quarter of a century ago—it sold for more than a million and a half. Interesting point: [here the professional painter takes over] they had to pay Almada, the old chap who painted it, some 300,000 escudos of the selling price. Under Portuguese law, if any work of art is resold at a profit above a certain figure, a percentage is payable to the artist—as much as 20% in some cases.' Apart from this portrait, I never found anything very attractive about the Irmãos Unidos, whose atmosphere must have evaporated with its refurbishing.

Helle de Freitas

FRIDAY

The Brasileira is a famous café, a late nineteenth-century survival, standing in the Chiado—a little square at the top of the Rua Garrett, the street running up the hill to the west of Rossio, where the best and most expensive shops congregate. It is a smaller edition of the larger and even more rococo Café Brasileira at Oporto, and furnished in the same style—black mahogany panelled walls, heavy-browed mouldings, elaborately carved mahogany chairs, mottled marble tables. The atmosphere is of Victorian starched wing-collars, black pince-nez ribbons and bourgeois *ton*, of solid mercantile respectability hankering after Art and Bohemia (*vide* the smoke-blackened canvases set high in the panellings). A true period piece, yet with no suggestion of camp, such as one finds in over-restored 'Victorian' pubs in London. Here we found Swift reading the *Diário das Notícias* over a cup of black coffee.

'Lima's palace is over the way,' he said. 'Have a coffee and I'll take you there. Oonagh won't be coming, she's at the pensão, resting.'

Oonagh was due to have a baby any moment: it was one of the reasons why the Swifts were in Lisbon.

'The Palácio de Quintela is really interesting,' he went on. 'It belonged to Monteiro dos Milhões—a millionaire who married into the Pombals, descendants of the famous Marquês de Pombal who ran Portugal in the eighteenth century and rebuilt Lisbon after the big earthquake. The old marquesa still lives in part of the palace, all alone but for her maid.'

The Palácio de Quintela, he explained, originally belonged to the Baron Quintela e Count de Farrobo. It was built on the site of an older palace of the Counts of Vimioso which had been destroyed by fire in 1726.* In the nineteenth century it became the property of the capitalist Carvalho Monteiro, known as Monteiro dos Milhões. In his time it was a place of political activity—it is said that *o Milhões* used to bolster the tottering government of the day with vast loans of cash.

A few yards from the Brasileira is the Largo de Chiado, at the top of Rua Garrett. It merges into the Praça Luis de Camões, where a tall pedestal supports an effigy of the Portuguese national poet—much appreciated as a roosting-place by the thousands of city pigeons who inhabit the two squares. To the left, the Rua do Alecrim runs down a steep hill to the waterfront, past the famous monument to Eça de Quieroz, perhaps the most magnificently absurd of memorials. Quieroz was a nineteenth-century novelist, one of the great ones, in the class of Stendhal and Flaubert. His stature is still unappreciated in the English-speaking world as only a few of his novels have so far been translated, and those badly. The best is Roy Campbell's version of *Cousin Bazilio*. This book has much the same theme as *Madame Bovary*, and is to my mind a more penetrating because more sympathetic study of a woman. But to return to the statue: it is slightly larger than life and portrays Quieroz impeccably dressed in a lounge suit and half supporting a lady wearing nothing to speak of, whose arms are gracefully outspread to reveal all—which all the novelist examines with an expression both quizzical and

---

* One of these Counts of Vimioso had much to do with the origin of the fado: see p. 109.

amused. It was to this monument that Swift led us, for the Paláçio Quintela stood directly opposite.

'Monteiro dos Milhões couldn't stand that statue,' remarked Swift. 'He thought it indecent. He couldn't bear having it in front of his house, so he left and went to live in another of his palaces.'

'He had more than one palace?' I asked.

'Half a dozen at least. They used to call him "Six millions"— he was so rich that the government used to borrow money off him when they ran short.'

The solid and imposing portals of the palace stood open. Inside, we found a large hall occupied by carpenters hammering away, at work constructing a wooden platform. Shavings littering the stone floor, brand new plywood desks and chairs stacked here and there, adzes, trestles—all witnessed a frantic last-minute scurry.

A beaming Lima greeted us.

'As you see, we're a bit busy—the official opening is tomorrow.'

He escorted us up a vast stone staircase illumined by stained glass windows to the first floor, where lavatories and washbasins were being installed in one corner. The main lecture room was a grand affair decorated with murals one of which was a self-portrait of the artist who had painted them. An inscription declared that they had been completed in 1822 and restored by the same hand in 1878; constituting, I suppose, some kind of record. The windows of this room, I noticed, overlooked the famous, or infamous, nude statue; it which might come in handy for the life class. In this palace, Lima told us, Marshal Junot had signed the so-called Convention of Sintra after his defeat by Wellington in the first round of the Peninsular War. Then he took us down to the basement to see the huge kitchens with their gigantic tiled fireplaces, reminiscent of the enormous monks' kitchen we had seen at the monastery of Alcobaça on our way to the Minho.

'You must come to the opening tomorrow,' Lima invited as we said goodbye outside the heavy doors of the palace.

This evening the Irmãos Unidos served once again as a

rendezvous. A young South African novelist, Desmond Greig, had introduced himself to me by letter as a friend of a friend, the architect Michael Sutton. Greig and his wife Barbara—an architectural sculptor in ceramic—were visiting Portugal. Could we meet? I suggested the Irmãos Unidos at seven; and went there a little before time, in order to absorb the snifter that I find necessary before social encounters. Unfortunately I spotted a bottle on the shelves labelled *Absinthe,* a liquor it has been my lifetime ambition to sample (according to the *Encyclopaedia Britannica* it 'acts powerfully upon the nerve-centres and causes delirium and hallucinations, followed in some cases by idiocy'). So I ordered an absinthe, rather to the waiter's nonplusment (he had to consult the manager to find out how much to charge). Arriving at this point, the Greigs decided to try one too. Pip followed their example when she turned up a moment afterwards. A bit bothered, the waiter made some remark of disapproval, or so we thought. When, twenty minutes later, Swift found us all drinking absinthe, his eyebrows disappeared.

'It doesn't seem to have all that much of a lift,' I told him, 'but at any rate it's got the waiter dead worried, though we don't know why.'

Swift turned to the waiter and asked him what the trouble was. The waiter explained in rapid Portuguese.

'He's worried all right,' said Swift. 'He doesn't know why you're wasting your time on the stuff. He says it's only twenty degrees proof.'

After this descent from the sublime we decided to go to the Alfama for a meal. We looked expectantly at Swift: he was the habitué, the expert.

The Alfama is a warren of little pubs at almost any of which you can get a dish of food of some sort: the problem is to find one that is able to produce something really out of the way in the shape of a meal yet has not at the same time prostituted itself to the tourist image (candles stuck in chianti-bottles, and fancy-shirted fado-singers yodelling in your ear).

'We'll take a taxi,' Swift announced. This is his solution for most problems; but for once perfectly correct. The Alfama is a wonderful place to wander about in, but confusing if one is going anywhere specific. In such a case it is best to take one of of the incredibly cheap Lisbon taxis—even if the driver doesn't know the place you want to go to, he'll find out where it is a good deal quicker than you will.

So we drove in style to Swift's choice, which was situated in one of the hanging lanes and alleys that zigzag up the hill overlooking the Tagus. Unable to go further our taxi came to a halt in a little square half-way up the hill. A couple of guitar-bearing waiters advanced to escort us to their touristified nosh-house, but we gave them the slip. Led by Swift, we found his quarry—a little place called the Parreirinha, up an alley not far away. His 'tipico' pub-restaurant consisted of a small narrow bar with a chest-high counter and, beyond it, a slightly ampler space almost filled by a couple of check-clothed tables.

Here we ordered the speciality of the house—called, somewhat off-puttingly, 'chicken-blood'—and a litre each of red and white wine. The 'chicken-blood' turned out to be an immense and truly magnificent dish: a concoction of chicken, black-puddings, and rice in a dark wine-coloured gravy. We told the Greigs, who were returning to South Africa the following day, that we proposed to visit the Lisbon Flea Market next morning (a Saturday, one of the two days of the week when it is open; the other is Tuesday).

'We've seen it,' they told us. 'Very disappointing. All plastic rubbish.'

We wound up with coffee and brandy: the bill came to around fifty escudos a head—say seventeen shillings—which we thought very reasonable.

SATURDAY

In the morning Pip and I walked to the Feira da Ladra— 'the fair of the women-thieves', so called because it was once thought of as a market for stolen goods. It is held in the Campo de Santa Clara, which name derives from a Franciscan convent, one of the biggest and richest in Lisbon till it was utterly destroyed in the 1755 earthquake. The fair has an ancient history; its venue has changed from place to place in the course of the centuries. In the time of Dom Afonso III it was held in Ribeira Velha; in Dom Manuel's time in the Praça Ribeira; while in the sixteenth century it was situated in the Rossio. After the great earthquake it moved to the Praça da Alegria. Finally, after various other shifts, it was definitely established in Campo de Santa Clara, where it has been held ever since 1882.

Our way to the Feira da Ladra took us through the Praça do Comércio. This is the great square on the waterfront, variously known as 'Terreiro do Paço' or 'Black Horse Square'. The last is a nickname given by English sailors because of the prancing equestrian statue of Dom José. This green-bronze artefact dominates the great open square, backed by three colonnaded sides and the gigantic triumphal arch over the Rua Augusta, where a huge stone effigy of Glory may be seen crowning the heads of Virtue and Valour. The statue was unveiled by the Marquês de Pombal, the reforming and iron-handed eighteenth-century statesman. His own portrait in a medallion was affixed to its pedestal. But not long afterwards Dom José died. Pombal fell from power, whereupon Dom José's successor ordered the destruction of the medallion. According to the story this task was assigned to the artist who had made it. Rather than destroy his own work the man hid the medallion and only on his deathbed revealed its whereabouts. He had bricked it up in a wall of the Arsenal. Thus, sixty years later, it was recovered and put back in its original position. The square has grim associations—the two marble pillars on the water-front mark the spot where the Tagus swallowed up thousands of people in the 1755 earthquake, while in 1908 its north-west corner became the site of the murder of Dom Carlos, the last but one king of Portugal, together with his eldest son.

Leaving the square, we turned to the left, following the Tagus upstream and passing the Casa dos Bicos. This is an odd-looking sixteenth-century house with more doors than windows. It presents a saturnine knuckle-duster façade of pointed diamond-shaped stones. About to climb the hill in the direction of the church of São Vicente, behind which the Flea Market is situate, we were seduced by a glimpse of the courtyard at the back of the Artillery Museum. Cannon, culverins and bombards dozed like huge tranced lizards in front of its azulejo-faced walls. On going inside, we found the usual fan-shaped arrangements of swords, pikes and bayonets. Though we have no particular weakness for military bric-à-brac, some of the items—like the eighteenth-century matchlock twenty feet in length—fascinated us. In a glass case was a scale model of the lines of Torres Vedras, rather like that of the Battle of Waterloo which used to stand in the Banqueting Hall in Whitehall. One large chamber devoted to the Great War displayed a rather effective bronze setpiece of a mounted gun team bogged in the mud of Passchendaele. The museum is housed in the old eighteenth-century Arsenal. Some of its numberless rooms—e.g. the Sala de Dom José II—are superb examples of carved gilded baroque decor. Its vast collection of arms, armour and uniforms of all periods we found a trifle overwhelming. But there were all sorts of surprises. Down in the basement, we came upon an enormous wooden cart or carriage whose gigantesque proportions dwarfed even those of Wellington's funeral car in the crypt of St. Paul's. The wheels alone were some twelve feet in diameter. This monster had been used to transport the enormous pedestal for the statue of Dom José in Black Horse Square; eighty span of oxen had been required to shift the load. The statue itself, designed by the famous sculptor Machado de Castro, was cast from 84,000 pounds of bronze in eight minutes by Bartholomeu da Costa, who was rewarded with military honours for this feat. He eventually became Governor of the Arsenal. The Artillery Museum, we agreed, is one of the sights of Lisbon.

But having an appointment to keep with the Swifts, we could not linger. The Flea Market, they had told us, was behind the church of S. Vicente—a grand Renaissance edifice of white limestone, half-way up the hill, overlooking the river. Here canvas-roofed booths and stalls, their wares overspilling the cobbles, cluttered a broad tree-lined promenade. In the middle of all this stood a small but elaborate nineteenth-century meat

S.Vicente

and vegetable market, a beautiful specimen of period ironwork.
 The Greigs must have been unlucky when they visited the Feira da Ladra. Plastic there was, but hardly visible in the splendid flood of ancient junk and kickshaws offered for sale—bottles, bedsteads, lavatory seats, old primuses, oil lamps, door-knockers, boots, combination-locks, revolvers, car registration numbers (now who wants those?), rusty keys, cutlery, bottles, steam-irons, empty Alka-Seltzer tubes, old telephones, ivory billiard-balls, kitchen scales, motor-horns, spurs, second-hand harness, and job lots of ancient clobber. But quite a number of the stalls had genuinely interesting and

often beautiful antiques and objets d'art on sale—African carvings and masks, Victorian wax dolls, antique azulejo tiles, and old church carvings and statues. One we saw was of the Virgin pregnant—rather like the famous fourteenth-century effigies of 'the Virgin of O' that we had seen some years before at Lamego, on our way to the Minho. We very nearly bought an old powder horn beautifully decorated with scratched 'primitive' drawings by its owner, doubtless some eighteenth-century rustic farmer.

We had found the Swifts in the course of drifting round these booths and stalls. Presently we adjourned to a little taberna next to the market. Sitting at a table outside on the terrace in the October sun, with brandy in front of us, the bustle and bizarrerie of the market all about, and, far below, the broad bosom of the Tagus dandling its boats and steamers, was euphoric. I wanted very much to lunch at this taberna, dingy though it looked. Already a number of workmen were having their midday meal (and a pretty substantial one, at that) in the bar. But I had to be content with sampling a

Flea Market

A LISBON DIARY

prego (sandwich) of roast sucking-pig, for the Swifts were engaged to take the daughter of a friend to the Zoo that afternoon, and had arranged to lunch at the restaurant there.

The Lisbon Zoological Gardens are one of the most renowned in Europe. I am ready to bet they are among the most beautiful. Though almost more garden than zoo—its rose-beds are famous—the Lisbon Zoo has an enviable record for the breeding of animals in captivity. It stands in the north-western outskirts of the city. You can reach it by tram or bus; but as Swift was in charge of the expedition, transport was by taxi.

Having picked up the small girl en route, we lunched off rather leathery beef and chips at the little restaurant in the gardens. As it looked like rain we had a table in a latticed alcove covered with creepers, not far from an aviary of jaunty little parakeets. Lunch over, we wandered through the park-like grounds to the old pink palace of Laranjeiras, once the home of the Count of Farrobo, and for a period a maritime museum—a giant block and pulley, with two enormous ship's propellers like Hepworth sculptures, lay abandoned in one of the courtyards.

'This Count of Farrobo was also the owner of the Palacio de Quintela, where Lima is opening his art school,' Swift remarked. 'It was his father, the Baron Quintela, who built the place. The Count de Farrobo added to it a grandiose theatre with room for nearly six hundred spectators and a ballroom lined with mirrors. It was illuminated with gaslight, a wonder of its day. That was around 1830. Then it burned down in 1862. For years it had been legendary for its luxurious festas attended by royalty. In the gardens were labyrinths, lakes and hothouses, cages with wild animals and aviaries full of exotic birds. It was the obvious place for the zoo, which was installed here in 1905.'

Turning away from the palace, we climbed up a wooded hill where deer have an open-air enclosure to themselves, as at Whipsnade. A broad gravel walk took us past the cages containing the big cats. The only pair of Siberian tigers to breed in captivity are at Lisbon Zoo. But more remarkable to look at were the lynxes; and two sinister black pumas, their fur the matt gleam of Whitby jet, glooming in a corner of one of the dens. Below this was a poolful of frisky seals; further along, a great iron cage with a population of baboons. There may have been sixty or seventy of them, all living together, though some were divided into separate family groups. Many of the unattached bachelors—rakish and not very reputable characters they looked—had lost their paws, perhaps in fights. I was startled to notice that the infant baboons could, and of course did, slip through the bars of this cage to mix with the audience and accept buns and bananas from admirers. Then they would scamper back to their parents. Personally, I would not care to risk a bite from those infantine yet powerful dog-jaws. A day must come, I reflected, when the young baboon would discover that he had grown too big to wriggle through the bars—but on which side of them would he find himself?

Not far from the baboonery we came upon a line of open enclosures, moat-defended—the home of a pair of Russian bears. They were the biggest, most formidable carnivores any of us had seen—massive beasts, huge as houses; quite unlike the comparatively chubby brunos one finds in Regent's Park. It must be said that the Lisbon Zoo, unlike most other zoos, manages to make its cages aesthetically appealing—at least for the human visitor—largely through the decorative use of azulejos on their inside walls. One of its oddest features is a sort of canine suburb: row on row of pens containing specimens of almost every breed of pet dog in existence. Next to it is the Dogs' Cemetery—a memorable repository of sculptured kitsch, decisive proof that English mawkishness in respect to man's best friend may be easily outdone by the sentimental Portuguese. This graveyard of little marble tombs, some faced with coloured azulejos, some with photographs of the defunct animals, some with effigies, and a good many inscribed with heartbreaking verses, is not to be missed.

During our visit to the zoo I temporarily lost the rest of the party. While looking for them (the gardens are very extensive) I came upon the ape-houses. I have never seen so complete a collection of the great apes in any zoo. Besides the usual chimpanzees and gorillas were a pair of orang-outangs, covered with long, silky red hair. One of them was standing erect, motionless, clutching the bars of the cage. The face expressed so concentrated and profound a boredom, despair, and contempt that it was like a personal accusation: I fled.

This evening we were due to attend the official opening of Lima's art school at the palace. Unfortunately, or perhaps fortunately, we were a bit late and could not get seats in the main lecture hall, which was packed with notables and prospective students while speech after speech coruscated from the platform. We stood in the passage outside, wedged among the other latecomers. The confusion and débris of the carpenters and plumbers had been abolished, it seemed, overnight. It was one of those unbearable muggy nights of damp and clammy heat—made no cooler by the fact that everyone had turned up in formal subfusc. Eventually the speeches came to an end. The crowd in the lecture room and passageways began to disintegrate like the breaking of a log-jam. Lima discovered us and brought us in to the lecture hall to shake hands with friends and VIPs. There was to be a celebration, he said. We were invited to a party being given by António Quadros, then on to dinner. Swift said he would take us to António's house.

On the way there we stopped at a café for a couple of brandies —after that vigil in the passage we needed them.

'António Quadros is a very distinguished writer and philosopher,' Swift explained. 'He knows a good deal about Pessoa too.'

Though Senhor Quadros lived just off the Rua do Século, a handsome street on the fringe of Bairro Alto, barely a couple of hundred yards from our café, Swift bundled us into his inevitable taxi. We rang the bell of a porticoed mansion; a pretty maid in cap and apron let us in. António and his wife inhabited the large ground-floor flat of the house. Like the uniformed maid, the furnishings struck the note of 1920, with their blend of the modernistic and the Victorian. Very good paintings hung on the walls; one that I particularly admired turned out

António Quadros

to be by Lima himself. There was a good and unusual Picasso drawing. But most of the pictures were Utrilloesque and Braque-like paintings by Portuguese artists I had never heard of. We were offered an excellent madeira. I asked Senhor Quadros if he had known Pessoa.

'But he died in nineteen thirty-five,' he exclaimed. 'I was only a small boy. It was my father who knew him—he was connected with Pessoa's magazine, *Orpheu*.'

I asked if I could see a copy of this famous 'little review' which had been one of the pioneers of the 'modern movement', like *The Egoist* and Eliot's *Criterion*. Alas, someone had borrowed António's files of the magazine.

His bookshelves contained an enviable library of contemporary and classic literature, French and English, as well as Portuguese. But Pip and I were fascinated by a collection of exquisite clay models or figurines to which António drew our attention. He had picked them up for almost nothing; but they were, he thought, the work of Machado de Castro the great eighteenth-century sculptor who was responsible for the splendid equestrian statue of Dom José in Black Horse Square. These little statuettes put me in mind of a series of curious painted earthenware figures we had seen in a shop in Lisbon on our last visit. They were remarkable, stylised representations of daily life and rural occupations: e.g. a woman carding wool, another washing clothes in a tub, another at an ironing-board; butchers killing a pig, or making sausages; a milkman with his donkey and panniers; and so on. We described them to António and asked if he knew anything about them.

'They come from Estremoz in the Alentejo,' Antonio told us. 'There they still make them to a traditional design and style that has hardly changed over the centuries. My father could have told you a good deal about them—he founded the Museum of Popular Art at Belém. You ought to visit it if you're interested in these things.'

There were perhaps fifteen or sixteen other people in the room, nearly all of whom spoke English. But I did not have time to exchange more than a word or two with a few of them before we were summoned to the grand dinner. This was to be held in one of the big new hotels at the top of the Avenida da Liberdade. The guest of honour, it turned out, was a Spaniard, and our Portuguese hosts were on their mettle. They were out to show their Iberian cousin that things can be done in style in Lisbon no less than in Madrid.

The Hotel Rex, where the dinner was held, turned out to be one of those glass and cement palaces, the last word in luxury and expense, with the kind of carpet one needs a machete to traverse. The dining room, dim with concealed lighting, was sumptuously centre-set with a table bearing a pair of gigantic brass market-scales whose panniers overflowed with melons, breadfruit, oranges and bananas, while around it lay, in harvest-festival profusion, decorative bunches of giant turnips, carrots, and so forth. For the party a great round table had been prepared—not large enough, as it turned out, for the last-minute additions represented by Swift and ourselves. We were accommodated, however, at a small side-table illumined by flickering candles.

The dinner began at nearly 10 p.m. and wound a slow and magnificent progress through the early hours of the morning. Course after course appeared to the accompaniment of different wines. The dish that remains in memory was what they called 'Portuguese steak', a steak covered by a thick slice of ham, braised with potatoes and served sizzling in the earthenware pan in which they had been cooked. Champagne was served in tall deep glasses, far better than traditional vessels. I am afraid I was a dead loss socially at this party: but that was the fault of the wavering candlelight—which inhibited my ability to lip-read—not of our kind and courteous hosts.

SUNDAY

After a restless night—steak weighing on stomach, social failure on conscience—uneasy dozing turned into true sleep just before dawn. Feeling better than I expected or deserved. I awoke. The Swifts had suggested a day at Sintra, where a famous fair is held every other Sunday. This was one of the operative Sundays; we determined not to miss it.

We found the Swifts at their pensão in Santa Catarina near the Bairro Alto, and walked down the hill with them to pick up their car. They had had to park it nearly a mile from their pensão. Reflecting the heavy and comparatively recent increase in traffic, parking is now almost as much a problem in Lisbon as in Rome. The Swifts had not brought their Mini-Morris but had borrowed an estate car for the sake of more leg-room. We drove along the boulevards that run parallel with the shipping docks and quays, past the great ivory-yellow monastery of the Jerónimos, to stop outside a long low concrete-modern building not far from the Torre de Belém.

'This is the Museum of Popular Art that António was talking about,' Swift announced. 'It was founded in 1940. His father had a lot to do with it.'

The whole museum is laid out on one floor, though upper galleries run above to some of the rooms. Each province of

Portugal—Algarve, Minho, Trás-os-Montes, and the rest—
has its own sala filled with the artefacts, costumes, vehicles,
tools, pottery, and utensils peculiar to itself. As most of these
are still made and used today, walking through the museum is
rather like making an instant tour of Portugal. We kept coming across, and greeting like familar acquaintances, the regional
objects and artefacts we had seen in various towns and villages
during our journeys to the Minho and Entre-o-Douro three years
before: the strange and beautiful black pottery of Bizalhães,
or the carved ox-yokes of the north. This museum was probably
set up in the nick of time, for within the next few decades many
if not most of these traditional regional artefacts will probably
cease to be made. Some, like the elaborate floral banners borne
in religious processions, are ephemeral in their nature, while
others, like the different kinds of wicker- and wattle-work
baskets and containers, are perishable. Among the more
remarkable objects preserved in the museum one could list
the carved and painted wooden saddles—those for women
resembled elaborate armchairs—stone sundials (one in the
shape of the bust of a man wearing a top hat, very like Hugh
Lofting's drawings of Dr. Dolittle), decorated shoes, lanterns
and ornamenal wax candles; carts, carriages and carrinhas of
all kinds (some of them the actual vehicles, though most were
models); spinning-wheels, looms, examples of tapestry and
intricately patterned bright coloured cloth; a strange, primitive
harrow—a flat sledlike board in which rows of sharp flints had
been fixed. Outside the museum, in the open, various types of
fishing boat—the shapes and design differ from village to
village—lay on their sides. One was a fine specimen of the
gondola-like *moliceiros* of the lagoons near Aveiro.

The museum absorbed us for almost two hours; we could
have stayed twice the time. But we still had to get to Sintra.
So we returned to the car, taking the coast, or riverine, road (it
is hard to tell where the Tagus ends and the sea begins) via
Estoril and Cascais. On the way we passed some of the miniature
forts that defend the coast of Portugal—there seems to be a
chain of them running along the entire Atlantic seaboard. We

admired the blue and tawny water of the estuary, the little yachts with ballooning spinnakers dancing on the waves. This is the Portuguese Riviera, which antedates the French Riviera as a fashionable refuge from the northern winter by a couple of centuries.

I was agog to see the plutocrats' villas and their architecture of ostentation that I had heard so much of. But little of that kind of thing was evident; perhaps it is hidden away in gardens, behind the pines and feathery palms. Estoril and Cascais are now one town rather than two villages. If anything, I was reminded of the seaside resorts of the Cape rather than what I have seen of the French Riviera. One building we laughed at: a signboard announcing the English Bar, outside a perfect if incongruous specimen of ribbon-development mock-Tudor with painted beams ...

Beyond Estoril the houses and villas faded away. Nothing was to be seen but blue sea on the one hand and green scrub on the other till we came to Cabo Raso. Here two estalagems overlook a half-moon beach uncluttered with tourist-holiday umbrellas and similar litter. Either could prove a magnificent place to stay, for their situation is superb. In the distance lies Cabo da Roca, a dramatic rocky headland with a lighthouse. This cape is in fact the westernmost point of Europe. To the right we could see the jagged woody peaks of Sintra, with the roofs and white walls of the town lying on its slopes. Dotted here and there, on eminences to catch the wind, stood round-barrelled windmills with tiny triangular canvas sails.

Our road now began its ascent to Sintra, winding and climbing steadily past hills capped with naked granite rock sculpted and polished by rain. Up and up wound the road till it entered the green damp mountain-forest. Soon we found ourselves above the cloud-line. Clouds swirled about the weird Gothic boulders that crowned the peaks of the Serra do Sintra. Then down we went to the little town which lies or clings half-way up the sides of the mountain.

Sintra has been rhapsodised enough by Byron, Beckford, and Southey. It is easy to see why: the place might be a creation of the Romantic imagination. There are castles on every hand—roosts of Valkyries, some of them; particularly Pena, which balances its crenellations on the highest pinnacle of a conical mountain. Horrid crags, sunless glens, torrents that from cliff to valley leap—if one may borrow from the write-up of the place in Byron's *Childe Harold*—all are there. By the by, Byron is said to have begun this poem (the apotheosis of sentimental romanticism; its publication made him famous overnight) at Sintra when he was staying at the Hotel Lawrence (now the Estalagem dos Cavaleiros) in 1810. Ten years earlier Southey had written to his brother a description of Sintra which is still valid: 'There is no scenery in England which can help me to give you an idea of this. The town is small, like all country towns of Portugal, containing the Plaza or square, and a number of narrow crooked streets that wind down the hill: the palace is old—remarkably irregular—a large, rambling, shapeless pile, not unlike the prints I have seen in old romances of a castle,—a place whose infinite corners overlook the sea...'

This palace, the ancient royal palace, one of the oldest in Portugal, stands in the central square of Sintra. It was built in the fourteenth century by Dom João I, the Master of Avis, but much remains of an older, Moorish edifice. Looking at it from the outside, one is struck first of all by two enormous conical pointed domes rather like the roofs of Kentish oast-houses. These are the kitchen chimneys; on the inside they are blackened with the soot of centuries. And the huge ovens and rows of grills to be seen in this kitchen give one some idea of the sheer work and organisation the palace must have required when it was a going concern. It is now a museum. Though almost worth visiting for the furniture alone, many of the rooms are of exquisite beauty. A fountain plays in the middle of a Moorish dining room, whose walls are faced with very old blue, green and white azulejos. In fact the azulejos in this palace are among the oldest and most remarkable in the peninsula. There is a grander and later dining room with great chandeliers and a painted ceiling of blue magpies, each holding a rose in its beak and the legend 'por bem'—'for good'. This is the motto of Dom João, but the story goes that he excused himself with these words when his prim English queen caught him kissing one of the maids of honour. Nearby is an enormous throne room, the Sala dos Cisnes, or Hall of Swans, so called after the swans painted on the ceiling From this room you are offered a splendid view of the castle of Pena, which perches on the topmost peak of the serra like a Rhineland castle or one of Arthur Rackham's fairy-book illustrations. One small room with a barred window, floored with azulejos, has a depressing impact, and a classically romantic history. In this room Dom Alfonso VI was imprisoned for nine years by his brother, Dom Pedro, who not only stole his throne but his wife. Here he died in 1683; the guide still points out the path worn on the azulejos by the steady pacing of his feet.

As I learnt from Swift, the palace of Sintra is considered one of the richest museums of 'mudejar' Moorish azulejos in the whole peninsula. It is also an important showpiece of the development of the Manueline. Most of the decorative features of the palace date from the reign of Dom Manuel. The azulejos start with the transitional fifteenth- to sixteenth-century tiles still in mosaic (as in the chapel) and the Seville type in 'corda seca' and 'cuenca' techniques of the sixteenth century. Made by Moorish potters in the Alentejo, these have a thicker glaze and more pronounced relief. The decoration (the Hall is the last of the Manueline, 1518) shows domestic Manueline-Moorish techniques and style, and beautiful examples of the carpentry of that period are the ceilings of the Hall of Swans, the armorial room, and the chapel. Altogether, it can be regarded as the most important example of Moorish-Gothic that exists. It was probably from this centre that the 'Moorish' influence spread south—but most of these elements (ajimeces, mosaics, azulejos, afarjes and chimneys) are of Manueline construction.

For me Sintra has the faded seduction of now unfashionable watering-places like Buxton, though no vulgar up-dating or touristification as yet afflicts the curiously genteel charm of this white-walled, ivy-creepered, oak-embowered and cobble-stone-laned little town. But, as happens all over the world nowadays, trippers are liable to some gentle milking, if our lunch-time adventure here was typical. We were too hungry to look around for a place to eat, so stepped into the first restaurant that presented itself in the centre of the town. The menu promised a dobrada, which we ordered. This is a famous peasant rib-sticker—a monumental collation of tripe with its bits of chicken, ham, sausage, and any amount of spiced and seasoned beans. Ours was served up on a single large dish. The quantity, however, was not nearly enough for our sharpened appetites.

'This place is not up to much,' said Swift, surveying rather gloomily the depressed faces of the other diners, who seemed all to be visitors rather than locals. 'Let's give it up and find somewhere for a *real* lunch.' He went over to pay the bill while we gathered up our impedimenta and made for the door.

When we had settled down in the car, he said, 'I told the patrão that we thought his dobrada was a bit skimpy. He seemed rather surprised to hear me speaking in Portuguese—and explained he'd given us three portions instead of four "because you are foreigners".'

From the main square we took a turning to the left, following the road that climbed further up the mountain to the little village of São Pedro de Sintra, where the sometimes-on-Sunday fair is held. (In fact, it is always held on the second and fourth Sundays of the month.)

Near the church in this village is a big, shady, slightly sloping square. When we arrived, we found it densely packed with people, with canvas booths, tables, and makeshift counters protected by tarpaulins or sheets of plastic rigged from trees and poles. Beside the church stood two restaurant-pubs close together. Of these we selected the humbler and more retiring—a little rural taberna called 'O Cantinho de S. Pedro'. Its dining room was a sort of glassed-in arbour, a verandah covered with creepers (now why are such places always the pleasantest to eat in?). Our appetites must have been whetted rather than blunted by the hors d'œuvre at the tourist restaurant. It is with shame I record that we got through, without the least difficulty, four huge plates of pork and chips, followed by some magnificent apples, pears and peaches, washing down the whole with a litre of vinho verde.

Substantially refreshed, we threaded our way to the fair. (En route we had to step over the recumbent form of a happy customer sleeping it off outside the pub.) The Swifts, who as residents in Portugal have vast experience of fairs, thought it one of the best they had so far encountered. At the head of the square stood stalls of rural earthenware pottery, stands overflowing with brightly-coloured handwoven country rugs and blankets. Old women waylaid the entrances, selling smoking chestnuts roasted over charcoal embers in perforated earthenware bowls; there were hucksters with trays of combs, lighters, razor-blades, laces, and glittering trinkets. Narrow lanes of booths, some overflowing with haberdashery, or forming groves and thickets of boots, leather attaché-cases, saddlery and harness; some displaying wooden spoons, tenderisers, mortars, rolling-pins, bread-boards and kitchenware, horn-handled knives and forks, fire-irons and cheap wooden bellows, pots and pans. Half a dozen stalls sold antiques and junk—two or three we recognised, for we had encountered them at the Lisbon Flea Market the day before. Nor was the inner man—or come to that the inner child—uncatered for: there were stands selling candyfloss, while others exhibited whole roast sucking-pigs, split open and spreadeagled, of which portions were sold by the kilogramme to those who felt in need of a snack. In the middle of the fair stood a canteen under a canvas shelter, where fresh sardines grilled over an open stove. Near it a similar establishment, but distinguished by firkins of wine propped on trestles, dispensed bom vinho tinto and bagaço. Most of the customers at the fair were country people, though some were visiting townsfolk from Lisbon. Now and then we caught glimpses of a party of conspicuously German trippers in Bavarian uniform—plumed green hats, black leather shorts and white calf-socks. Good though the fair was, I could not help noticing that, in contrast with the fairs I had visited in Portugal three years before, nothing was particularly cheap.

'They say it's really more economical now to buy in the shops,' Oonagh told me. 'But the countryfolk don't like change

—they still flock to the fairs even though things cost the same, or perhaps a little more. That's because, as an old peasant once explained, "Here we can examine things and make up our minds 'á vontade'—'at our ease' ".'

We were now ready to visit the castle of Pena, which so romantically and aptly perches on a craggy pinpoint of rock overlooking the town of Sintra. The car took us up a steeply winding road that found its way, like a needle threading a thick rug, through luxuriant, damply moss-grown forests—mimosas, cork-oak, pines, magnolias—to the rock-strewn heights. Again we reached the cloud-line. Our first near glimpse of the castle was thus appropriately sinister, for we caught sight of its Gothic curtain-walls swirled about by shimmering opaque skirts of racing cumuli. It might have been the residence of Frankenstein's monster in a Hammer film. The road wound on and up till at last we reached the summit with its fairy castle. It was a Teutonic-Lusitanian fantasy, complete with drawbridge over a dummy moat (a moat on a 1600 ft. mountain peak!). Wild twistings of Manueline rococo embellished the gateway.

Byronic and Beckfordian as it looks from the distance, the castle of Pena did not exist in their day. It was built as late as 1840 on the site of the 'tottering convent' Byron celebrated in *Childe Harold*. What's more, and even more appropriate considering its strong links with Scottish baronial Gothic, the place was built by a cousin of Albert the Prince Consort. This was Fernando II, one of the nineteenth-century Saxe-Coburgs who did so well in the royal marriage-market; he drew Maria II, the already widowed, seventeen-year-old Queen of Portugal. A German baron was his architect; one can believe it. His Teutonic jumble of Manueline, Renaissance and Gothic styles is consummated by the presence of an Arab minaret. All this is built round and above the fourteenth-century cloister and chapel of the original monastery, which yet survive. The mixture is so incongruous that it achieves a kind of mad congruity.

A guide showed us round the apartments. These retain most

of their original nineteenth-century furniture. All the rooms lead one into the other, imposing a purely medieval lack of privacy that must have embarrassed the proprieties of the Victorian period; and each has its own peculiar gimmick— one room being made of cement disguised as wood, another furnished in porcelain, another counterpointed in yellow and black. Their impact is fantastic but effective, rather like the rooms of the Pavilion at Brighton, though without their exquisite Regency balance and proportion.

We went out upon the parapets but, owing to the wreathing clouds, missed seeing what must be one of the most spectacular views in Portugal. However, I was much taken with an ingenious device for summoning the denizens of the palace to luncheon: a small brass cannon fixed to a sundial of polished steel, with a burning glass above it adjusted so that at noon the sun's rays focus on the touchhole of the cannon and automatically fire its charge of gunpowder.*

Being at Sintra, we could not return to Lisbon without calling on Mary Campbell. Her house, which we had visited a few years before, stands somewhere on the serra, isolated among the pines and blue gums. With some difficulty we found it at the end of an unmetalled but negotiable track that branched off from the main road to Lisbon. She had built the house for her husband, the poet Roy Campbell, but he never lived in it. They were driving there from Spain in April, 1957, when a tyre burst near Setubal; the car hit a tree, and Campbell was killed.

The situation of the house, half-way up the boulder-strewn serra whose vegetation (particularly the eucalyptus trees) is so reminiscent of Africa, brought powerfully to mind my own childhood home on a kopje outside Johannesburg, with its panorama of the high veld. I found it difficult to remember that Campbell had not in fact lived in this house, for his presence impregnated it as if he were in the next room or about to come in from the garden. Partly, it was the books and furniture

* Perhaps not an uncommon gadget in the nineteenth century. I have since seen another—in the Georgian mansion on Derwent Island on Derwentwater.

I remembered from his old home at Kensington, where I used to go every Sunday afternoon to have tea with him and listen to his outrageous stories—which would be interspersed with unexpected maxims and apophthegms (e.g. 'a sense of humour is the conscience of poets'); partly it was Mary Campbell's remarkable portrait of him as a young man (what fine luminous eyes he had before the flesh began to mask the structure of his face) that dominated the room from its position above the hearth. Here we were given tea. The conversation was about Laurie Lee's autobiography, which contained an account of his stay with the Campbells at Toledo just before the outbreak of the Spanish Civil War. Mary Campbell spoke of Laurie Lee with affection; and I was surprised to learn that his beautiful wife was a niece of hers. Just before we rose to go, Mary's elder daughter Teresa appeared. We asked them both to come to Lisbon to lunch with us.

MONDAY

I invariably breakfast at one of the grimly masculine cafés on the other side of Rossio. There is nothing wrong with the hotel breakfast; it is just that I like the walk across the square in the morning sunshine. The flower-sellers are beginning to hide the bronze figures of the fountain with their stalls, their baskets of roses, and tall feathery pampas grass; the Italianate National Theatre at the north end, for long used as government offices but now being reconverted to its original purpose, gleams white and elegant; the bulb and neon advertisements, turned off at dawn, surmount the other buildings like a faded, somewhat rakish wreath, suggestive of some reveller's morning-after-the-night-before. Above are the hills of Lisbon with their climbing houses, the shell of the Carmo church dominating the skyline. In the centre of the square stands the bronze figure of Dom Pedro IV, perched stylite on a tall column of fluted marble. Rossio's official name is in fact Praça Dom Pedro IV, but no one has ever called it anything else but Rossio—which simply means 'open space'—except perhaps the

English sailors who once used to call it 'Turkey Square' because of the flocks of turkeys that were sold there.

But to return to my morning: in the café I read my day-old *Times*, bought at the next-door news-stand where all the papers of Europe are on display, drink my café-com-leite and eat my 'tost' (hot buttered toast, which this particular café does rather well) while the traffic outside begins to warm up—the early-morning trickle of cars, bicycles and the odd tram swelling into a positive flood, a moving wall of manic vehicles.

Pip does not take breakfast. When I have had mine I pay the bill, pick up the newspaper, take my life in my hands, and re-cross the traffic-beseiged square to buy her some apples in the Rua Dom António Vaz de Almada—the grandiose moniker of a very ordinary little street behind the Rossio. The apples are ambrosia. At first we supposed they must be a special variety; but no, 1969 had been a particularly good year for apples in the peninsula. All were distinguised by an unusual, exquisite flavour.

This morning we meandered. We strolled from Rossio towards Black Horse Square by the Rua Aurea, looking at the goldsmiths' and silversmiths' windows, full of trays of delicate and intricate filigree metalwork brooches and earrings for which this street is famous—Portuguese filigree work is a hangover from the Moorish occupation. Pombal, when he built the Baixa, decreed that each street should be devoted to one trade, and this is still largely the case—at least in the Rua Áurea ('Golden Street') where, besides the goldsmiths and jewellers, you also find most of the money-changers. There is the street of the shoemakers, of the leatherworkers, of the gilders, and of the drapers. But their names are now not much of a guide to the kind of shop you may expect to find in them—for instance, the Rua dos Correeiros ('Leatherworkers') is almost entirely occupied by small, cheap restaurants.

Near the Rossio end of the Rua Áurea rises, like some tall palm with a foliage of extravagant ironwork, the ascensore or street lift to the Largo do Carmo on the hill opposite. This tower is pure Emmett to look at: and irresistible. The fare costs only a few centavos. When you get to the top the view is almost as vertiginous as that from the final stage of the Eiffel Tower. Barbed wire enclosing the platform shows how tempting it is to suicidal impulse. From the tower a fairly

Carmo

narrow iron bridge takes you high over the Rua do Carmo and deposits you at the top of the hill. The ruined church of the Carmo is just round the corner.

The fifteenth-century church, shattered and roofless ever since the 1755 earthquake, stands out on the hill like the broken incisor of a sheep's jawbone. It is now an archaeological museum. Its Gothic shell encloses a green lawn where the nave used to be, and where are now preserved stone pillories, Moorish fountains and basins, statues, sarcophagi, Roman inscriptions and carved capitals. At the eastern end, those chapels whose roofs remain have been furnished with showcases. Here we saw broken pottery from the prehistoric Celtic citania which I had visited with Swift at Viana do Castelo in the Minho; painted wooden statues, mosaics, and two or three royal tombs; and—a rather exotic touch—some Peruvian mummies.

From the Carmo we made our way by side-streets to the Bairro Alto, passing and admiring the fine eighteenth-century façade of the São Carlos Theatre. The Bairro Alto ('high quarter') is, second to Alfama, my favourite district of Lisbon. Like Alfama, it was not much damaged by the great earthquake. The Bairro Alto is not so old as Alfama, for it dates mostly from the seventeenth century, and it is as European as the Alfama is Arabic. The streets are straight, narrow and cobbled, inclining steeply up the hill. Beautiful ironwork balconies embellish the windows, themselves enhanced with potted geraniums, ferns and hanging creepers, canary-cages, and washing hanging out to dry; spotless white sheets and coloured underclothes.

At ground-level the shops and doorways are fascinating. There are greengrocers, cobblers, carpenters, blacksmiths, tinsmiths, ironmongers; shops selling cheap earthenware casseroles, bowls and baking-dishes; brightly-coloured handwoven carpets, blankets and rugs, or wickerwork baskets, plaited straw bags and the like—all for daily use, none of your tourist-bait here. Almost every third house seems to be a pub. a dingy little cavern with a high counter piled with plates of fried sardines or fresh crabs, a counter defending huge and blackened wine-barrels under rafters which are hung with smoked hams and strings of garlic. Sometimes one finds a parrot or a cockerel, often as not granted the freedom of the establishment. In one pub I remember seeing a magnificent golden pheasant roosting on top of the refrigerator. In the streets you even come across stumpy little parrots nonchalantly perching on the open windows of their owners' sitting-rooms.

Perhaps the most attractive street of the Bairro Alto is the Rua da Rosa. This steep cobbled lane is an open-air vegetable market, pleasing the eye and enchanting the nose with edible greenery arranged in bouquets and garlands at every corner.

At the top of the Rua da Rosa, on the broad summit of the hill climbed by the Bairro Alto, we saw and hailed a taxi. Our destination was the Jardim da Estrêla—the Estrêla Garden, which is both park and square. This is half a mile or so to the west of Bairro Alto. We could have walked; but, having stopped at three or four of the little tabernas in that quarter, I was feeling a trifle relaxed.

The Estrêla Garden is one of the many green, shady and flowerful oases of Lisbon. It is enlivened with melodramatic nineteenth-century statuary (for which I have an unassuageable weakness). An exotic placidity emanates from its strange South American trees, fountains shaded with white heavy-scented moonflowers, and pools haunted by pink-tinged flamingoes.

At one end of the gardens stands the huge domed basilica of the Estrêla, one of the landmarks of the city. This great church was built at the end of the eighteenth century. The façade is splendid and the interior imposing. Some of its baroque sculptures are by the great Machado de Castro, whose enormous Christmas crib behind the sacristy should not be missed—it is better than the famous but rather disappointing one by him in the Sé Catedral. The tomb of Queen Maria I, who built the church to fulfil her vow when she bore a son, is to be found beside the altar. In the sacristy is the sepulchre of her confessor, Fr. Inaçio de São Caetano, who began his extraordinary career as a circus clown and died in 1788 as Archbishop of Évora.

But, being Anglo-Saxon, heretic, and a scribbler, my object in going to the Estrêla ditsrict was not so much to see the basilica as to seek out the English Cemetery and the grave of Henry Fielding. The English Cemetery is at the north side of the Jardim da Estrêla, behind a high white wall. Here one steps out of Lisbon and Portugal into eighteenth-century England—or so it seems for the first moment or two, as the eye gathers in the English and Augustan contours of its stone urns, tombstones and obelisks, which stand lichened and calm, as if in some old print to illustrate Gray's *Elegy in a Country Churchyard*. But, after the first surprise, you detect the heavy Portuguese sculptural panache of these locally made sepulchres, though they do their best to imitate an English and alien reticence. Then the Judas trees and other subtropic foliage dispel the illusion of England created by shade and greenery. It is a strange and beautiful spot, more suggestive of sadness and exile than even the Protestant Cemetery at Rome. Most of the inmates, like Henry Fielding himself, are British invalids who came to Lisbon as a last hope—for in the eighteenth century it was the fashionable wintering-place for consumptives. Among the newer tombstones I noticed that of Huldine Beamish, authoress of *The Hills of Alentejo* and of the only English book on Portuguese tauromachy. That of Henry Fielding, an orotund white structure raised by subscription long after he was laid to rest, is somewhat unpleasing.

We found it out of character among the nostalgic melancholia of the sepulchres of forgotten clergymen, retired army officers and exiled rentiers.

By now it was lunch time. We took a taxi to the Francfort-Rossio, and after a wash and brush-up strolled towards Alfama. I wanted to walk to the great church of Madre de Deus, which I knew was near the waterfront, somewhere to the east of the Flea Market. As we began to climb towards Alfama I noticed, on the right-hand side of the street leading up to the Sé Catedral, an old-fashioned taberna-restaurante that called itself 'Estrêla da Sé'. Just beside the bar was a little wainscotted, partitioned-off dining room containing three or four tables. At one of these we were served grilled salmonete (red mullet) with a bottle of vinho branco. Behind this dining room, as we discovered before we left (while having a bagaço at the bar and chatting up the patrão), were a series of little wooden dining alcoves, each elaborately partitioned off from the other, giving a markedly Edwardian charm to the place. I liked the atmosphere so much that I decided to make it a regular port of call in future.

It was a torpid afternoon. Predictably, we got lost in the further reaches of Alfama; and eventually emerged at the church of S. Vicente near the now deserted Flea Market. But the Madre de Deus, I knew, was a good deal to the east of this. On we went, climbing cobbled streets that gave us delusive glimpses of the river, of church-domes that we thought must be our quarry, but to which the streets—either by doubling back on themselves to return to Alfama, or by terminating in some cul-de-sac—never seemed to lead. Finally we found ourselves in an area occupied by recently built tower-block flats. It was a desolate and depressing quarter, as all such engineered pigeonholings of communities seem to be, whether in London, Leeds or Lisbon. There were no shops, and no pubs—perhaps the planners were anxious not to spoil the orderly look of the place. We were now on the brow of one of the many hills we had climbed. Below us we could see a little valley through which an unmetalled dirt road wound between what seemed a dense congregation of vegetable-allotments—a rookery of tumble-down wooden shacks surrounded by cabbages, maize, vines, creepers and roses, divided one from the other by rickety fencing. As we descended the hill we realised that we had stumbled on one of the shanty-towns of Lisbon.

Reaching the dirt road we found it disgraceful with rubbish. Old pots and pans, tins, tyres and refuse lay anywhere, just as they had been dropped or discarded. I had my camera with me, and could not resist taking a snap of one of the shacks, though I felt it rather an intrusion on the poverty of the inhabitants. To my astonishment this action caused great and pleasurable excitement. Heads popped out of windows. An old lady with a brilliant gold tooth ran down one of the scruffy little alleys and seized my hand. She began talking rapidly in Portuguese, far too fast for us to follow; we wished we had Swift with us to interpret. Still holding my hand she led or dragged me up the hill to a miserable little shed about ten feet high made of warped planks roughly nailed together. By now we were in the centre of a group of people—men, women and children. A pleasant young man who spoke some English introduced himself to us. He told us that the old lady wanted us to photograph her 'house'.

The old lady had flung the door open and stood poised at the entrance. There was very little light to see in, but what furniture we could glimpse seemed made—and made badly—out of old packing-cases. As I took the photograph I could not help thinking of the coachload of Russian trade delegates visiting Cumberland who had asked their guide and interpreter 'Are these the workers' hovels?' as they passed a collection of hen-houses. This shack would hardly pass as a hen-house, even in Russia. But the owner regarded it not with indignation or shame but with evident and cheerful pride. It was hers.

This hut, be it said, was the smallest and crudest of the dwellings. The others were much larger; some quite complex and elaborate, with corrugated iron roofs and improvised verandahs. Their tin roofs and rickety home-made balconies were rescued from the squalor by luxuriance of the vines and creepers that grew over them, by the giant cabbages and sunflowers trained against their tin or wooden walls. This ensemble of makeshift cottages had more character, humanity, life, warmth, visual charm and *appearance* (I only say appearance) of comfort and livability, than the geometric desert of towerblock flats on the hill above.

Our young man now insisted on our coming to see his own house. It stood about twenty yards from the old lady's hovel, a little lower down the hill. The building was a corrugated iron shanty running to three small rooms. We entered through a tiny kitchen, spotlessly clean, though it looked as if a meal had just been eaten—plates and glasses had not yet been cleared away. There seemed no shortage of food or drink in this house. Indeed, none of the people we had seen looked anything like underfed, and except for our old lady, all were well and, in some cases, even smartly dressed.

The next room rather took our breath away. It was the sitting room, decorated in true Portuguese style with frills and furbelows and bobbins and bibbins in every nook and corner. The note was of Victorian over-ornamentation. Tiny shelves supported sprays of plastic flowers and little china bibelots—all very feminine, crowded and pretty. The young man's wife had now joined us. Like the old lady, if with far more reason, she was obviously very proud of her home. There was no lack of furniture or carpeting. She lifted a curtain screening an alcove at the end of the room and invited us to peep into the bedroom. It was small, neat and elaborately cosy, though mostly occupied by a large double bed covered by one of the usual brightly-coloured handwoven Portuguese rugs. I noticed a couple of small nail-holes in the tin roof and wondered why they had not bothered to stop them (a couple of dabs of cement could have fixed the trouble). We could see oil lamps and stoves, but no sign of electricity or running water.

But quite apart from the lack of these amenities the great drawback of the little dwelling, though not evident at the time, must have been the summer heat. I have lived in corrugated iron houses in Africa and remember too well the unendurable oven atmosphere the sun generates as it beats against the ribbed sheets of tin—which can even raise a blister if you put your hand on them. Pip asked the young man if he would like to live in one of the new blocks of flats we could see on the hill above us. He threw out his arms: 'Not possible! No money!'

When we came out of the house I was asked to take a photograph of the young man and his wife outside their front door, a group photograph of the neighbours, and yet another snap of another of the shanties till I ran out of film. We exchanged addresses, and I promised to send prints of the photographs when they were developed. Which I did, on my return to England.

While in Portugal, I made many enquiries about these shanty-towns (they are not peculiar to Portugal; similar ones may be seen outside Rome and Athens). From what I could gather, it seems that these settlements are permanent and likely to remain so. Nearly always they are to be found on the outskirts of some big new housing-estate. The reasons have to do with Portuguese law. It lays down that no one with a roof over his head may be evicted. Thus all these shanties were originally run up overnight and *sub rosa*: once the roof is fixed, the inmates cannot be turned out. Moreover, they automatically go on the housing-list of the nearest local authority: that is why the shanties are built near the new estates. And when the local authority eventually finds a proper house or flat for one family, they pass the word to friends or relations, who move in at the back as the original inmates are leaving by the front. As the new inhabitants are *ipso facto* immune from eviction, the shanty cannot be pulled down. But as these hovels are illegal they do not officially exist in the eyes of the municipality: for which reason no water, electricity, or even sewage or street-cleaning services are afforded. On the other hand there is neither rent nor rates to pay. This situation will, of course, continue till enough houses are built to shelter everyone; which is as much as to say, the Greek Kalends.

Since my return Swift has written to me: 'According to a note in Francisco Keil Amaral's *Lisboa: Uma Cidade Em*

Transformação (Publicações Europa-America, 1969) there are 50,000 people living in these "barracas" (the figure for Rome, for comparison, is 72,000). There have been a number of full-scale newspaper enquiries—recently the *O Século* newspaper ran a series with big photos. The municipal authorities of Lisbon have announced a plan to rehouse the people of the "barracas" by 1977. A typically optimistic plan. According to Amaral, the provincial in search of work in the capital provides the main source of tenants. Once they are established in the city they move on to different forms of slums or to council houses and flats, but their place is taken by others.'

It was now latish in the afternoon. Pip and I decided to give up our quest for the Madre de Deus. We hailed a taxi (another paradox of the shanty-town: plenty of taxis were to be seen plying in its rubbish-strewn dirt road). 'Praça do Comércio,' I told the driver. Four or five minutes' spinning along the riverbank road took us back to Black Horse Square, where the evening rush was just beginning.

'Let's go over to Cacilhas and perhaps have supper there,' I suggested. Pip was agreeable. Cacilhas is the town, or large village, on the other side of the Tagus, where the coach and bus terminus for the south is to be found and to which the car ferry operates. There are also, especially in the rush hour, very frequent ferries for foot passengers (about as frequent as tube trains from Tottenham Court Road to Barnet, if this encourages anybody). One of the inexpensive pleasures of Lisbon is crossing the Tagus on one of these ferries—they are huge old tubs, nearly as big as one of the Newhaven–Dieppe packets. The fare is only a penny or two.

This evening the crossing was magnificent. A huge black thundercloud to the south, brooding over Alentejo, lidded half the sky and helped a gaudy rainbow spanning the wide reach of the Tagus to display to advantage its iridescent ordering of the spectrum. Against that dark backdrop, a couple of transocean liners glittered in the sun's last rays. Which illumined, too, the wide arcaded square retreating from the stern of our ferry: Dom José's equestrian figure on his tall pediment, framed by repeated colonnades and the great triumphal arch;

the hills rising behind with their white houses, palaces, domes and battlements.

Cacilhas, however, has a seedy atmosphere—bus termini, unlike railway stations, seldom raise the spirits. Though there were some active little pubs and much bustle. Blue smoke from roasting chestnuts rose to the sky from the vendors' charcoal braziers of earthenware; old women stood at corners with baskets of boiled crabs. A row of fairly garish restaurants, most of them specialising in seafood, stood on the waterfront. We were tempted to have supper in one of them—you can sit in the upstairs rooms and watch the night falling over the Tagus, and the lights of Lisbon picking up. But it was really too early; and there is nothing more depressing than an empty restaurant. These would fill up later in the evening. A ferry just about to return across the river decided us. We ran for it, did what almost qualified for a pierhead jump, and returned to the city for an early night.

TUESDAY

Sintra is only twenty-six kilometres from Lisbon, but in that radius are dozens of objectives for the sightseer who wants to get outside the metropolis and into the country: fishing-villages, palaces, gardens, churches, castles, aqueducts, monasteries, forests; even a submarine Roman city. Almost all can be reached by bus or train, one way or another; but we had the advantage of a car.

The Swifts proposed an expedition to Máfra, the immense palace built by the spendthrift Dom João V in fulfilment of his vow when his queen bore him an heir. (This queen was the Dona Maria who built the Estrêla church in fulfilment of what you might call a side-vow; the birth of this child, who became the Dom José whose effigy dominates Black Horse Square, must have been a bonanza to the Portuguese building industry.) We would go by way of Queluz, another royal palace, built (or at least begun) in 1758 by Dom José's younger brother Pedro, who—having somewhat incestuously married his late brother's daughter—became Regent of Portugal when she went mad.

Queluz lies more or less on the north-western periphery of Lisbon, being fifteen kilometres out on the road to Sintra. When we saw it, the palace looked somewhat scruffy and forlorn. It stands just outside a drab little township of the same name. A new and obviously important road or carriageway running past the palace was under construction, with all the circumambient desolation and devastation these undertakings seem to generate. The pink and white façade of the long low palace was surprisingly reticent; I had expected something considerably more rococo.

In 1934 a fire seriously damaged the interior, but it has been so carefully restored that no trace of this calamity is to be seen. One of the rooms that the fire did not reach we admired very much. Its walls were decorated with azulejo chinoiserie, light blue and yellow tiles depicting Chinese figures, Negroes, and palm trees. The throne-room, or Sala dos Embaixadores, struck a note of elegant splendour—its great windows let in plenty of light, and mirrors were everywhere. Octagonal pillars panelled with looking-glass; pilasters on the walls were mirrors, surmounted by painted capitals; even doors constructed to look like windows, but with mirrors instead of panes of glass.

However, the real attraction of Queluz is less the palace than its famous gardens. One of them was laid out by the French sculptor J. B. Roubillon in 1762. Its baroque fountains and rococo leaden statues standing among arabesque topiaries form an architectural extension of the palace. From the garden side its façade is certainly not reticent; the palace roof is sentinelled by flowingly carved decorative effigies and figures. Below Roubillon's 'Neptune Gardens'—so called after the rumbustious fountain in front of the palace, presided over by the bearded sea-god with his trident, who manages to look remarkably like Allen Ginsberg—is a geometrical creation of hedged alleys and ponds, said to be the contribution of Marshal Junot. He stayed here during the French occupation—the man certainly had an eye for a good billet. Beyond these formal alleys we were delighted by a strange kind of artificial waterfall topped by a gigantic and grotesque sculptured head. Water trickled down by half-eroded carvings and the lush growth of a dozen varieties of rock and water plants that had contrived to become integral with the sculpture.

But the charm of these gardens is threatened—or at least the perfection of their eighteenth-century image is being tarnished—by modern blocks of flats that have been built on the skyline of the hill behind the palace, and whose cubic heads are now to be seen peering over the elegant, placid frivolities of Queluz.

Before we left we visited the old kitchens, which occupy a separate building. They have been turned into a sumptuous restaurant. A giant chimney-piece occupies the centre of what is now a dining room, and there is another of those vast marble tables that seem to have been standard culinary furniture in the kitchens of all self-respecting Portuguese palaces. A lunch here, we were told, would come to 100 escudos a head. But we did not feel like facing too heavy a meal while we had yet to get to Máfra (for the menu promised a repast as sumptuous as the restaurant itself).

Instead, we drove on to Sintra and settled for a simpler but still delicious meal in the rustic surroundings of the Casinha de S. Pedro, where we had lunched on the day of the fair. This time we were treated to braised rabbit and a remarkably good cheese called ílhas.

Sintra is twenty-six kilometres from Lisbon; Máfra is almost as far again to the north-east of Sintra. Our road took us through a countryside of low, rolling, bosky hills. We passed several marble quarries. Marble is found all over Portugal, and is one of its important exports—we were told that some of it is even exported to Italy, from whence it is re-exported as Italian marble!

The Palace of Máfra is said to have 4000 doors, 5200 windows, to contain 866 rooms, to measure about a fifth of a mile from north to south and a sixth of a mile from east to west, to have taken 50,000 workmen thirteen years to build, and to have cost more than £4,000,000. None of these statistics is reliable; almost every guide-book one consults gives a different figure for each item. But all agree in leaving you with the impression that Máfra is large, lavish and lunatic. The architect, Frederico Ludwig, was a German, and his orders were to go one better than Philip of Spain's Escorial. It is a palace, church and monastery in one—the king's apartments lie to one side, the queen's to the other, with the church in the middle and the monastery at the back. According to the terms of Dom João's vow, it was built as a convent for the poorest friary of the kingdom. This turned out to be a wooden building that sheltered a small settlement of Franciscan monks in what was then the village of Máfra. One wonders what the brothers may have felt about their new home when it was finally completed in 1730.

In a dust-hung café in the dust-hung township we sat contemplating that solid block of mirror-balanced masonry—twin cupolas at either end, pediment in the middle, and the great single dome of the church mathematically at centre. The regiment of 5200 windows stood to attention.

'It just doesn't add up,' remarked Swift after a while.

We drank brandy and water and contemplated the monster, while behind us three or four locals played, inexpertly, some form of Portuguese billiards on a baize-covered table.

'Somehow it doesn't *look* big,' I said, thinking of all those statistics.

Eventually Swift and I rose to our feet to do our duty and inspect the prodigy. The ladies elected to stay in the café and wait for us. We entered the building by the great central doors. A guide showed us straight into the church. The cathedral-like interior, if a trifle chill, was certainly impressive, with a very grand inlaid floor of coloured marbles from all over Portugal. Swift particularly admired the grotesquely heavy bronze lamps that hung in a row over the altar, while I was more taken with the decorated interior of the dome, and the bas-relief dove high up on the ceiling of the lantern cupola. When we had finished admiring these matters our guide escorted us to the base of an immense marble staircase and, after accepting a tip, handed us over to another, with whom we made the ascent to the first floor. Here we found ourselves in a gallery running the entire length of the building. I found myself muttering, 'Is there a bicycle in the house?'

The rooms were endless; after every dozen or so salons we would be handed over to a fresh guide—which meant, naturally, a fresh tip. By the time we had done with the palace, or the palace had done with us, we were completely cleaned out of loose change. But the rooms were not without interest; it was just that there were too many of them. We were surprised by some unexpectedly good royal portraits and fine paintings. (Portuguese sculpture of whatever date is almost always good or at least interesting, but this certainly cannot be claimed of most Portuguese painting.)

One of the rooms contains perhaps the most grotesque furniture in Europe—it is a dining room, spiky with antlers and trophies of the hunt. The chairs are made of antlers and upholstered with the hides of stags. The final monstrosity is an umbrella-stand fashioned from antlers, with a stuffed boar's head as centre-piece. Another room has a charming kitsch fantasy in the form of a guitar shaped like a boat with mast and sail. We saw the monks' cells, each furnished with a wooden slatted bed (I remembered sleeping on exactly the same kind of bed for five weeks in an old furnished house at Carvoeiro, when I first came to Portugal), and finally the great marble library. This library, a narrow room of prodigious length, is in its way quite incomparable; as fine, though nothing like as grandiloquent, as Dom João V's more famous library at the university of Coimbra. We were only allowed to look at it from the doorway; entry was prohibited.

As a consolation the guide offered to take us up one of the twin church towers and show us the famous carillons that were brought from Antwerp in 1730. But—though perhaps we had seen no more than half the palace—we were already worn out with our long walk; unanimously we refused to have anything to do with the 114 bells made of 45 tons of bronze.

These giant carillons still work and are sometimes played on Sunday afternoons in summer, when they can be heard for miles. Reading the diary of William Beckford, who visited Máfra in 1787, I find that he too refused to inspect the bells, though he got as far as the roof: 'A fresh balsamic air wafted from the orchards of citron and orange fanned me as I rested a moment on the steps of the dome, and tempered the warmth of the glowing ether. But I was soon driven from this peaceful situation by a confounded jingle of the bells; then followed a most complicated sonata, banged off on the chimes by a great proficient. The Marquis [Beckford's guide] would have me approach to examine the mechanism, and I was half stunned. I know nothing of chimes and clocks and am quite at loss for amusement in a belfry.'

From Máfra we turned west to the coast, to the little fishing port of Ericeira—famous for its lobsters—from which the last king of Portugal embarked for Gibraltar after the revolution of 1910 to begin his exile. His last night in Portugal had been spent in the chilling splendours of the palace of Máfra. Here the beach, like all the beaches of this coast, is splendid. Altogether it is a pleasant little resort, with hotels and pensoes. We had a good view of the sea from the cliffs before again turning inland (for the road does not follow the coast) on our way to Praia das Maçãs. Every now and then we caught glimpses of the palace of Máfra, isolated on its plain, and in the distance contriving to look far huger than it does when seen from close to.

Praia das Maçãs is not far from Sintra. Soon we were in sight of its wooded, boulder-strewn peak crowned by the castle of Pena, while to our right lay the sea and the dramatic Cabo da Roca with its white lighthouse. Set on cliffs above a magnificent sandy beach, with huge sad combers thundering in, the little village of Praia das Maçãs is very taking. But these are dangerous waters for swimming, at least for the foolhardy, because of the currents. The beaches from Cabo da Roca to Estoril are the most famous in Portugal; to me they looked fabulous. We drove along their fringes as the evening came on. The sun became an enormous red disc and began to sink into the sea—not to sink so much as to disappear into a slot above the horizon. Nothing was left but a one-coloured sky and sea and sands of pearl, sadness and solitude. Though so near to Lisbon, these parts are strangely unspoiled. There seem to be hardly any hotels or villas or bungalows—none of the shoddy junk that testifies to the urban appreciation of a seascape.

At Cascais we stopped near the harbour to make a telephone call. Sophisticated as Cascais is, its original character of a fishing village still manages to survive, though faintly. Like a ghost a fisherman in rough jersey and jeans walked past our parked car carrying two long silver fish—they were espadas— quite oblivious to the glittering neon of the flash cafés and bars, the Mercedes-Benzes sweeping by.

WEDNESDAY

One of the pleasures of Portugal, and therefore of its capital city, is gardens. Either the climate of Portugal is such that almost anything will grow there, from cacti and tropical trees to most plants of the more temperate north, or the Portuguese are such good gardeners that they can grow anything. Probably it's a bit of both. But if every race has a peculiar genius for one of the arts—the Germans for music, the French for painting, the English for poetry—then the Portuguese forte is for the plastic or three-dimensional, which includes pottery, sculpture and architecture, and also the making of gardens. Nor are gardens a necessarily ephemeral form of art—one might instance the Jacobean topiary garden of Levens Hall in Westmorland, which was laid out in the seventeenth century and retains its original form to this day.

But apart from the purely decorative, there are two gardens in Lisbon that we visit every time we come to the city. One is the Botanic Gardens, perhaps the finest of their kind in Europe. They lie on the slope of a hill to the north of the Avenida da Liberdade. If you approach from this, the lower entrance, you have the advantage of the grand introduction afforded by the magnificent and famous avenue of palms—almost every one a different species—that marches up the verdurous hillside. This avenue is now almost a hundred years old—the gardens themselves date from 1873. It would seem that there is scarcely a species of tree in America, Africa or Australia that is not represented—for the Jardim Bôtanico of Lisbon is more of an arboretum than a garden. One seldom sees anyone in the dense shady paths and alleys, where you brush against conifers, plantains and arborescent dicotyledons (trees to the non-botanist). There is a placid melancholy, a dilapidated peace, emanating from these walks and groves. At the heart of it is the dead water of an embowered pool crossed by a rusting, rotting iron bridge, dark water reflecting the darker leaves overhead; a quiet, secret, and soothing place.

The other garden is not far away. It is a corner of the Edward VII Park at the top of the Avenida da Liberdade, where you find the really posh modern hotels. This garden is called the Estufa Fria—'cold hothouse', according to the translation given by one of the picture postcards they sell outside. It is, in fact, an enormous conservatory comprising several acres. Instead of being protected by glass, the trees, ferns and flowers that grow therein are covered by a vast trellis of thin wooden slats painted green. This is to protect the plants from the direct rays of the sun and to reproduce the shade and coolness of a tropical forest. Inside the Estufa Fria, stone-paved paths lead you through ferns and feathery leaves to pools and fountains embellished with stone nymphs. You cross the water on stepping-stones made of natural rock, and the path takes you up to terraces where you can look down on the greenery, which now enfolds you on every side, above as well as below. One might be drifting, in some dream, along the floor of an immense sea

> Annihilating all that's made
> To a green Thought in a green Shade.

Coming to Lisbon: Santa Catarina and District

PATRICK SWIFT

Oonagh was going to have a baby. It was heavy September in the Algarve. Tiresome encroachments on our 'long planned half solitude' at our home there had been increasing. But at last the long summer ended. Our daughter Katty departed for school in Sussex. Mr. Jones opened up his English School of the Algarve for the new term. Our younger daughter Julie was to board there. Lisbon beckoned us, rather as Moscow beckons the characters of a Chekov play.

There was the baby and there was the book. David Wright, after an innumerable series of obstacles, found he could manage to be in Lisbon with Pip in October. We closed up the house with some relief and set out for the city.

For the first time we were to abandon our old favourite, the Francfort Hotel in the Rossio. I felt a certain pang about this. Oonagh however, vastly pregnant, was not prepared to walk half a mile to the lavatory. Our neighbours the MacIntoshes had recommended the Santa Catarina, a small pensão located in the old part of the town, hard by the praça of Alto de Santa Catarina. For myself, the name Catarina already prejudiced me in its favour. Other reasons combined to make us choose it. And a good choice it proved.

It also proved to be a difficult place to find. We drove into Lisbon late in the evening. Dusk was falling over the city like a mist. Lights were coming on. I had worked out that our route lay up the Rua do Alecrim, a street that runs from the river sharply uphill to the Chiado.

River from Alecrim

We entered Lisbon via the bridge; as always a surprising experience. Like a vision, exotic and mysterious, the city rises along the riverside on both sides. Monsanto crowns it, and one can see out towards the sea. Below, a huddle of huge liners cram the quays. What looks like a maze of sweeping motorways as one comes off the bridge, reminding one of a scene from a Hollywood gangster movie, turns out to be a logical and orderly arrangement once one has summoned the nerve to follow the signs. We had no trouble getting as far as the riverside. To get from there to the Alto de Santa Catarina turned out to be more difficult.

It was the first time I had attempted to drive directly to the door of our destination in Lisbon: our usual plan was, like cowards, to park the car and take a taxi from some suitable suburb—the airport, for instance. This will only make sense to the reader who has driven about Lisbon either in a car or by taxi. It is, to say the least, an exhilarating experience. No quarter is given, and the weak go to the wall. Everyone drives as if there was a demon chasing him, and in a sense there is—the motorist behind. Pedestrians hop and skip through the mêlée with cheerful agility. A friend who has lived and driven all his life in Lisbon has described driving there as a good-humoured game of chance, played without rules, between the motorist and the pedestrian. Things have, I think, improved in the years since the use of the motor horn was banned. Previously, the taxi men would blast the klaxon and roar round blind corners in narrow streets, relying entirely on the hearing of anyone who happened to be in the way.

When, finally, we did reach the pensão in Santa Catarina, we found every inch of space full of parked cars. All our efforts had been in vain. We drove off to a quiet part of the town, parked the car and took a taxi. I am able to give the visitor who arrives by car in the evening a piece of categoric advice: park at the first quiet square and take a taxi.

The pensão is tiny. It has about it an immediately sympathetic air. At the desk a small stout man—red faced and smooth and clean—was expecting us, our friends having booked us in. This was Mr. Menelli. A man, as I was soon to discover, who

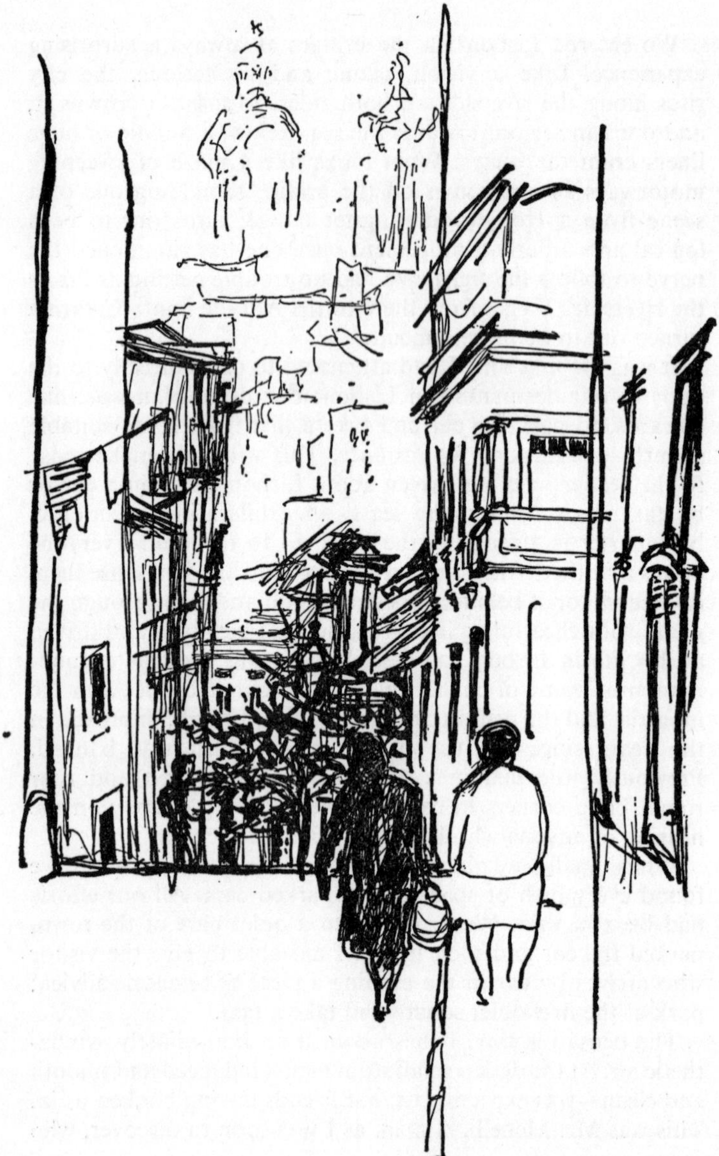

looked upon the world at large with something little short of terror. He sat behind his miniscule reception desk and pondered the risks that lay in the world beyond the glass doors, He rarely ventured into it.

This little street, the Rua Dr. Luis de Almeida e Albuquerque, turned out to be a haven of rest and an endless pleasure. It looked straight down a narrow defile of picturesque houses. These framed a theatrical view of Estrêla. The Lapa district rose up before us, tier upon tier, in shades of pale green, pink, white and yellow—the whole conglomerate crowned by the flamboyant structure of the domed and turreted basilica. In the changing light from morning to night, this view assumed every possible gradation of dramatic effect: at times clean and clear like a Canaletto painting, at times a misty romantic haze that evoked the later Turner. It was never the same and it never palled. It was a pleasure to walk the few yards down the street every time we came home to the little pensão and to Mr. Menelli, who seemed to await with some anxiety our escape once more from the awful world that lay beyond the Rua Dr. Luis de Almeida e Albuquerque.

Our room was excellent. I had a small table where I could do some drawing. If we looked out of the window, it was into the tree-shaded quadrangle of an old eighteenth-century building which houses the newspaper *Jornal do Comércio*'s editorial office. The oldest newspaper in Lisbon. A paper with an interesting literary association as it had formed a connection between Teófilo Braga and Eça de Quéiroz (I was deep in my readings of Eça at this time). When Braga first met Eça at Coimbra he found that the future novelist had been collecting his short stories then appearing in the *Jornal do Comércio*. The great trees hanging in heavy profusion of greenery over the cobbled courtyard, the ponderous wrought-iron gates, reminded one of nothing so much as a school or place of learning. The comings and goings of those who entered and departed, most of whom looked more like dons than journalists, enhanced this impression. Hard to think such a vulgar thing as a newspaper was produced in so venerable an institution.

As we discovered when we took a walk about the district

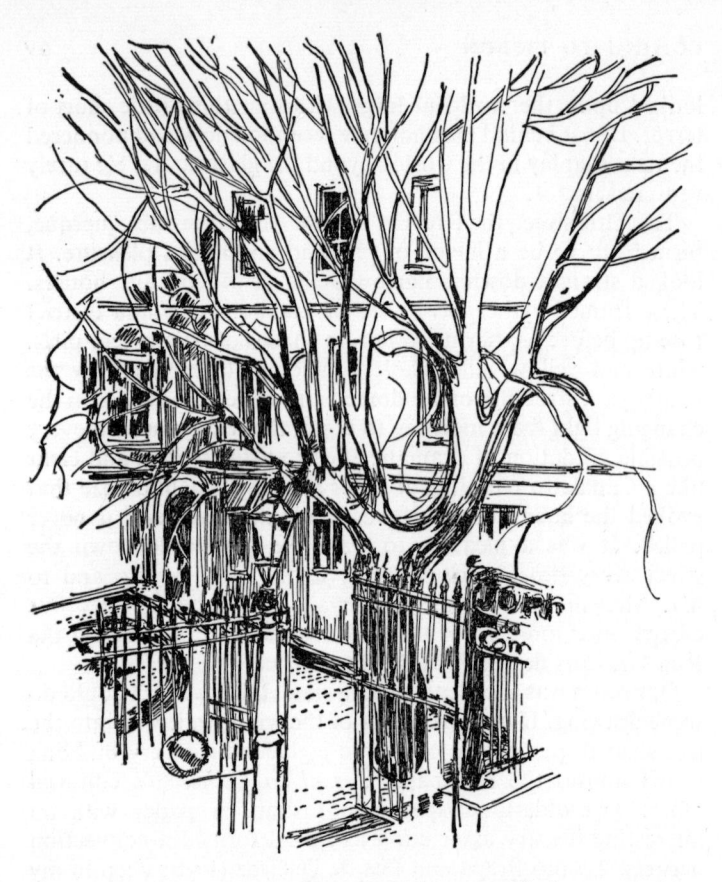

next morning, this quiet almost countrified atmosphere is the chief characteristic of this endearing quarter. The square itself, the Alto da Santa Catarina, is round the corner from the pensão. It tends to be lined with parked cars at all hours. But somehow this does not disturb the quiet and the silence of the tiny park. There is a statue of Adamastor with lines from Camões inscribed on the stone, an impressive carving in limestone, but the effect is spoiled by a tiny bronze figure intended to emphasise the scale of the giant. It makes it look a little silly, diminishing rather than enhancing the sense of the gigantesque. There is an absorbing view of the river over a jumble of rooftops. This square was always a place where the people came to watch the shipping. Known earlier as Monte do Pico, or Belveder, it had at one time a curious role to play as an observatory; for astronomers, observers of the moon, came here for this purpose. There still survives in common use the popular lisboeta saying: 'ver navios do alto de Santa Catarina'—'seeing ships from the heights of Santa Catarina', meaning daydreaming and wishful thinking, or a Mr. Micawberish attitude to life. It was obviously an ideal place from which those awaiting the return of the caravels could watch the river.

The district has a most unusual configuration. From the square on all sides the streets descend steeply. It forms a small platform jutting out from the Calçada do Combro via the streets Travessa da Santa Catarina and Marechal Saldanha.

Below the Rua Marechal Saldanha one looks directly down into the Rua da Bica de Duarte Belo (commonly called simply Rua da Bica). This is a gorge—an unnatural fissure running down to the river. It came into being as a result of a cataclysm in the sixteenth century. On the 21st of July in 1597, at eleven o'clock at night, the ground opened and a large part of the hilltop was swallowed up, taking three streets with it. One hundred and ten people were killed.

Most of the houses that now crowd this area, built steeply down the sides of the hill, are from the time immediately after this disaster. They are all humble houses, and almost all date from the beginning of the seventeenth century. It makes it one of the most fascinating bits of ancient Lisbon—full of life, a maze of small pubs and restaurants and tiny shops. As we settled down in the pensão, we came to know the area like a village.

The only buildings here that do not belong to older Lisbon are the great nineteenth-century houses that face the square itself. They have French-provincial façades, shuttered and sad, and one has a superb overgrown garden. There are two fin-de-siècle lamps at the gates—ecstatic ladies holding aloft ornate lanterns—which add considerably to the charm of the place.

It was on a sleepy autumn morning that I first walked about

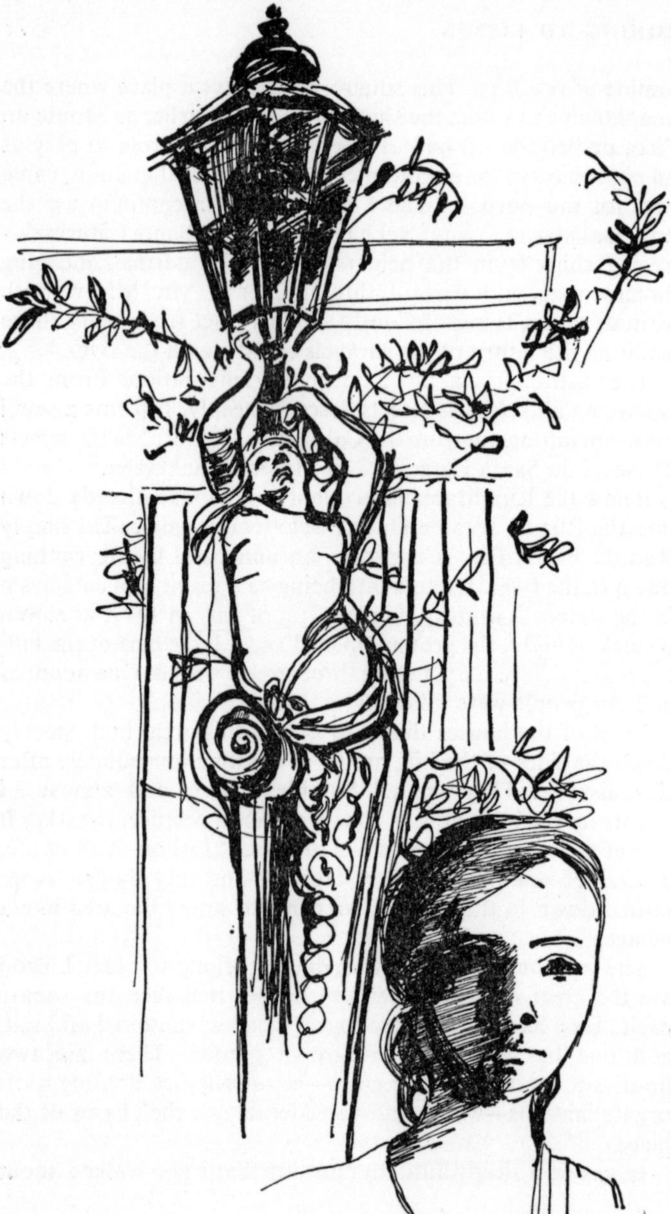

the little park and sat among the elderly peaceful folk who were taking the morning sun. Some children played about the statue of Adamastor. A village-like restful place. This is how I always think of Alto de Santa Catarina.

I had that morning phoned the Francfort Hotel seeking our friends David and Pip. Typically they had vanished into the thick of the city at an early hour and had not been seen since. They had however left a note. There would be no seeing them until lunch time at the earliest.

While Oonagh rested at the pensão I went to look at the church of Santa Catarina, curious to see the building which gives its name to the district. It had once been a convent—indeed, one of the great convents of Lisbon.

I made my way down the steps of the Travessa de Santa Catarina and into the Calçada de Combro. The busy street, the rattling trams and the dangerous taxis make it all but impossible to see the enormous flat façade of the church. It is known as the church of the Paulistas; what we see today is the post-earthquake reconstruction. The original foundation goes back to the mid-seventeenth century when it was built for the hermits of Setta de Ossa. As it is now, it is one of the more impressive of Lisbon's churches. If it were set off as well, say, as is S. Vicente, it would be seen to be beautiful. The only place with anything like an adequate view of the façade is the slope of the Travessa Condessa do Rio before one descends on to the street. It has equilibrium and majesty in its proportions that do not seem to belong to so late a date as that of the post earthquake reconstructions.

Inside is worth visiting for anyone who likes ornate baroque carving. It is enormously rich in this art form: a line of altars on each side of the nave presents a prodigious amount of intricate workmanship. The two most important items to see are the organ and the high altar; the choir and the organ, in particular, must come very high as works of art in their genre.

For the more curious there is another reason for looking into Santa Catarina. It contains a considerable amount of painting by two of Portugal's better known public or official eighteenth-century painters: Viera Lusitano, whose real name was Matos, and Bento Coelho da Silveira. Faded Italianate painting that is not without its quality.

But more interesting perhaps for the modern taste (not many of us, I imagine, are prepared to look for the charm in Portuguese-Italianate eighteenth-century church painting) are the azulejos in the remarkable vaulted ante-chamber to the left of the main entrance of the church proper. This is a vaulted room with the lower parts of the walls panelled with azulejos, all of the blue eighteenth-century Lisbon type. The work is so fresh and the quality of the tiles so sensitive that this is a place to linger. It is run-down, the walls above the tile panels peeling. There was once painting on the ceiling. In one corner, on this autumn morning when I wandered in, there were some dozen old ladies receiving soup from some sort of soup kitchen. Completely out of our times, it created a nineteenth-century atmosphere: each of the old ladies was dressed in a long-skirted costume, with cloak or fur collar, and wore a large hat. There was something very gentle, perhaps genteel, about the scene.

Although at ground level occupied by shops, cafés and little restaurants, the buildings round here are largely composed of great houses and palaces. Looking up, one can see many fine stone balconies, many large elegant windows. Once in a while I wandered into some of these old hallways, one-time entrances to palaces; here it is possible to find some remarkable azulejos. Now dingy business places, they still contain the splendid tile panels and carved stonework of their days of glory.

Santa Catarina is very much a self-contained district, very much a 'bairro'. We found we had every convenience at hand in the area. The regionalism of Portugal as a whole seems to be reflected in the city. Areas tend to have a character—can one even say a culture?—of their own. They are self-sufficient. On our corner there was a greengrocer, the smallest greengrocer in the world; one tiny room crammed with fruit and vegetables. Our local taberna was a few yards further down the Rua Marechal Saldanha. The telly was available every evening. The proper grocer was next door. At the end of the street stood our café, our respectable café with nice chairs and tables and cakes and snacks available at all hours. From here, we would bring back to the pensão—with Mr. Menelli's blessing —a bottle of Dão wine and some fresh sandwiches. Or if we felt like a more ambitious dinner, a grilled chicken hot from the charcoal in our local restaurant 'The Prince of Calhariz'.

Another element in our day's pleasure at the Rua Dr. Luis de Almeida e Albuquerque was the morning arrival in the street of the criers of various goods for sale. The street cries of Lisbon are worthy of record; still very much alive and still performing a practical function, they also have a poetic dimension, a musical and emotional shape. This pregão das ruas is most effective in the old narrow streets. After a few days at the Rua Dr. Luis de Almeida e Albuquerque we began to make out the words, at first utterly incomprehensible. Not only did the long drawn out musical phrase tell us that, for example, there were carapau (little fish like sardines) for sale but it also added that they were fat and would be excellent for grilling. Even the newspaper vendor, usually the first to arrive in the street, called out his presence in this musical way. That the system works can be observed any day in the old quarters: the seller pauses now and again as he or she makes the slow length of the street. A head appears from a window high up. A basket will be lowered on a long string. The fish, or whatever it may be, will be put into the basket and the cash lowered when the goods have been retrieved by the housewife. I was glad to hear the street criers in modern Lisbon too, though there they are less in evidence and the acoustics of the old streets are missing. The rhythm of the cries can be exotic. Some sound as if part of a complex Eastern song. The voices are frequently out of the ordinary. Not all are mere raucous calling; we heard, from time to time, musical notes of great beauty.

Many of these street criers are 'varinas'. The varina of Lisbon is a famous character—a figure much admired by the foreign visitor in the nineteenth century. She is the fish-seller of the streets. Of fine upright carriage (undoubtedly due to the fact that she carries her basket of fish on her head), she traditionally

Varinas

wore long brightly coloured skirts. This costume is slightly modified now. No longer the sweeping skirt down to the heels. But she is still a striking character and has an arrogant graceful way of striding through the streets. And the scarf, and the basket of fish, with its brilliant yellow oilcloth, make a pretty exotic get-up for modern times.

There is a lot to be said for staying in a small quarter. One has the sensation of taking part in the life of the city. We found this at Pensão Santa Catarina. And the people at the pensão itself quickly became friends. There were, however, certain matters of protocol and behaviour. Mr. Menelli was very circumlocutory when it came to such things. In order to explain that I could not pay him with a cheque on an Algarve bank he left me an elaborate written explanation about his partners with many apologies. He lived in fear that I would make international phone calls from the first-floor phone without his knowing: he had once, he explained at length, had a Swede who kept phoning Stockholm—a fact that did not come to light until the bill was delivered a month after the Swede had left.

When I returned to the pensão after my first exploration of our bairro I found Oonagh settled in. She loved the place. It was lunch time and we sallied forth, walking the distance from Praça Camões down to the Rossio to look for the Wrights. We found them ensconced in an old haunt of ours, the Irmãos Unidos, under the large portrait of Fernando Pessoa.

Lima de Freitas

Visit to a Hidden Lisbon

PATRICK SWIFT

It was a brilliant spring morning in 1968. My window in the Francfort Hotel looked out on to the Rossio. The early bustle of the day was beginning to die down. Blinding sun glinted on the endless stream of cars as they whirled about the square. An island of colour, the flower sellers' stalls clustered about the white sun-spray of the fountain made an exotic centre-piece for a theatrical scene. I was in Lisbon to meet Lima de Freitas.

Lima is a painter whose general outlook on the gloomy situation of the art of painting in an over-organised art world is close to my own. This alone forms a common bond. He also happens to be the sort of dedicated man that I admire. He has written a book with the superb title *Pintura Incomóda* (Uncomfortable Painting). We both agree that only the highly developed personal vision of a serious mind is worth bothering about. In other words, we both hate fashions.

However, my reason for meeting Lima on this occasion was

VISIT TO A HIDDEN LISBON

not to talk about art—that had never specifically figured as a reason for our meeting. It was something much stranger. Stemming from our basically sympathetic viewpoints, we had embarked on a scheme so foolhardy that, looking back on it, I do not know how we had the temerity ever to start.

This was nothing less than to try to rescue and resuscitate the local potting industry in our part of Algarve. Lima is a neighbour of ours. Like myself, he was living in Algarve on and off long before disagreeable suburban development began to encroach on our village of Carvoeiro. The potters of Lagoa in those far-off days (nearly ten years ago) were many and active, yet at the time I am speaking of only the master potter and his brother were still working. The others had taken a variety of jobs—some as roadworkers, some as farm labourers, one as a watchman in a tourist motel. Lima and I, by some chemistry of mind and circumstance, simultaneously came round to the idea of attempting to do something about this sad decline of a very charming local, not to say ancient, art. To understand the point one would have to have seen the simple beauty of the ordinary household objects that these potters were making as a matter of course up to about 1962; from then on, the decline was fairly disastrous. Plastic came into its own.

The story of what we did and how we set about it is only incidentally relevant here. But when I rang up Lima on this superb spring morning my aim was to visit with him some ceramic experts in Lisbon who were to help in the mad venture.

As usual with Lima, a certain gay energy communicated itself over the phone. 'Let me take you to lunch in a really típico place,' he said. 'Somewhere tourists never go.'

I took a taxi to the Praça Pasteur and there boarded Lima's venerable Skoda. We tootled off by way of the big roundabout at Praça da Espanha passing the elegant Spanish Embassy— one of the more beautiful of Lisbon's old palaces. The restaurant (called 'Coral') turned out to be quite nondescript, tucked away in a tiny square full of parked taxis behind the Zoo. Here we secured a table with a view of the gates of the Zoological Gardens, a view not to be despised: amusing ironwork with very naturalistic looking leaves in metal, the sort of gates a garden deserves.

It was an eating place where professional working people of the area lunched. Nothing fancy, no catering to luxury. But the food was extremely good and the price in inverse ratio to the quality. There was, however, one item of interest. It was a ceramic wall decoration of quite imposing dimensions, technically perfect though of no great merit design-wise. It had this peculiarity: it had been made in the Lisbon gaol. Lima told me that in the gaol the prisoners can learn a trade (and earn a small wage). One of the things they have is a ceramic works. The decoration looked professional, even too commercial. I was reminded of a carpenter I knew in the south who had told me he learned his trade in gaol, though I did not grasp what he meant at the time.

Having lunched, our destination was Viuva Lamego, an old ceramic factory with which Lima had some connections. He frequently undertook commissions for azulejo panels for a number of architects who tried to adapt this traditional Portuguese type of decoration to modern buildings. We made our way westwards from the Travessa das Boas Águas, out by the Estrada Benfica. It is a ragged part of the city where the new and remnants of the old appear to struggle in a jumble of streets, lanes and countryside. Here and there, an old square with a fountain asserts the quiet feeling of another age. Round the corner a seven-storey block shatters it at once.

Lima drove us up a little laneway with the true careless abandon of your Lisbon motorist, into a dingy yard through a wonky gate. At once we were in a different atmosphere; a world apart. This was the factory of hand-painted majolica ware. Through a large hallway, packages were stacked by the grey walls. It seemed dark and dungeon-like after the bright daylight. In a truly Dickensian office, dimly lit and heavy with the afternoon's sleepy air, we sought the manager. In vain.

The whole place was nineteenth-century in atmosphere. We wandered through cavernous places where work seemed to proceed with interminable silent leisureliness. There were ancient-looking bottle kilns where several aproned men carried

VISIT TO A HIDDEN LISBON

in saggers. Others piled them high round the circular interior. At the centre of this conglomerate of different ages and methods, there was an enormous tunnel kiln with azulejos rolling out at one end on a trolley, to be checked and stacked by women. We found our way to a high and kitchen-like room where, at a vast table, a white-robed young man with slow and solemn movements dipped jugs in a great basin of glaze, after which girls took them away on their journey to the painting room. Here, a host of youngish women were painting at long desk-like benches. The designs were all very much in the Portuguese tradition, and even those added recently were strictly in the same style. But the profusion of different motifs and patterns was astonishing, as if nothing was ever discarded, nothing abandoned or betrayed.

One felt the building had been added to throughout its history without any previously existing part being interfered with. We went up and down stairs through narrow, devious, passages and along wooden galleries; passed precariously by large tanks full of liquid clay and beside huge mills where clay was washed through various filters. Finally we arrived at a remote silent studio at the heart of the whole thing. This was the master painter's room. Here we sought the man whom we had come to see—Mestre Rogerio. Not there. It appeared that the master no longer attended every day. Just as we were about to leave, someone informed Lima that a panel of his had emerged from the kiln that very afternoon. We all trooped off to yet another hidden section of this rambling works to a room where, on a huge easel-like structure, the azulejos were being set out.

Lima's panel had come beautifully out of the kiln with that pleasant irregularity here and there that showed that it was truly a hand-made object. One or two of the azulejos had small bubbles and the workers wanted them discarded. The factory had already rung up the architect. While we were still looking at this golden landscape being put together—an adumbration of deep greens merging to form a spreading symbolical tree of life—the architect arrived. Typically Portuguese, he was immaculately neat and slightly dandyish with a trim beard.

He loved the bubbles and the workers were slightly puzzled. We all stood about to gaze into this awesome symbolic world fixed in the vitrified oxides and silicas of the mysterious ceramic.

The architect was a man of charm and culture. He had a new project which he discussed with Lima. It involved a story not without relevance to understanding the Portuguese enigma. A big Swedish industrial combine was building a factory. It was a multi-million project and the architect was hoping that they would have some typical traditional azulejo work incorporated in the scheme. He had however run into a difficulty with his clients. The living quarters for the factory personnel were so designed that the Portuguese workers' section formed part of the same block as the management. The Swedes it appeared were horrified at this. Impossible to have management cheek by jowl with the workers! The architect was equally shocked, declaring that he would not alter his scheme on social segregationist grounds. Besides, in Portugal such distinctions were unheard of. It was a deadlock. So much for the socialist Swedes.

We left the factory of Viuva Lamego to pursue our quarry, the Mestre Rogerio, and headed back towards the Benfica road. There in a newly built-up district of tall blocks of flats, we found our man's house. It was a gem—a tiny frontage with ornamental Edwardian windows, and a decorative porch covered with a fancy tiled roof supported by little Ionic columns. There was a small garden, jasmine tumbling over the fence and a path up to the porch. The striking and incongruous thing was that this little house was tucked directly in between two seven-storey apartment blocks. It had a lost and pathetic air—crushed by the crowded modern world, engulfed in a harsh concrete wilderness.

The master was greying, middle-aged, shy. He took us through a side gate into a garden covered in vines. The walls held innumerable ceramic bits and pieces set into the plaster. Other faience objects cluttered the spaces under the vine trellises. All was neat and orderly in spite of the air of miscellaneously accumulated pieces.

VISIT TO A HIDDEN LISBON

There was a shed at the end of the garden. It was in reality a tiny ceramic factory. A laboratory and a workshop. Modelling, painting, chemistry, engineering—all were carried on in a space not bigger than an average living room. Here were rows of bottles filled with oxides, neatly arranged files on tested glazes, small electric kilns in the making—others firing. It was a world that had grown around one man and his obsession.

He told us how his little house came to be forlornly sandwiched between the tall blocks. The developers had bought the rest of the street, only he would not sell. Nothing they could do, no sum of money they were able to offer, could move the master. His house was his private world, had grown with him and his family over twenty-five years. He was not going to give up his carefully built-up workshop, his azulejo panels, his home improved and extended by his own hands.

This part of the city put me in touch with the real Lisbon. A testament to a personality and a way of life—it made a profound impression. Mestre Rogério is exceptional, I need hardly say. I have seen him on holiday in the south, hunting out a perfect seam of white silica sand here, an excellent clay there, and afterwards sending us an analysis of these materials. But to know such a man, such a 'lisboeta', changes one's ideas of the town, affects one's notion of what the city adds up to. His home is full of books on his favourite subject. His little den, where he did his reading and his accounts, was redolent of a methodical, cultured mind. Yet the master was a simple craftsman who showed not the slightest sign of pretension or arrogance. He paused and considered any remark before answering. If he found it silly he would merely smile, making a non-committal gesture. His living room, to which we retired to partake of a glass of port, was equipped with a hi-fi record-playing machine. When we entered, his son was listening to Mozart. It was an island of sanity in a modern chaos; impossible not to be moved.

We were to see another aspect of this kind of Lisbon that afternoon. It was necessary, for some reason which I have forgotten, that we contact another gentleman of the ceramic world. This time the master led the way and we found ourselves driving through laneways that not long ago had been pure countryside. We drove down narrow roads between high walls of old farms and quintas, passing an occasional crumbling palace with heavy wrought-iron gates. We were heading for Camarate near the airport. Bougainvillaea and morning glory filled the walks before solemn eighteenth-century façades with shuttered windows. Here and there we passed new developments but ended up in an old village or township. This was Camarate, now connected with Lisbon, so that the people there consider themselves lisboeta. Yet it remained obviously a self-contained community. It appeared that nearly everyone living there was in some way connected with the ceramic industry or related activity.

We pulled up by the side of a big and gloomy old block, probably seventeenth century to judge from the smallness of the windows and the scale of the principal entrance. Now occupied by people in small flats or rooms it looked as if it had been a great house in its heyday. The failing light increased the impression of grimness created by the grey façade.

We had to go to the local café to search for our man. The café was a perfect example of its country-town type. The telly was already on. Excellent draught beer from the barrel was served. Our man, Toneca, was down at the club. It transpired that although only a humble ceramic worker—his speciality was moulds—he was a man of consequence in his own community. He was president of the Bombeiros Voluntarios— the fire brigade—and this occupied his spare time. Or did it? We were later to see his workshop, which once again opened my eyes to a way of life so industrious, so dedicated, that the financial side seemed incidental. Here, when he had finished at the factory, he continued to experiment and carry out all manners of complex mould work with various clays. He had a little kiln, built of special French-designed bricks and to a plan provided by our friend the master. 'Oh,' he said, 'we are all indebted to the master.' Toneca was a humorous small dark man with a constant twinkle in his eye; every sentence a joke. But he was a consummate expert. When he showed us his work and spoke of technical problems, the master weighing his remarks and the two pondering the subject, one saw the confidence and authority of a man who knew his business.

I suppose one could call Senhor Toneca (short for António) a 'soloio'. He looked like my concept of one. But he had a sophistication and a natural charm that was really urban, if not urbane. Also one gathered from his conversation that he identified himself very much with the working classes. He too was a master to the ordinary ceramic worker. But in the presence of Mestre Rogério he gave all deference to the superior skill, education and wider knowledge of the latter who, after all, was a professor in the technical school.

This was a Lisbon that the foreigner seldom sees. A world that concerned itself with a craft and gave one an impression of being curiously self-sufficient. It was a village associated with the city but living its own private way within the greater complex. I only realised how very city-conscious and sophisticated our Senhor Toneca was when we brought him down to Algarve to help instruct our local and very country potters.

Lima and I had made various peculiar discoveries about country red-clay potters soon after starting up our venture. They are an old, stubborn breed. I can recall scenes of mutual and utter incomprehension when Senhor Toneca confronted our potter—a giant of a man nicknamed 'The Barrel' who used to shout 'I am an artist' if ever asked to vary his technique by a hair's-breadth—and tried to explain that in Lisbon he expected a man on the wheel to work within millimetres of his specification. There was gradual erosion of the patience of both—the difference between the slow, dogged, countryman and the factory-trained expert. Toneca could not grasp that a man would not execute orders to precise instructions. 'I could bring you a potter from Lisbon,' he would sigh, 'who would make you three hundred pieces in a day, and there would not be one millimetre divergence from first piece to last.' The sad thing was that the Lisbon efficiency was too efficient for me. The perfectly turned work, the immaculate moulds of Mestre António had a coldness and a perfection that was almost mechanical. The rough-turned pots of the maddening 'Barrel' had a charm more valuable than efficiency.

The world of Lisbon's craftsmen, where our friends had worked all their lives, is in some ways an anachronism. It is difficult to see how, in a modern city, and in the awful competitiveness of modern production, these communities of patient workmen, who attach far more importance to the object well made than to the economics of the market, can survive.

It is a privilege to enter and to observe here the sanity, gaiety, pride and confidence in skills. It would be tragic if this vanished. For the moment the ceramic industry is healthy; the market for hand-made majolica is an expanding one. Some of the factories making it have orders for years ahead. So the position is not too gloomy. Wages for these craftsmen are not bad. A potter can earn about two pounds a day—more if he is first class. In terms of 'take-home' money, and the cost of living in Lisbon, I put this at the equivalent of three times as much in England.

Praça Figueredo

Notes and Observations

PATRICK SWIFT

Lisbon exists on a series of ever receding levels. Apparently accessible, and small as capital cities go, it appears to offer itself unselfishly to the casual visitor. As one goes deeper, as one knows it longer, it proves ever more elusive and mysterious. A recurrent pattern of my days in Lisbon has been to set out to do or see something specific and end up utterly absorbed in a quite different place and object. The contours of the town are such that I find it still possible to get lost, even after eight years' visiting there on and off.

One moves on to a wavelength, a level, of the city's life, quite by chance, and finds a world somehow ready to receive one, as if the accidental visit were expected. I recall a peculiar circumstance of my first acquaintance with the city; the very first day, indeed, that we spent in Portugal. My brother James had undertaken the strenuous task of moving me and my family from London to the south of Portugal. We had reached the last stage of the journey and had driven from Madrid, with a stop over at Merida, with the idea of spending a night in Lisbon before heading for Algarve. Portugal had made an immediate and profound impression. Out of the dust of the long broken road, potholes and poverty all the way, we seemed to enter a garden-like world of freshness and cleanliness. At Estremoz the wide open square was full of flowering trees, gay with piles of brightly coloured ceramics displayed on the pavements. Setubal had seemed less attractive, but the ferry gave us our first view of Lisbon and proved an unforgettable experience. At that time (1962) there was less traffic about and the city seemed gentle and welcoming. In Madrid I had been balled out in the middle of the Avenue José António by a bad-tempered policeman—all traffic stopped, myself and the family standing forlorn while we suffered a flood of unintelligible abuse. By contrast Lisbon was a haven.

We drove down the quay, and all being thirsty, looked for a café. There are no cafés along the quay front in Lisbon. But we saw a pub. Rather like an Irish or English pub—closed on the outside, with an entrance door half glass but curtained. We all bundled into this pub, where we had sandwiches and beer; the children had mineral waters and orangeade. It was a quiet, dull pub with a number of women and a few groups of sailors about at wooden tables; clean yet shabby at the same time. We were made welcome by a barmaid who fussed over the children. All was well. As an introduction to Lisbon I found it, even then, a little odd. We had expected open cafés of a southern type, but this was a dull drinking pub. Nondescript. Yet we felt very welcome; felt as if we were known and liked. Even our total inability to communicate did not affect the ease with which we were able to settle down and enjoy our beer. It was a long time afterwards that I realised where we had been for our first beer in Lisbon. It was a sailors' pick-up bar; hence the ladies and hence the traditional closed pub atmosphere.

This silly episode has a significance for me. We had moved in on a certain level of Lisbon, barged into a world where we had no place. But we had found a welcome and a courtesy—a charm even—that ever afterwards has seemed to me the chief characteristic of Lisbon's response to the visitor. And I have found since that one can move with similar ease from any level of the city's life to another, finding this easy-going unobtrusive welcome everywhere.

Rossio

One gets to know the city in a certain way. The feeling of being made part of it, of being welcomed into it, is so strong that one continues in this way, in this groove, for some time. Then something happens to break the mould and a different Lisbon is discovered.

For a long time, the Rossio and its immediate environs seemed to me the very heart of Lisbon, the Francfort Hotel our world. Here we would return from abroad, or arrive up from the country, to be received like old friends. It did not occur to me that for a true lisboeta the Rossio was a place not much visited. True, the Café Suiça is famous for its cakes and many a housewife when shopping in central Lisbon will call there to take home pastries. There is the main shop for the lottery tickets. There is the smart Loja da Meias, mostly French women's fashions. But in spite of all, I discovered at a certain point that the Rossio is not Lisbon's centre as far as the life of the Lisboner goes. For me it will never lose its old magic, because it was here—among fountains and cobbles of delirious patterns, among the miscellaneous crowd of the pavement cafés and the paper-stalls, with the hot sharp sun slicing through the air—that I conceived my first palpable notions of what being in Lisbon means to me. I can recapture this concept of being by sitting in the Rossio any morning before lunch and drinking my aperitif on the pavement at the Café Suiça or outside the Irmãos Unidos.

But if I am in Lisbon with friends, it's ten to one I will find myself somewhere in or around the Chiado. This is far more a centre of Lisbon life than the Rossio. Although today it is a sort of Piccadilly Circus of the city, the Rossio has a history as the true heart of Lisbon in older times. Before the 1755 earthquake, it was very different from the present busy quadrangle. The important part lay roughly round the area where the National Theatre now stands. Here was the Paço dos Estaus, a palace built on three floors with towers and turrets, constructed at the order of Dom Pedro, the regent, in 1449 to house foreign princes and members of the court who did not have town houses. A great deal of the more pompous and elaborate ritual of court life took place here. Festivals and celebrations marked its history throughout the sixteenth century, when it was the seat of João III. It was here that Cardinal Henry handed over the reins of government to Dom Sebasteão. The Court of the Inquisition was installed here in 1751.

Throughout this time the great square of the Rossio was simply beaten earth and the principal feature was a famous fountain, chafariz do Rossio, situated to the west of the National Theatre in front of the Largo de S. Domingos and consisting of a stone-carved Neptune figure dating from the end of the sixteenth century. It was the scene for most important public events such as the auto-da-fé and other public executions, bullfights, military reviews and parades, court festivals and popular revolutions. It saw Garcia Valdez, the conspirator who tried to overthrow the House of Avis, burned alive. On a hot August day in 1641 it saw the Duke of Caminha, the Marquês de Vila Real, and the Count of Armamar, all beheaded for conspiracy against João IV.

During the Liberal–Miguelite struggle, in 1831, three hundred men died there when the 4th Infantry division made an abortive proclamation of a constitution. And finally, around the beginning of the nineteenth century, the Rossio had a period of social brilliance as a café centre where the literati and artists of the time forgathered. Bocage, Milhão (the painter of big historical pictures), Pato Monís, Santos e Silva, José Bernardo da Rocha, and all the dominant artistic lights of the day appeared regularly at the cafés Nicolau and Parras; and here many of the famous satires of Bocage were first improvised.

Today, the Rossio is lined by Pombaline façades nearly all altered and disfigured by commercial encrustations. Only the National Theatre of Dona Maria II presents a formal noble front to the square. This is a nineteenth-century building which owes its existence to the efforts of the writer Almeida Garret. The architect was the Italian Fortunato Lodi, whose magnificent use of the six ionic columns in the imposing peristyle taken from the old church of S. Francisco da Cidade makes the façade. The entire building was gutted by a disastrous fire in recent years, but fortunately it is now being restored to its original condition.

The other charming architectural feature worthy of note in the Rossio is the Arco do Bandeira, so called because it was built, towards the end of the eighteenth century, by a business man, Pires Bandeira. Above the arch is an elegant window of the same period.

The statue which dominates the centre of the square—Dom Pedro IV dressed in general's uniform—is not in itself a notable work. Taken in conjunction with the fountains on either side and in the context of the busy scene, it has nevertheless a fine air about it. It is nineteenth century (inaugurated 1870), though numerous plans to erect a monument to Dom Pedro IV in the centre of the Rossio seem to have been considered and abandoned from an earlier date. One of these stood for a long time, started and unfinished—a pedestal awaiting a statue known ironically to lisboetas of the time by the nickname galheteiro (the container for holding oil and vinegar bottles on a table). This was finally removed* and Lisbon was probably

* It served for a while as base for a provisory statue of Hymen commemorating the marriage of D. Pedro V, which was destroyed in 1864.

lucky in getting the present sculpture which has, at least, the right scale for the setting (it is 27½ metres high). The pedestal of the monument is surrounded by splendid allegorical figures—Justice, Prudence, Strength, and Moderation. The King stands on a Corinthian column holding out in his right hand the Charter of the Constitution.

When I say that Rossio is not a centre of lisboeta life I am not endeavouring to deny its truly Portuguese character: I am even aware of a life that goes on there not at once obvious. For instance, it is *the* place in central Lisbon for catching a taxi. Yet the uninitiated may find great difficulty in grabbing one of the innumerable cabs that pour in and out of the square. The reason will be that a small boy, who will have been commissioned by some experienced denizen of the area, has already booked the taxi before it reaches the rank in the Rossio. The technique is simple: the boy lies in wait at the entrance to the Rossio, probably by the Praça dos Restauradores. Similarly, it is possible to discover after a few months that there is a regular life, a regular clientele, about the cafés here: it is not quite all turismo, But who are those people? Apart from odd friends from the provinces, who inevitably take the evening passear round the square before dinner, I have never seen anyone I know in these cafés. It is, I suppose, as in London. Nobody makes a centre of Piccadilly apart from foreigners and visitors. It is Soho or Mayfair or Kensington that constitutes a social scene.

Chiado

For this sort of thing the Chiado and surrounding area is the rough equivalent to a Mayfair with, at the same time, overtones of Soho and Chelsea added on a small scale. It is the fashionable shopping centre par excellence. Its heyday as a social scene was in the nineteenth century. It is where people bump into each other by accident in the novels of Eça de Queiroz. There are tea-rooms unchanged from that era. These are a joy for anyone who has a feeling for the poetry of the tea-room. None of your snack-bar vulgarity. Instead the charm of the silver teapot and sugar bowl, a pervading sweet scent of cream buns and, for me, the shadow of W. B. Yeats is already knocking at the door among the gossiping ladies at eleven in the morning. In the Pastelaria Marquês the decor is fresh, white, with mirrors and a faintly baroque air. Mountains of cakes and chocolates are consumed here every morning. Superb cakes and chocolates they are too. If one takes some home the attendant spends a leisurely five minutes on the delicate task of wrapping.

The Chiado has its café too: the Brasileira. But this, unlike the tea-rooms, is somewhat rough. Always crowded from morning till late night, it is—and has been for a hundred and fifty years back—a gathering place for journalists, writers, artists, students, and such as keep their company. I like the atmosphere. But there is nothing about it to encourage the casual or the curious visitor. In many ways its ambience is not unlike that of the French pub in Soho, with the difference that it is a café where, as is usual in such places, many people sit over a coffee for hours immersed in flurries of papers and manuscripts. And there is the continual coming and going of people looking for people.

There are three bookshops of note in the Chiado. One, the bookshop owned by the newspaper *Diário de Notícias,* is also an art gallery. As a bookshop it is excellent, though small; as a gallery it is as well made and as fine a place to mount an exhibition as anyone could wish (I have shown my own work there). But the big bookshop, and the famous one, is down the street; the Livraria Bertrand. This is legendary and has its special place in literature and life of Lisbon over a long period of the town's history. It is also a publishing house. As a bookshop I would rate it very high.

But almost every shopping facility is available round the area: fancy jewellers, photographic shops, clothes shops, some smart stores—such as *Sopal*—and some old gloomy department stores that have so far succeeded in ignoring the twentieth century; for instance Grand Armazem do Chiado: an antediluvian institution where some incongruous efforts to bring it

Café Brasiliera

up to date overlay a truly nineteenth-century attitude to shopping. If this persists a little longer it may enter the mysterious phase where the ornate gilded lettering on its façade will become Art. Even now it is beginning to suggest that it should by rights be a national monument.

Eça de Quieroz

What I am talking about when I speak of the Chiado and its immediate environs is *fashionable* Lisbon. And it is just as fashionable now as it was when it was the show place for the janoto, the dandy, of the world of Eça de Queiroz. I cannot pass through this district without thinking of Eça. All these streets, from the Baixa up to the Chiado and the Bairro Alto, and down to the river, make up the Lisbon of the books of Queiroz. The street names evoke those encounters the novelist so frequently arranged for his characters with devastating poignancy or intolerable angst, accidentally on the pavement. In a way, Eça did for Lisbon what James Joyce did for Dublin. He brought to life and defined a whole world. His prose is very like the early Joyce in character. It is clean, hard, and real, with a capacity for romantic and sensuous evocation. His spare but moving use of place names is also similar. This will mean nothing to the English reader, however, for Eça still awaits a translator of genius. It is certainly not good enough to suggest, as I have heard Eng. Lit. gents do, that he is a poor man's Flaubert. Although this is not the place, maybe, for disquisition on the work of Queiroz, it must be remarked that it would be impossible, or utterly blind, to treat of Lisbon and not bring in his work at some point. It is possible that there can be no real understanding of the Portuguese character without reference to this writer. Nor is this any accident. His influence has been vast. It is unlikely that any interesting writer in Portuguese has escaped the shadow of his satiric yet wise and comprehensive vision. He re-created the conscience of the race (to use Joyce's phrase) to such a degree that in a certain sense his work *is* Portugal.

Dealing specifically with Lisbon his novels cover a truly Shakespearean range of life. In *Os Máias,* for instance, we find a picture of the rich and noble, the sensitive successful hero with all the upper-class background of the period; in *Cousin Bazílio* the scene is the world of the moderate professional middle class of the time with vivid scenes of low Lisbon too. In *A Capital*—for me one of the most fascinating books as far as the portrait of the city goes—we see the world of the cafés, the newspapers and journalists, the political underworld, Socialists and Royalists, fanatics and spongers, poets and tarts, the fashionable salon and the low hotel.

The book moves through all the levels of Lisbon life in the late nineteenth century. Eça with brilliant, sometimes savage, comic strokes takes his hero (or anti-hero) through the gamut of experience, starting with the innocent excitement of the provincial would-be writer arriving with his small inheritance to conquer the literary world of Lisbon to the brutal end of real vision. Personally I can never walk down the Rua do Século past the gloomy façade of the newspaper of the same name without seeing the ghost of the wretched Artur seeking out the depraved and outrageous Melchior, the hack journalist who had ruthlessly sponged off him, looking for his fare back to the country and his dying aunt. It is not that Eça has endowed the town with character, it is that his vision sharpens the eye and adds a new dimension.

The fact that Lisbon is physically much the same today as it was then is important. Unlike London, where the transformations are so drastic that it is becoming futile to look for those places hallowed in literature (even modern literature—Pound's Kensington, or Eliot's City for instance), Lisbon can still offer almost intact the stage on which Eça's characters are made to act out their tragi-comic roles. This is a privilege we can enjoy in Lisbon.

It was the conscious aim of Eça de Queiroz to create a full-scale portrait of Portuguese life. In letters to his publisher he sketched out such a scheme. And he had the attitude of a modern artist: there would be no room for explanation and philosophising. There will be no digressions, he said, nor declamation nor philosophy, 'something you will read in a night but will impress you for a week' he added modestly. In a way, although he never fulfilled his scheme and the Portuguese *comédie humaine* was never published, his complete work does add up to the sort of portrait of which he spoke. It is a comic vision that understood the passion, the gloom, the tragedy of the race. Having read him, one can never again be happy with the superficial, the trite and picturesque view of the Portuguese, found so repeatedly in English travel writing about the country from the eighteenth century onwards.

But as I have remarked earlier, it is the fact that so much of old Lisbon has survived intact into our day that allows us to enjoy these insights. And this applies to other eras and other parts of the town aside from the world of Eça

It is remarkable given the rate at which the city has expanded in the last twenty years, that so much has been preserved. It is also encouraging to notice that in spite of the pressures of big business there is a high degree of awareness of the value of the city's heritage. A typical example of this is a recently published book by one of the country's leading architects, Francisco Keil Amaral, surveying the dilemma of a rapidly expanding metropolis: *Lisboa: Uma Cidade Em Transformação* (Lisbon: A City in Transformation). This writer draws attention early on in his book to an interesting aspect of life in a city not yet overwhelmed by the demands of modern mass-housing and concomitant problems. People in Lisbon, he points out, were Portuguese and Lisboners in a special way. In a concrete and real manner were inhabitants of Alfama, of Madragoa, of Bairro Alto, of Campo Ourique, of Poço do Bispo, of Alcântara of Belém ... or in a more concrete way still, of certain patios, streets, or sectors of these quarters. The customs of the neighbourhood, habits and communal interests—whether of hate or of love—moulded the district into a real community: a situation where even the football clubs—Benfica, Sporting, or Oriental—were basically clubs of the quarter, the bairro, supported by local enthusiasm and expressing a local cohesion. Much of this is passing under modern pressures. But for those of us who visit Lisbon, coming from places where this process is so much more advanced, where nothing, or nearly nothing, has escaped brutal levelling progress, Lisbon still presents a picture of how more pleasant life can be when the scale is not utterly shattered, wherein human beings can converse, communicate and care for each other.

The old self-contained quarters of Lisbon are a joy. In one district we will find ourselves in an atmosphere belonging to a certain era: in the Bairro Alto, for example, we are in the seventeenth century. Down below, it is all eighteenth century, Pombal's Lisbon. This is very much French influenced; while now very lisboeta to us, it was a foreign intrusion when first built. To the east the rising hillside of Castelo de S. Jorge brings us back to ancient Lisbon, to the world as it existed before the disaster of the earthquake. Baixa in that pre-earthquake period was also a dense mass of alleyways and lanes—becos in Portuguese—very much in the style of the Alfama. It is hard to imagine how it must have been: a maze of antique buildings, all on different levels. But that venerable monument of Lisbon, the lift which will take you up from the Rua Santa Justa to the Carmo, gives a clear view of the great drop between the Alfama and Castelo de S. Jorge on the one side and the Bairro Alto on the other. Where now there is a flat bed, with its straight streets criss-crossing in orderly fashion there was a mass of unruly detail. There was the heart of ancient Lisbon. This included in its time the Jewish bairro, Judiaria Grande, with its synagogues, and its extension the Judiaria Pequena. The river covered much of what is now the Praça do Comércio. At that time the palace (from which the square gets its other name Terreiro do Paço) did not reach more than half-way down the length of the present space.

Looking at this cityscape from Eiffel's lift at Santa Justa, one is presented with a paradox—a curiosity of town architecture that must be among the most fascinating of its kind. Here is a perfectly self-contained and largely untouched expression of the eighteenth century stuck artificially in between two almost equally untouched sections of a medieval city. The one is an elegant exercise in logical reasoned town planning. The others express the organic growth of a city over its centuries of existence, the natural higgledy-piggledy charm of an unplanned conglomerate obeying laws and embodying a personality not susceptible to the operations of the ruler and drawing board.

The intrusion of the eighteenth-century logic on such a

drastic scale into the character of the city also symbolises the powerful effect of foreign influence in Portugal at that time and subsequently. Somehow the older city holds more of the soul of the true Portuguese. I do not find the spirit of Portugal in the Baixa.

There is some confirmation of these notions in the writing of many of the nineteenth-century generation of Portuguese poets and philosophers, who found that the national identity was being undermined by essentially French influences, and who were responsible for what can properly be called a Portuguese renaissance. Men like Teófilo Braga, Antero do Quental, Oliveira Martins, Leite de Vasconcelos, Alberto Sampaio and not least of all, Eça de Queiroz himself. The latter gave fairly strong expression to the sort of dilemma this generation felt when he wrote in an essay entitled *O 'Francezismo'*: 'I have been accused with bitterness in the periodicals, or in those pieces of printed paper that in Portugal pass for periodicals, of being *turned foreign*, of being Frenchified, and more, by my writing and my example trying to *de-portugalise* Portugal. But this is an error of the salon . . . Far from being guilty of de-nationalisation I was one of the melancholy products of it. No sooner born, hardly having taken my first steps, still wearing little crochet boots than I began to breathe France. All round me was France only . . . All of my generation with the exception of some superior spirits like Antero do Quental or Oliveira Martins, we have all turned fatally French in the midst of a society which was frenchifying itself and which throughout every part from the creation of the State down to the taste of the individual had broken with the national tradition, divesting itself of all its Portuguese clothes in order to put on—in thinking, legislation, writing, teaching, living, cooking—rags brought from France.'

Eça played his role, of course, in the re-creation of the national image. And although he may have exaggerated in this essay he does express the dilemma—essentially a dilemma of identity—that preoccupied his generation, and most Portuguese writers since. I feel that Eça left out of account the degree to which the Portuguese can absorb foreign influence and make it their own. A great and obvious example is the Italian architect Nazzoni, the master of the Portuguese baroque in the north of Portugal. And one of the sculptors of the Jerónimos was a Frenchman, Nicolau Chanterene.

These writers and thinkers of the nineteenth century in Portugal (even the more journalistic of them like Ramalho Ortigão were brilliant and witty writers) introduced in an acute way the whole question of what ultimately *was* Portugal and where Portugal was going. It was a sort of nationalist renaissance comparable to the Irish literary revival of a slightly later date.

Fernando Pessoa

In modern times, a poet has demonstrated again that this is a basic concern with the thinking Portuguese. Fernando Pessoa was obsessed with the question of identity. He also shared the messianic character that repeatedly asserts itself in Portuguese literature and life. Pessoa was a major European poet. He was a complex personality to begin with. So much so that his own thought and work led him to an assertion of the impossibility of a simple identity. A man is now one thing and again another. One expression is as valid as the next, and there is no simple truth. He developed four separate personae for himself. Each a poet, publishing under his own name, each with a history, a profession and even a horoscope for himself. They not infrequently wrote critiques and introductions one for the other.

Without a knowledge of the poetry this sounds fairly crazy. But the world Pessoa created by this device is utterly convincing. In it, he can range from the romantic and heroic to the wry, satiric, and comic.

Pessoa applied his notions to the analysis of the Portuguese character in general and, for the purposes of the present remarks, this is where the interest lies for me: for Fernando Pessoa, like Eça, haunts Lisbon once one gets to know his work.

It is worth quoting some of his earliest statements on this problem of identity written in 1915, 'I do not know who I am, what soul I have.' 'When I speak with sincerity I do not know with what sincerity I speak.' 'I feel myself multiple. I am like a room with innumerable mirrors that turn into false reflections a single anterior reality which is not in any one of them and in all of them.'

He wrote: 'Being Portuguese it is as well to know what we are.

a) adaptability, which in things of the mind gives instability and therefore diversification of the individual within himself.

b) a predominance of emotion over passion. We are tender and little intense, the opposite to the Spanish—our absolute opposites—who are passionate and cold. Never do I feel myself more Portuguese than when I feel different from myself—Alberto Caeiro, Ricardo Reis, Alvaro de Campos, Fernando Pessoa'

(The names of his various 'personae'. N.B. his own name comes last.)

It seems to me that Pessoa's note on the national character here is enlightening. It even seems to me, too, that the city expresses this feeling: diverse, tender, poetic, rising in tiers of pastel shades from the warm hazy river where dark triangular silhouettes of sails move gently through the afternoon. This is one face of Lisbon.

O Fadista!

PATRICK SWIFT

The fado belongs profoundly to Lisbon. Nobody can visit the city without hearing this sad song. The fatalistic amorous notes float out from café and bar as one passes through the streets. In a quiet corner of the town one hears someone singing from a kitchen window or a garden terrace with all that rich indulgence in lugubrious sentiment that is the essence of the fado. It can be very moving. In the right mood and setting it can be heart-breaking. It is a difficult thing to be detached about or to make any sort of rational analysis of. But in its way, it *is* Lisbon.

O FADISTA!

For all practical purposes it is now the national song. Musicologists will never accept this; nor is there any direct demonstrable ancestry to support the popular role the fado has assumed as Portugal's national musical form. But as such it will be taken by any casual visitor. And not without reason. It is ubiquitous and dominant. In Lisbon it is not merely a song; it is an attitude to life, a philosophy, and one might even say a manner of living.*

There exist innumerable attempts to explain, to justify, to denigrate or to extol the fado. The word simply means 'fate'. Or at least it did mean this. Certainly when it occurs in Camões, say, one reads it as 'fate'—usually invoked with a capital letter ... *quando seu Fado o consentia* (when your Fate permits) or *Ah! Fortuna cruel! Ah! duros Fados* (Ah! cruel Fortune, Ah! harsh Fates). Now, however, the word fado conjures up a whole idea of life, an outlook at once an acceptance of the inevitable agony of doomed passion and rejected love, and yet bitterly complaining. It is lyrical and sentimental, but with an acrid flavour. In this form, and with this sense and implication, the word cannot be more than a hundred and fifty years old. And yet, having listened to many efforts to knock the fado, and having gone through anti-fado phases myself, I am convinced that the form must have preceded the word: that, after all, such a strange and compelling phenomenon cannot but have an ancient history.

The exotic character of the fado tended to make apologists look for an exotic origin. Descriptions of songs occurring in the sixteenth-century work of D. Francisco Manuel de Melo—a flamboyant character who certainly would be called fadista today—were invoked: descriptions of the tarambote, and the sarambecque and, even more, the references by the eighteenth-century Tolentino, a satirical and ironic versifier; or the doce lundum chorado, the sweet weeping lundum had the added exotic flavour of Negro influence since it came to Portugal from

---

* Here is a dictionary definition of *fadista:* 'Name given in olden times in Portugal and especially in Lisbon to a certain class of individual of low condition, disorderly ruffians who frequented tabernas, had their own special vocabulary and used their spare time to play and sing the fado.'

Brazil. In Brazil it was called the lumdu and was a dance reported to be extremely erotic and amorous by writers in the eighteenth century. There is no doubt that there seems to be a relationship between the syncopated Afro-Brazilian rhythms and the fado of today.

This relationship of the lumdu of Brazil to the fado of Lisbon has never been convincingly proved in any historical way. But I have come to the conclusion that it contains the germ of the truth, though in a curious manner. Your serious folklorist or musicologist will almost certainly agree that the chula of the north of Portugal is the national musical form par excellence. It is at once demonstrably ancient, original, and unique to Portugal—or to a certain region principally composed of the Entre Douro e Minho district. The chula is a dance-cum-song with a musical (instrumental) opening and a ballad section in which the dancers, who can be male and female, or all male, exchange verses amorous or bantering, frequently rude. The dance form can be complex but the dancers always face each other with hands raised above the head and snapping their fingers in time with the rhythm, which is slow and archaic with many grace-notes reminiscent of the bagpipe.

The more classic of these songs are said to echo pure Celtic music (the Chula Rabela is taken by Cesar das Neves, the father of Portuguese musicology, as a perfect case in point). I find this absolutely convincing. And the chula, of course, went to Brazil—not surprisingly since, apart from the fact that the chula in any of its innumerable variations is a nation-wide popular song form, most of the emigrants, from the seventeenth century onwards, were from the Minho and the north.

As frequently happens, the simple logical solution may well be the correct one. It seems reasonable to believe that the fado is descended from the chula but with Afro-Brazilian influences. Further, it may be that the lascivious and obscene overtones were developed in Brazil to a greater extent—for the country songs, while sometimes rude and always amorous, are fresh and simple and hardly ever sentimental in the manner of the fado. For me, at any rate, this is a satisfactory notion of how the fado came about. And it would explain how it has managed to instal itself in Portugal as the most commonly heard song, indeed, whatever the musicologists may say, as *the* national song.

Reactions to the fado are variable because it is the type of song that strikes an intimate personal note. It can be depressing at first. It can appear mawkish. It requires to be well sung if it is to work at all. Frequently it is not at all well sung. It demands a great deal of the voice, and many fado singers sing on long after their voices have been destroyed by the demands made on them by the song.

The singer most responsible for the popularisation of the fado is undoubtedly Amália Rodrigues. She is, beyond question, an artist of tremendous personality. What she sings is sometimes fado but just as often merely song—canção. There is a vast and important difference between the canção and the fado. Your true fado singer (Amália's sister, Celeste, for example, less famous but a truer fadista though an inferior singer) despises the mere canção which for her does not partake of the mystique: and really the mystique is *all*. Amália, however, is a great singer and she puts the fado and semi-fadista songs on the map in an international way. Her most famous song, *Uma Casa Portuguesa,* is not fado.

When I first listened to the fado it was to some records of Amália's. I had just arrived in Algarve and was being entertained in the village of Carvoeiro by a French poet and his wife (he was writing an interminable Rimbaudesque epic and she was painting little pictures of an exquisite sensitivity) and my reaction was completely negative. In fact, for a long time I did not get the message at all. It seemed to me a facile and sentimental performance—I was being priggish: but then a sunny afternoon in a simple seaside village is not the place or time for getting the message of the fado.

I discovered it eventually. The place was the Alfama and the time around midnight. I recommend this to anyone who does not see the point of the fado. Go to a little Alfama fado house and submit to the strange atmosphere—the gloom of dim lights, the smell of rough brandy, and of piri piri sausages (chouriço) being grilled in alcohol on the tables.

I was in Lisbon at the time with my old friend the cinéaste Jacques Darribaude. It was spring. Lisbon in the company of Jacques had blossomed into a fantasy world in which we passed our days rolling about with laughter. Jacques had a large number of odd introductions cutting right across the social scale of the city. One moment we were being entertained to lunch by a marquesa and admiring her Leonardo in a small town palace; next we were hurrying off to some café to meet a member of the theatrical profession, or some opposition political writer.

One of Jacques' contacts was a little poetess who lived on the edge of town, in a desolate block of flats. Here we met her and sat in a parlour that seemed to form part of an endless complex of rooms through which wandered a variety of characters whose presence or relationship to our poetess was never explained. It was late in the evening of this encounter that our literary lady, waxing lyrical about the beauties of Lisbon at night as we wandered through the dim lights of the Alfama, led us to the tiny fado house, the Guitarra de Alfama. It was tucked away in a miniscule square. There was a door, rather like an old garage gate, blankly closed and bolted. It was drab and covered with smears of paint, as though someone had cleaned a variety of paint brushes on its fading planks. We knocked at the sort of closed porthole in the left corner of the gate. After some persistence, a pale small face appeared at the little round window, and after a silent interminable survey its owner rattled open the garage gate and bade us enter.

We found ourselves in a cave-like room of stygian tenebrosity. A curtain divided the entrance from a long crepuscular corridor lined with small tables. Candles flickered dimly, throwing light on glasses and red earthenware mugs. Shadowy groups occasionally sipped what smelled like the roughest bagaço. At the end of this smoke-filled space a young man, hands in pockets, head thrown back, was singing a slow keening song to the accompaniment of a sweet somniferous medley of guitars. We groped our way to a table aided by a youth dressed in an open-necked red shirt. He had a pale poetic face that seemed to glow in the dark. The poetess was determined that we were going to have the full treatment. Choriço was ordered, together with a large jug of wine. All this was transacted in whispers while the singer carried on with some heart-breaking ballad quite impossible to follow. When the song ended murmurs of approval and handclapping went through the tables and here and there a cry of 'O fadista!' rose above the general clamour. The guitarists struck up another tune and after some consultations with the singer they were launched on a new fado.

Our choriço, reeking of that distinctive piri piri garlicky tang, was grilling on flaming bagaço in a small earthenware barbecue on the table: the very smell was intoxicating. Our red wine was dark frothy stuff of the type that comes from Arruda dos Vinhos and stains the lips deepest crimson. The mélange of sensations was intense: the dark broken by the flickering candles on the dimly-lit circle where the singer sang on, the dense palpable odour of the food and drink; the intolerable yearning in the music of the guitars; and above it all, the sharp sad cutting notes of the fado.

The decor of the place was fascinating. At the end of the long room were two painted screens. They depicted typical street scenes of Lisbon, with enchanting primitive figures lounging by the corners of dreamlike squares. Azulejos seemed to line the upper half of the walls. Numerous odd pictures of singers, bullfighters, and famous characters, together with a variety of caricatures and primitive paintings, completely filled what space was left. The azulejos were actually imitation, being painted with oil paint on commonplace white cheap tiles. In the gloom all this was utterly successful as decor.

Then the lights went on and we were able to observe the clientèle. They were mostly young people. There were some old chaps with a prosperous air, smoking cigars. We speculated on the company. Our poetess, who evidently loved the atmosphere, said it was basically a student's place, that one frequently had the opportunity of hearing beginners at the fado game, or even amateurs, here. As the evening progressed we discovered that the young men and women who served at the tables were also singers. Each singer sang three songs, then the lights went on for about five or ten minutes. In the intervals the singers talked with the clients and sometimes took a drink. Everyone smoked like mad. The air grew thicker as the evening went on.

The best singer, and she was something quite special, was a youngish woman, quite cross-eyed. Somehow this oddity failed to matter the moment she started singing. She had a superbly casual air when she started. As part of the ritual the female fadista wears a short black shawl. This she manipulates to express emotion; but to begin with she drapes it correctly and with a certain grace round her shoulders and starts the fado with a solemn composure.

Some were duets in which a man and a woman answered one another in alternate verses. Sometimes the clients joined the choruses from the tables. And on that evening the most strange and moving thing was a young boy who sang twice: his thin pure voice not yet tuned into the weary plaintive notes of the fado. It was a rare and fine voice which seemed to give a different dimension to the song.

After this evening out I became a fado addict for a time. For two years or so, I frequented the fado houses of Lisbon on every visit I made there. On each successive return to the Guitarra de Alfama (where I never failed to recapture the strong flavour of that first experience) the young boy sang. His voice changed: he grew tall, he acquired all the mannerisms of the fadista; the pure edge went from his high notes; and for me there was strange experience of watching the transformation of the incongruous purity of the youth I first heard, so out of place in the atmosphere, into a perfect denizen of the fado world.

The Guitarra de Alfama is not in some ways a typical fado house. It closes too early, for one thing. Shortly after midnight it locks the doors, and not long after that all is over. Your true fado joint is just getting into its stride by one or two in the morning. At three the feeling is so strong that one may get a great performance. It is tremendously a matter of inspiration, of mood. Of all the places I frequented during my fado phase,

O FADISTA!

I found the strongest fadista feeling at the Solar da Madragoa—well known but fairly low class—in the Madragoa district. Here when we first went there were two popular singers, the more striking of whom was a fat handsome lady rejoicing in the name of Zelia Maria. Many a night we listened to the end—one might say the bitter end—until at four or five in the morning the whole staff sang a rather grotesque song of the house, all the remaining customers joining in. The decor was superb. Lots of red satin and bobbins were employed. And although they changed the interior yearly it never lost a truly primitive charm. The patrão was a terrifying man of enormous dimensions. Though he could barely move his vast weight from one chair to another, he ruled the place with a rod of iron. Although basically a very lisboeta place, foreigners frequently found their way there; large parties of celebrating students occasionally took up a lot of space for a birthday or similar event. But, whatever the occasion, I never saw the outsize patrão smile.

The Solar da Madragoa gives the impression of being a tough place. This goes with the legendary character of the fado. Whatever may be the cultural arguments about the antiquity of the fado it is old enough a tradition to have its legends and its heroes. The original is the nineteenth-century fadista Maria Severa, who bewitched the rakish Count of Vimioso into a disastrous affair.

This legendary affair between Maria Severa and the Count of Vimioso is held by many to have been the vital factor in the rise of the fado in popular esteem. There could be some truth in this. The Count of Vimioso's great palace at the corner of Campo Grande and Alameda das Linhas de Torres was the scene of the most famous and spectacular bullfights of his time and his sponsoring of Maria Severa in society would have carried weight. It would have set the fashion.

At the Solar da Madragoa we learned that this traditional sense of belonging to a world apart—of being members of a confraternity with its own customs, mystique and slang—is strong among the fado singers and their hard-core followers. Night after night, at certain fado houses one saw the same characters, clearly enslaved by the atmosphere. And when we entertained Zelia Maria at our table (whisky, of course, being the drink on such festive occasions—and it always seemed to come in the same grubby Johnnie Walker bottle, no matter how much we ordered), we learned that she was immensely proud of her art: her great boast was that she could walk into a certain café near the Puerto del Sol in Madrid where artists and bullfighters drank and be recognised and accepted by all.

One night a group of rich and vulgar Spaniards vociferously demanded that they be allowed to see her home; perhaps she really was known in Madrid. But she begged me and my old friend Tim Motion to escort her to her flat. It was one occasion when I was grateful for the Portuguese law that insists that there be a policeman on duty at the door of every night club (at the expense of the management by the way). I was also impressed by the fact that when we pulled up outside the block of flats where the distinguished artist lived, the policeman on the beat saluted and escorted her to the door.

For the average visitor to discover this true fadista world is, oddly enough, not easy. The reason is that hotel clerks and taxi drivers will always recommend the tourist to one of the big popular places such as the O Faia, the Restaurante Folclore, or the A Severa, all excellent places in their way but strictly for the conventional tourist. Here it is the popular song, the canção parading as fado that you will hear, together with a mixed bag of country dances from various parts of Portugal. It is all rather stagy and gay but it is not fado. Among the fado houses proper are the Solar da Madragoa as mentioned; the Taberna do Embuçado, where Celeste Rodrigues can be heard, much smarter, and in the Alfama; the Parreirinha da Alfama; the Césaria, and—an unusual location for a fado house not far from the Avenida da Liberdade—Viela, where the famous fadista Sergio sings late in the evening. There is no use at all in going to any of these before eleven or twelve at night. And I merely name the more famous.

There are numerous little fado houses, each of which has its special background, its particular gimmick or history. The Bairro Alto contains many (traditionally the Bairro Alto was the night-town of Lisbon). Some of these are worth looking into

Bairro Alto

just for the fun of the atmosphere and decor—for the decor of the fado house has its mystique too.

Usually the interior tells the story of the owner's background or connections. A typical case is the Adega do Mesquita. David Wright and I, on one of our many peregrinations through the dense life of the pubs in the Bairro Alto, called in here by chance one evening. It was early, nothing was happening at all. At the bar a tall young man gave us a beer. It seemed a good opportunity to inspect in detail the exotic decor. Seeing we were interested, the young man emerged from behind the bar and took us through the fado restaurant proper. Here we found an incredible jumble of memorabilia, entirely to do with the bullfight and the fado, crowding the walls.

It transpired that the house was founded by and belonged to the young man's father, Domingos Mesquita, a Portuguese bullfighter. It was one of the older fado houses. In recent years there has been a rash of new ones. Our man was keen to let us know that this was none of your upstarts. It had been founded in 1938, when the bullfighter retired. He claimed that it was the first proper fado house in the Bairro Alto. Among its many distinctions was the fact that Amália Rodrigues was a friend of the old man and had many a night visited the house—though only as a friend, it appeared, and not as a singer.

On the wall a huge stuffed bull's head carried beneath it the legend: 'Head of the bull killed in the ring of Seville by Manuel dos Santos on the event of his taking the Alternativa.' While we were admiring this monster, a little dapper gentleman came bobbing into the room. It was the bullfighter father of the young man, Domingos Mesquita himself. Yes, he said, a fine bull; the head had been presented to him by the breeder the Marquês de Villamarta in 1941. Our attention was drawn to two azulejo panels. One showed Manuel dos Santos, who had killed the bull, and the other Amália. I noticed they had been made in Seville. Among other things was a picture of the last bull ever killed in Portugal. And for us, a particularly touching photo of the handsome cavaleiro Joaquim José, killed by a bull in 1968 on his twenty-first birthday. Wright and I had seen him in Santarém some three years previously. He was then a beautiful eighteen-year-old boy making a name for himself as an elegant and daring horseman in the ring. It seemed he had been a friend of Domingos Mesquita and frequently came to the fado house—the photograph was inscribed to the old man.

It must have been about eleven in the evening when we wandered into the Adega Mesquita; but there was no sign whatever that the business of the night was going to begin. Somewhat to my surprise, the dapper little ex-bullfighter announced that he was off to the theatre. He bade us good night and vanished into the Rua de Diário do Notícias in a slightly mysterious fashion. With our heads full of bulls and the tragic faces of faded stars of the ring and the fado house, we followed him into the dark street feeling somewhat fadista ourselves.

To slip into the fadista mood in Lisbon is all too easy. Once one has caught the fever of the guitars, and the romantic agony in the voice, there seems no reason to withdraw from the magic of a world where all is exalted tragedy. The night tends to draw one into the dark regions where only passion is respected and squalor becomes dignified through suffering. These ladies of the fado, all in black, a shawl thrown round the neck and over the shoulder, standing for that tense pause while the guitars set the scene, eyes closed and faintly quivering in anticipation of the tragic moment, can achieve obsessive fascination. For me, the difficulty is to get home at all. How many times have I strolled back to the hotel through a new, mystical Lisbon bathed in a fine clean light gently shedding dark tones of the night before.

In Lisbon it is possible, as in few other cities nowadays, to spend the entire night drinking in company until the cafés reopen in the morning. When the last fado house closes we make our way down to the Avenida where the all-night café bar (the Galo d'Ouro) is full of the flotsam of the city having breakfast, drinking beer, coffee or—as will usually be my case by that hour—bottles of that most blessed of Portuguese blessings, the mineral waters from cool northern spas. These late night, or early morning, cafés are great institutions. It would be difficult to describe the exotic heterogeneous confluence of miscellaneous humanity that awaits one in such places when the rest of the city has at last, as if reluctantly, subsided into peace, and the day not yet begun.

The music of the fado, is of its nature, a nostalgic kind of music. Once one knows this level of Lisbon life it becomes intensely nostalgic, full of saudades, evoking the city and its sad passionate undertones. The dark sentimental side of the character, gloomy but anguished with a sharp exciting edge to it. Anyone who arrives at an understanding of this emotional night-world will ever after be able to conjure it up through the music of the fado. There can be few forms so evocative and nostalgic. Recordings are innumerable and available at nearly all the fado houses: but for the poetry of this world it is still the old timers who can work the oracle, and among these the legendary Alfredo Marceneiro remains the greatest. An old man now of seventy-odd years, the only records available are from early seventy-eights reissued. Not long ago he was brought before the television cameras, in one of those cruel interviews with the heroes of the past, but his personality was so strong that he survived even the vulgarity of the telly. More than Amália at her most fadista, the voice of Marceneiro can recall Lisbon and its fado. The lights are low, the guitars are murmuring and someone is crying 'O Fadista' . . .

Bullfight

PATRICK SWIFT

For a long time it had been my ambition to attend a big night at the Campo Pequeno, the Lisbon bullring. Usually, however, I seemed to find myself in the city when somewhat less than classic occasions were scheduled. Special attractions such as Negro cavaleiros from Portuguese Africa, or the first appearance of female espadas in the Portuguese ring or, worse still, comic corridas with dwarfs on horseback, etc., were generally the advertised attractions when I found myself ready and eager to sample the Portuguese bullfight at its best. But one warm August I found myself with the family ensconced in Lima de Freitas' flat and my eye caught an advertisement in the *Diário de Notícias* announcing a great occasion at the Campo Pequeno: the Corrida da Imprensa (bullfight sponsored by the Press). I proposed to the family that we all go to see a proper bullfight. We were acquainted with the genre in the provinces, and at the big country festas had seen what passed for excellent displays; but the Campo Pequeno is something special, unique. My daughters, who were restive, having been dragged away from the delights of the Algarve in summer (particularly Katty who had reached the stage of boy friends with fast cars and surreptitious visits to the local discothèque) responded with enthusiasm.

We decided to go at once to the Campo Pequeno, happily within easy reach of Lima's flat, and buy the tickets. On the landing by the lift we met our neighbour, a large talkative lisboeta lady, and told her where we were going. Ah, she cried, wonderful, grande corrida. Our enthusiasm increased. On the way, Juliet became worried lest her age should rule her out of this treat. However, when we got there we saw a big poster for the corrida, which carried in tiny letters the legend: *m/ 6 anos* (over six years).

At the box office we were told there were seats for all parts. We looked at the diagram and the price list and received a slight shock. The best seats were 300 escudos (about £4 odd) and the only reasonable seats we could find were on offer at 130 escudos (a little less than £2). Still I was game for this. But my daughters whose economic sense is based on the relation of the cost of living to their pocket money were somewhat dubious. In the country we were accustomed to lording it with the local gentry for eighty escudos a seat for the best. I observed a gleam in Katty's eye and tentatively she came out with a proposition: if I don't go to the corrida may I have the money instead? It seemed irrefutably logical and so I ended up buying two tickets and disembursing cash to the children.

I decided to get a good view and bought a couple of 250-escudo second-best seats for Oonagh and myself. The bullring in Lisbon is divided into a number of sectores. The barreiras, being right up against the edge of the ring, are the most expensive; the contra barreiras come next, then the bancadas —still very expensive for the first seven rows (on this particular evening 200 escudos each, or about three pounds)—then the bancada geral at 130 per seat. The gallery went for 40 escudos a seat indiscriminately.

The bullring at the Campo Pequeno is something of a folly.

It was constructed in the late nineteenth century, a red brick building in pseudo-Moorish style with lots of arabic arches, onion domes and great arched entrances. It is surrounded by a spacious parking lot. Old trees and a profusion of shrubs encircle it in cool greenery, cutting it off from the busy thoroughfare that passes on all sides. The particular event we were going to was billed as the 17° espectáculo of the 79th época, or season. As is usual at the Campo Pequeno, it was to begin late in the evening, at 10 p.m.

It so happened we were invited out to Carcavelos to dine with the photographer Peter Neilson and his wife, Mizette, on the evening before the bullfight—this was to be held, as always in Lisbon, on a Thursday. Here was a chance to brush up on our background knowledge about the ancient art. Peter and his wife are passionate aficionados and carry the addiction to the extent of travelling about the country to see particular performances when anything special is on. I was determined to pick their brains and thus be ready to get the most out of the great occasion. Not only were we to see two masters of the Portuguese art of fighting the bull on horseback, David R. Telles and the legendary Mestre Baptista, but the programme was to include two leading Spanish espadas, one the new star Damaso Gonzalez, and the other an old hand in the ring, Antonio Chenel, known as 'Antoñete'. (The latter, according to the brochure handed out with the tickets, had 'filled the ring with rare perfumes for two decades and would bring Lisbon his satin muleta and his much written-of art of fine tourear'.)

When I mentioned the bullfight to Peter on arrival in his house he said, 'Let's leave that until *after* dinner', as though to embark on the subject would in some way impair our capacity to do justice to Mizette's cooking. In fact, the subject demanded such fine consideration that it would be necessary to retreat to his study in order to discuss the matter properly. There, as I saw after dinner, when we withdrew armed with a glass of excellent brandy, he had a vast collection of photographs of the bullfight covering every major figure in the game and every sort of situation in the corrida whether involving equestrian bullfighters or espada, or the forcados (the team of young men who tackle the bull barehanded and hold him to a standstill). The last in fact were his speciality. He was gathering material with the intention of producing a book on this aspect of the bullfight.

'Well,' began Peter, when we had settled down among his books and pictures, 'what do you wish to know of the bullfight?' I had hardly started to explain that we were off to the Campo Pequeno the next night for a corrida than he snorted, 'Campo Pequeno! It's the . . . ah . . . ah . . . Billy Butlin's of the bullfight! Go to the country, go to a small bullring where the audiences know their bulls, where they will not take any nonsense. The Campo Pequeno? There they do not have to try, they get the crowds, they get the money anyway. But let me see whose bulls they are tomorrow.' He looked over the announcement. 'José da Silva Lico. Ah, this is not bad, they will be very good bulls. Remember, it's the bull that counts. It is the bull, after all, that fights. A bull is a naturally wild animal. He will attack anything that moves. That is why the bullfighter likes to have the bull in the shade and himself in the sun—he cannot afford to have the sun in the bull's eyes, for he must not see shadows: that would be fatal. If it is not a spirited bull, a brave bull, then there can be no merit in the fight. The bull is the hero. Look at the bull when he enters the ring. If he goes down on his legs at once, if he stands and hesitates, it's probable that he is not a truly wild bull. No country audience will tolerate a bull like that. Look here, there is a bullfight in Coruche next Monday. Why not . . .' 'No! No!' I cried. 'I have bought the tickets, very expensive tickets too, besides it's the Campo Pequeno I want to see. Tell me about the Campo Pequeno.'

Seeing that I was committed to the Corrida de Imprensa, Peter began telling me what to look out for. 'Go early and see the museum,' he said. 'They have an enchanting little museum in the bullring and their own chapel. The museum has some marvellous pictures. And watch out for Sectore Number One, which is *the* club of the Lisbon aficionado. It exists for one sole purpose: to reintroduce the kill into the Portuguese ring. As you know the kill has been forbidden since the death of Marialva in the eighteenth century. There are, in fact, three such clubs whose existence is devoted to this end. I agree with them. The absence of the kill destroys the perfect cycle of the ritual. And it's so boring sometimes when they cannot get a bull to leave the ring. It's not dignified, and the bullfight is all about dignity. But let me see your tickets. Ah, very good. You will have a row or two of people between you and the barrier. Watch how many people they allow right in behind the barrier. Far too many. When a bull jumps the barrier it's impossible for them all to get out of the way; there are journalists and officials by the hundred, very dangerous!'

As I sipped my brandy and took mental note of these points, Peter proceeded to extract from his voluminous filing system a collection of photographs. 'Let me see . . . no; this is Barcelona, where I went last week to photograph . . . Ah, here is Telles, whom you will be seeing tomorrow—very fine, but lately a bit off form. Look, here he is at Beja two years ago, here he is at Santarém last year. Look at this blow-up of the placing of the banderilha. Can you see fear in that face? Now, here is Baptista—no doubt about it, he is the master. You will not see him at his very best. He lost his best horses in a tragic fire at his home a couple of years ago. Impossible to find such horses again.'

We looked over a host of pictures and then turned to the subject of the forcado, the team that wrestles the bull. 'The team from Santarém which you have for tomorrow is top rate,' Peter said. 'You know, the Spanish tend to look down on this part of the Portuguese bullfight. In truth it is the most ancient part of the entire corrida. It has survived here since the Romans; but, of course, it goes back without a break to the Minoan religious performance. In Portugal the old tradition was that these teams of young men went from village to village, town to town, offering themselves for the corrida at the big festivals. They had to be good, for there was competition. On some of the great occasions here they still enter the ring in the old preordained way: walking on each side of two donkeys carrying coffins. This is symbolic of the danger and undoubtedly originates in the fact that the coffins were often needed. Have no doubt about it, this is tough stuff and there is real danger.'

He produced some hair-raising photographs of young men being tossed all over the place. 'Look at this; here is a picture where the bull really was top class.' It was a dramatic photograph of a young man caught vertically above the horns of the bull, toes pointed straight to heaven. How he fell down one hated to think. 'Now unless the bull knocks these boys right and left you may not have a first-class bull. Even the best team will not find a raging bull—full of fire, as he will still be at the end of the Portuguese bullfight—easy to tackle. One day I mean to produce a proper study of this part of the corrida; it is in many ways the most extraordinary and the most significant.

'You can expect good work from the espadas,' Peter went on, 'but the Spanish matador is at a hopeless loss in Portugal because there is no kill. This is the great debate—to kill or not to kill. Even the director of the bullring is involved. You know the present director of the Campo Pequeno was one of the greatest bullfighters of the Peninsula. He was so good he could scarcely afford to fight in Portugal: his fees in Spain were so high. He still appears for charity corridas. His last appearance was in aid of the Peruvian earthquake victims. He is a remarkable man—Manuel dos Santos. You know, he felt so strongly about the question of the kill in the Portuguese ring that one night some years ago when he had played one spectacular bull before a jam-packed arena, he suddenly and without warning faced the bull and killed. It was a perfect kill. The great bull dropped at his feet. There was a total and absolute silence for two seconds. Then screams and uproar took over the Campo Pequeno. He was arrested, of course, and gaoled that night. Then, next day, he was fined thirty thousand escudos by the magistrate—a lot of money then. It is said that the club Sectore One paid his fine for him. That night is still talked about.'

Only one point still troubled me as I was taking leave of Peter. How the devil was I to gain access to the museum and the chapel—these being private, as I presumed—not to mention the infirmary which Peter seemed to think I should visit, as well as the stables? A young Portuguese doctor who was at dinner with us spoke up. 'Quite easy,' he said. 'You approach the policeman or the official on duty and you point to your wife and say, "It's all right, officer, this lady is with me," and then walk boldly past. This will work anywhere in Portugal. You can go where you like.'

I did not do this. I decided, instead, to attempt a more conventional ruse. I would ring up the Campo Pequeno before the bullfight and introduce myself as a foreign journalist. I felt a bit edgy about this. The last time Wright and I had tried it on, in a posh hotel in the north of Portugal, we had been ignominiously shown the door, with cries of 'Jornalistas, jornalistas', ringing in our ears like 'Wolf, wolf'. But, after all, it avoided the embarrassment that would ensue if the doctor's trick were to fail. I approached the phone and dialled the Campo Pequeno. As the instrument rang I pondered whether to take a risk and ask for the director or to seek some lesser light who might equally well be able to admit us to the museum which was our goal. At the mention of the museum the gruff voice at the other end of the wire said, 'Mas não ha problema, problema nenhum. No problem at all. It's open to the public. Come early.' Which we did.

Although we were there about half an hour before the opening time, the crowds were already steadily filling up the praça. Cars were rapidly covering the wide space around the ring and busy car-park attendants were collecting a small fortune in tips as the flood grew. We checked our tickets and found we were in the best possible seats up against the barreira with only one row in front of us, and directly below the president's box. It was Sectore One and, so far, the seats below us were empty. We went to look for the chapel and museum.

They turned out to be indeed open to the public. The chapel consisted of a miniature gilded baroque altar housed in a small room off a corridor. None of the crowd bothered to enter. It was a strange quiet corner—a carpet on the floor and two dusty old reproductions, one of the famous Virgin of Seville and the other of the Christ of the Passion. There was dignity, even solemnity, in the little shrine.

Next door we found the museum, where a small number of curious visitors were pottering about. It was certainly a poetic institution. Dusty old bulls' heads and horses' heads—the latter somehow more moving—hung high on walls above show-cases containing the faded eighteenth-century costumes of long dead cavaleiros. Some were dark stained with the blood of the final colhida that saw the end of their wearers. The resolute face of one Fernando Oliveira stared gloomily out of a mouldy oil painting at the stained costume in which he died in the ring in 1904. The photos in still sepia were even more touching. These recorded great occasions in the ring. There were many be-whiskered faces of the Edwardian period and a long list of honour: José Casimiro (pae), Vicento Roberto, and so on. We became quite engrossed in the little collection of sad memorabilia. By the time we decided we had better seek out our seats for the opening of the corrida, we were filled with intimations of mortality, of grave ritual, of life, of death.

The ceremonial entrance of the ensemble of the corrida in colourful costume, smiling and waving, to the blare of trumpets and the gay applause of a packed arena, dispelled this mood. The Ribatejo campinos were there, and the gang of young men who made up the forcado all wore the long green and red caps of the bull-breeding country. Then came the bandarilheiros and the espadas. Last of all the cavaleiros entered wearing the ornate eighteenth-century costume with the wide tri-cornered hat trimmed with white feathers. The horses—two handsome greys—pranced in time to the music.

There had been a last-minute change in the programme. Mestre Baptista was not to appear. In his place there was a striking young fair-haired Austro-Portuguese, Gustavo Zenkl —a flamboyant character who at once established a rapport with the crowd. He was eager and energetic, whereas the older man, David Ribeiro Telles, had a relaxed and suave style. After the cavaleiros, holding their tri-cornered hats aloft, had gone through the elaborate exercise of first saluting the president of the corrida and then each sector of the praça, the ring cleared and a trumpet-call announced the start of the bullfight. David Telles returned. He rode a small, dark, energetic Iberian horse with muscles rippling under its gleaming coat. At the entry there was an exchange of good wishes and handshakes all round among the participants. Then the first bandarilha was handed to Telles.

He now galloped into the centre of the ring. Silence fell. Horse and rider waited, quite still, for the vital moment. There was a blast of the trumpet and suddenly the bull was in the ring. A black thunderbolt, it rocketed violently into the flood-lit arena, charging against the stout wooden fence and wheeling about to seek anything that moved. The toureiros were waiting, waving pink capes to draw the enraged animal across the ring. Twice they ran the bull like this. Then the cavaleiro signalled to them to leave the fight to the horse.

These protagonists now eyed each other across the empty praça. The cavaleiro, holding aloft the colourful bandarilha, taunted the bull—'Eh touro!'—provoking him to charge. When the bull did so, he took off at an unexpectedly light trot rapidly gathering momentum as he went. As he came forward, horse and rider wheeled to the right moving across the vision of the bull, who was now charging at full speed. The horse galloped round the ring with the bull literally on his tail, the horns brushing the flying hair, and hoofs seemingly grazing the enraged bull as they ran. Horse and rider appeared one animal as they raced in a tight curve, a miracle of balance.

Now the cavaleiro resumed his original position and again taunted the bull into charging. This time as the bull took off Telles rode the horse straight at the charging black fury and, swerving vertiginously at the last second, placed the bandarilha squarely in the great shoulder of the bull, who stopped astonished in his tracks. The music struck up, as is the tradition when an exceptional pass has been made. David Ribeiro Telles was an elderly man, balding and not at all slim. Nevertheless, his style in the saddle was elegant and smooth. With grace and ease he achieved perilous and often impossible-seeming manoeuvres. Taking his mount within a hair's-breadth of the flying horns, he never betrayed the slightest sign of strain or anxiety. He made the whole performance appear an effortless exercise.

From our seats, close to the actors in this furious drama, we were able to appreciate the risks the horseman took, and the split-second decisions he had to make to produce this impression of effortless control. The reader unacquainted with the Portuguese bullfight must remember that the bull is all the time in top form. Unlike the Spanish bullfight, there is no picador in the Portuguese corrida to tire the bull and damage its neck-muscles. Towards the end of a fight, the animal is every bit as lively as when he entered. On some occasions his fury is even greater.

This seemed the case when, following David Telles' performance, the forcados entered the ring and prepared to wrestle the bull. The leader stood some ten metres or more in front of the rest, who arranged themselves at intervals behind him. He approached the bull, then stood dead still. Hands on his hips and head thrown back, he shouted at the bull to charge. As the bull did not respond, he danced a little closer. Again standing with his hands on hips, he taunted the glowering suspicious animal. Suddenly the bull charged with fury. As it advanced, gathering speed, the young man danced backwards. At the exact moment when the angry horns rose in an arc, looking as if they must surely catch him in the groin, he leapt above them and flung his arms round the neck of the thundering animal. Immediately, the boys behind threw themselves on the bull and the whole team was swept across the ring and up against the barrier in the inexorable momentum of the huge beast. Here they held on until the bull was incapable of movement. It was a perfect pega á cara. There was music and a tremendous ovation for the young leader of the forcados. Both Telles and the young man took a very deserved volta— round of the ring—though it was undoubtedly the young forcado who had won the real acclaim of the crowd.

The second bull was taken by Zenkl. His style contrasted sharply with that of Telles. Where Telles was suave and stylish, Zenkl was outrageous and provocative. He took tremendous risks. In the end, galloping for a gap between the racing bull and the sides of the ring, his mount was caught full on the haunch by the charging horns. By some miracle, the horse did not come down. There was a dead silence as the shock of the near tragedy swept across the bancadas. It was seen at once that the horse was injured. Zenkl signalled to the president of the corrida. The gate was opened and he took the horse out. Seconds later he reappeared on a smaller mount and, with even greater daring, took on the now immensely fierce bull repeatedly taking hair-raising risks. The crowd were tremendously taken with the handsome young cavaleiro and his evident bravery, In spite of the episode of the first horse, one felt he deserved acclaim; but for some (to us mysterious) reason he did not merit a volta of the ring.

The bull in this case was really vicious and when the forcados took him on we saw a terrifying spectacle. On the first charge, the leader of the forcados was carried across half the length of the arena on the horns of the bull, and he and his companions were tossed right and left about the ring. They reassembled and again were violently tossed. One was carried off, injured. Much bedraggled and blood-stained, the young leader faced the bull for the third time. When the bull charged, he made an immense leap and took grip, fair and square, of the great neck of the charging beast. This time he held on. He and the rest of his team at last brought this violent animal to a standstill. The battered team was wildly cheered as it hobbled off.

The next part of the programme was for the Spanish espadas alone. The legendary Antoñete came first. From the beginning there seemed to be something wrong. The bull was a particularly lively one. From the way he charged when being run by the toureiros while Antoñete watched, we could see what spirit he had. Later, when the bullfighter took over and began to play the bull in wide veronicas with the large pink cape, the audience began to show signs of displeasure. Murmuring and occasional whistles swept through the bancadas. At one point Antoñete tripped, but the waiting toureiros leapt into the ring to distract the bull. Bullfighters are notoriously superstitious. When things go wrong, or they feel crossed in their luck, the situation frequently goes from bad to worse. Thus it was to be for the unfortunate Antoñete; it simply was not his night. He managed to bring the fight to the correct end but in a most faint-hearted manner. The crowd was merciless. It was one of those dramatically touching occasions when a hero is dethroned.

A mere three months previously, on a memorable night at the Campo Pequeno, the same Antoñete had thrilled the crowd, produced some of the most perfect faenas ever seen in the ring and taken several voltas. Now he left in disgrace.

The unknown quantity, the young Damaso Gonzalez, billed as the new Spanish phenomenon, took on the next bull. One saw him watching the bull with evident intensity as the toureadors played it. After only two runs he signalled to the toureadors to leave the bull to him. He advanced with a slow impressive pace, arranging the cape with careful and leisurely precision as he walked. The bull charged. Gonzalez took him in a sweeping arc, drawing the cape across his head and, again and again with a careful and completely undemonstrative accuracy, playing the fiery beast in even tighter and finer veronicas. It was clear that he was in control. When he took the muleta—the small red cloth and sword—the crowd were already cheering. Soon his cold skill and proud, slow movements were sending chills down the spine as the horns, dangerous and lightning-filled, brushed past his thighs. Music played, the flag flew (the final honour for a beautiful pass) and the crowd roared, 'Olé! Olé! Olé!', as each superb pass brought the bull under control. The crowd gasped as Gonzalez stood in front of the snorting animal, still as carved stone, one hand resting on the bull's head, and looked slowly round the arena to receive a standing ovation. Then with a pat on the head he provoked the beast into charging again and took him through a series of classic faenas.

Even greenhorns like ourselves could appreciate that this was something out of the ordinary. At the end, it appeared the bull was literally tamed. Instead of placing a bandarilha in a symbolic 'kill', as is the rule in the Portuguese ring, Gonzalez leaned over the head of the now still animal and deliberately placed his hand on the exact spot where the sword must enter to finish the fight.

The flag flew above the president's box. The music played. It was a standing ovation and two voltas of the ring. Flowers and scarves and shoes rained in the praça as Gonzalez went round. The young Spaniard with the large dark eyes and the slight build of a ballet dancer had electrified the Campo Pequeno.

It was now the interval. We had certainly not been disappointed with our night at the Lisbon bullring. The forcados of Santarém were the best I had ever seen. Telles was in top form, and the unexpected bonus of Gonzalez had made it a remarkable evening so far. For myself, although I had often heard described the grace and dignity of a matador in action, this was the first time I had seen an unflawed performance (I am not an aficionado, but, as a visitor, I had often been depressed by the botching I had seen in Spain). The performance of the new star had raised the mood of the audience to one of high excitement.

The Campo Pequeno was packed. A high percentage of the crowd appeared to be foreigners. Television cameramen were getting shots of the more extravagant dressers, and one group of hippie-style youngsters was creating a great fuss. It was hard to say how many in such an audience appreciated the finer points of the corrida. The more sober part of the 'house' was directly below us in the Sectore One. All Portuguese, they seemed familiar with one another and proprietorial in their attitude. This, I presumed, was the club Peter had told us about. They appeared very pleased with the events of the evening, and we took this as confirmation that it really was an exceptional corrida so far.

The second half followed the same pattern as the first. Telles was in even better form. His control was extremely impressive. He was at one with the horse and never seemed to hurry or push his mount. All was masterly smoothness and elegance. Zenkl followed, showing as before a sharper and faster approach, in the gay and spirited, slightly erratic style that had marked his earlier appearance. Once, in a violent rush the bull suddenly had his horse at the flank and mount and rider were raised in the air. Incredibly, the horse refound its feet, the bull was distracted by the toureiros and Zenkl continued, ending with some superb displays of horsemanship. He was conceded an extra bandarilha by the president of the corrida.

The second half of the evening also saw some tremendous action from the forcados. The leader of the team that took on the fifth bull was a coloured boy who showed real bravery. He returned, having been tossed high into the ring, to tackle the raging bull a second time and execute a pega of impeccable style. Only after he released the hold and walked to the barreira did we see that he had been injured in the thigh.

Both the fifth and sixth bulls of the corrida seemed to be fiercer, and the atmosphere of the bullring grew increasingly tense. Telles, Zenkl and the forcado of Santerém received immense ovations.

The seventh bull was Antoñete's. He looked nervous. When he played this huge fierce animal, we got the impression that he meant to keep out of its way. We began to wonder if they kept the more fiery animals for the second part of the corrida. The violence of the bull that had caught Zenkl's horse on the flank, and the way in which the boys of the forcado had been tossed about by the previous two bulls, indicated that this might be the custom. Antoñete, after his poor showing in the earlier part of the evening, was now getting a bad time from the crowd. Nothing seemed to go right for him. One had the feeling that the bull was calling the tune all the time.

Antoñete moved across the ring to our left and was at last, it appeared, getting the situation in hand. It was clear that he was taking greater risks. Then, in the middle of a classic faena—of the wide and sweeping kind for which he was famous —he was caught. With a lightning movement that the eye could not follow, the bull appeared to turn fractionally. In a flash, Antoñete was raised high on the left horn—hooked, as far as we could see, in the groin. At once the ring was filled with toureadors and the hapless bullfighter was rescued from the savagely aroused bull, now trying to gore him. A deathly stillness fell on the praça.

Into this dead silence stepped the slight figure of Damaso Gonzalez, with the slow measured tread of one walking to some unheard music. He crossed the ring with an aloof air. He had gone almost half the distance before thunderous applause shattered the night air. In an atmosphere of high tension he proceeded with elaborate coolness to play the still furious bull, who charged with accumulated energy. In a matter of seconds, Gonzalez was master of the situation. Repeatedly he took the bull through a series of classic moves. As the evening paper had foretold, he was an exception to the run-of-the-mill current Spanish favourites, whose extravagant styles were not in the great classic traditions. His was a return to the older purity. The music played and the flag was flown as he put on a display of purest integrity, cold and fearless. He played the bull to a bewildered standstill. With agonising slowness he turned his back on it and carefully, indifferently, walked away to receive the applause of the now standing arena.

The tension and excitement generated by this electrifying display of skill and courage, following the tragic exit of Antoñete, left us feeling limp. But, in the event, it proved to be merely the forerunner to the greatest performance of the evening. Damaso Gonzalez took on the next bull, moving like a classic ballet dancer: formal, graceful, and totally devoid of any recognition of danger. Again the flag flew and the music played and the crowd, on its feet, roared 'Olé! Olé! Olé!' at each superb movement. In front of us, the members of the first row of Sectore One were up and applauding at each succeeding pass. For one moment tragedy again threatened. With a speed that made it impossible to tell what exactly had happened we saw Damaso for an instant on the sand. With consummate skill and speed he rolled in front of the bull as the enraged animal attempted to gore him. The toureadors jumped into the ring and capes flashed. But, rapidly on his feet, Damaso immediately resumed the fight. What followed was humiliation for a great and brave bull. In the end, standing with his hand resting on the head of the huge beast, exposing himself in still profile to the glaring eyes, Damaso coldly and slowly looked round the gasping crowd, which was spellbound and tense. Then, with a pat on the head, he took the bull through some perfect passes and again turned slowly to the tense, packed bancadas. In all this his grace of movement was formal and smooth as if of a dance whose choreography was so familiar that he moved without thought. Only when the bull hooked with violent life did one recall that this animal was still a dangerous beast, whose slightest movement could rip the slight frame of the matador to pieces with its deadly horns.

Nothing could restrain the enthusiasm of the audience at the end of what had proved to be a great night at the Campo Pequeno. Above all, it was the night of this frail looking young Spaniard. Flowers, shoes, handbags, scarves, hats, showered into the ring as he took several voltas. There was no doubt about it—the Campo Pequeno had found a new hero.

Eating in Lisbon

PATRICK SWIFT

Lisbon abounds in restaurants and eating houses, not to mention cafés and tabernas (pubs) where some sort of a meal can be got if need be. There are roughly between six and seven thousand places where one can eat and drink. In the face of this profusion, I can only suggest a few of those that experience and chance have led us to.

But, to start with, it is perhaps necessary to say that there is such a thing as *Portuguese* cooking. In Eça de Queiroz's book *A Cidade e as Serras* can be found a splendid description of a Portuguese exile returning to the country and discovering the joys of his native cuisine. The sophisticated Jacinto, sated by city civilisation and the rich cooking of Paris, where he lived the luxurious life of nineteenth-century high society, has arrived unexpectedly at his country estate in the mountains. He is appalled at the primitive scene. Queiroz evokes perfectly the great, abandoned crumbling manor. In this setting, a typical Portuguese meal is presented.

'A formidable girl, whose enormous breasts trembled in the foliage of her crossed scarf, still flushed and hot from the hearth, entered stamping across the floor with a steaming tureen. And Melchior, who followed bearing a jug of wine, hoped that their excellencies would pardon him as there had not been time to strain the soup . . . Jacinto occupies the ancestral seat—and for some minutes (with anxious gaze at the excellent housekeeper) energetically rubbed with the corner of his napkin the black fork and the rustic spoon. After suspiciously tasting the broth, which was of chicken and steamed aromatically, he tried it—and looking towards me, his comrade in misery, his eyes shone, surprised. He returned to savour another spoonful, this time more considered. And smiled, with amazement—"It's good!".

'It was a precious brew: it had liver and it had giblets; its perfume melted the heart; three times I fervently attacked that broth. "Me too," exclaimed Jacinto with immense conviction—"I have such a hunger. . . . Good God! It's years since I felt so hungry."

'It was he who finally finished off the tureen. And I was watching the door, awaiting the bearer of the hors d'œuvre, the strong lass with the trembling breasts, who finally emerged, more flushed, clattering over the boards— and placed on the table a dish over-flowing with rice with beans. What a let-down! Jacinto in Paris always abominated beans! . . . However he tried a timid forkful—and once again pessimism in his eyes evaporated; they sparkled, seeking mine. Another large forkful, concentration, with the slowness of a monk gourmandising. Then a shout.

' "Superb! Ah, these beans, yes! What beans! A delicacy!" And for this saintly feeding he praised the perfect art of the gossipy women who rattled about among the pans below, and Melchior who presided over the feast . . .

' "This rice with beans . . . not even in Paris, my friend Melchior." The good man smiled, completely relieved.

' "Yes, here it is the food of the men of the farm. And

here Senhor Dom Jacinto will fatten up and grow strong."

'The excellent housekeeper really believed that in those remote Parises, the Lord of Tormes, far from the plenty of Tormes, suffered hunger and grew thin. And it looked as if my friend in truth were satisfying some old hunger, some old nostalgia for abundance, breaking out in more copious praise at each succeeding dish. In front of the golden grilled chicken off the spit, and the salad from the garden, now tempered with olive oil of the mountain worthy of the lips of Plato, he ended up by crying: "Divine!" But nothing drew more enthusiasm than the wine of Tormes, flowing high from the fat green jug— a fresh wine, expert, nourishing, and having more soul, entering more into the soul, than many a poem or holy book. Staring at the tallow candle my Prince, his face resplendent with optimism, cited Virgil:

' "*Quo te carmina dicam, Rethica?* Who is worthy to sing your praises, friendly wine of the mountains?" '

For me, in every good Portuguese meal something of the spirit of this description of the joys of simple country food lingers. And as all the worthwhile pleasures of life stem from the particular, the local, the personal, it is this element, essentially an element of simplicity, that I look for in Portuguese cooking. The joys of Portugal are not the joys of France nor, for that matter, of Italy or of Spain. So crude and obvious a remark has nevertheless to be made. Portuguese cooking can be complicated, but always in a strong and healthy way. Robust and plentiful, fresh and tasty. It is not Mediterranean, it is not Provençal or Florentine. It has its virtues; and frequently its so called defects are merely its proper characteristics. It is disastrous to come looking for the wrong thing. What there is is so superb that to miss it by seeking some form of cuisine that belongs elsewhere is simply tragic.

And Lisbon is a great town to eat in. For my money, it is one of the best places left in Europe for eating out on the average, not too expensive, level. But it must be pointed out that, as in most capital cities, there are the first-class international restaurants where top-standard food in essentially French style is available. I have heard gourmet friends say that the Avis (in the Chiado) is still one of the greatest restaurants in the world. It is legendary and said to maintain the highest standards. Some of the newer hotels are also up to this level: certainly the Lisbon Ritz must come very high. But this is not the sort of thing I am talking about, nor is this the sort of place that David Wright and I and our wives sought out when we went forth to eat of an evening. On the contrary, we looked specifically for the true Portuguese eating-places—such as for instance the Parreirinha, in the Alfama, whose speciality is the chicken in rice cooked with its liver and blood: *cabedal* as it is called. The word means 'a mixture of precious things'. This is a great and true Portuguese dish; the rice is dark, wine coloured, mixed through with pieces of chicken, liver and giblets. It is distinguished from other forms of risotto by distinctive spicy flavourings that come from various added herbs. A dish for a hungry man. When, as in the little restaurant Parreirinha*, it is a speciality of the house, and done with all the love and lore of the countryside, it is something worth travelling to taste. The Parreirinha is the sort of little gem that Lisbon can uniquely offer. Its charm is a combination of atmosphere and good will, plus an honest love of solid tasty food in large quantities. It should be remembered by the visitor that the scale on which food is served is gargantuan, of the old school. In this kind of genuine lisboeta place the portions are formidable.

For me, there are perhaps four clear categories of eating-house. First there is the ordinary little restaurant where the people of Lisbon—those in the city to work—eat their daily lunch. Lunch-time trade in these places is the big trade. All is bustle and fuss, and the service is rapid. Typically, though, no one is going to suggest that you should not linger a while over the coffee. These restaurants (the Rua dos Correeiros that runs from the Praça de Figueira, behind the Rossio and down towards the Praça do Comércio, has many such) are cheap,

---

* Not to be confused with the Parreirinha da Alfama—a fado house.

business-like, and redolent of the city as it lives its daily life. But they are immensely enjoyable for anyone who wants to get the feel of the workaday town. One can meet interesting people—civil servants and clerks, shopkeepers and salesmen. It is amazing how many can speak tolerable English or French. Quite passable conversation is possible. The food is fairly rough but always fresh.

When the restaurant belongs to someone from the country there will occasionally be regional specialities. It is pointless to single out one from the rest. They are so numerous throughout the Baixa, and keep such a similar standard, that it would be difficult to recommend one over another (the restaurant X in the Rua dos Correeiros, referred to by David Wright in our book on Algarve, is typical). Perhaps there is one which is such an institution on this level that it should be mentioned. It is called João do Grão, and you find it on the left-hand side as you enter the Rua dos Correeiros from the Praça de Figueira. Being a most popular place it is always full except at certain hours in the evening. The interior is brown-panelled and divided into a number of connecting rooms crammed with small tables. It usually serves *sopa de Grão*—a chick-pea soup, and the menu is fairly typical of these small restuarants. There will be *canja de galinha* (chicken broth) or *caldo verde* (cabbage and potato soup), there will probably be *sopa de mariscos*, a shellfish soup (something most of these small restaurants seem to do well), and frequently *sopa Alentejana* will be on offer. The latter is a great favourite: a clear soup with garlic and coriander, with an egg poached in it.

Apart from soups a pretty varied range of hors d'œuvres is available too. The ham, of course, whether from Chaves or Lamego, or merely from some place in the Alentejo (this is cured Parma type ham), is practically always on the menu and first rate. In season one eats it with melon or with figs. But melon by itself as well as artichokes (*alcachofras*) and asparagus (*espargos*) are frequently offered as starters. Tunny fish or sardine salad and some kind of shellfish will be there as well, even in these small workaday places.

Main dishes vary with the day, and some restaurants have

their different special dishes for different days. A notice will usually be seen in large letters on the wall informing the customers that, for instance, the *bacalhau* (dried cod) done in the particular way of the house is available on such a day. There is a fairly wide range of fish and the names you will see repeatedly on menus are *linguado* (sole), *pescada* (whiting or hake), *cherne* (sea bream), *robalo* (sea bass), *lulas* (squid), *choco* (cuttlefish), *salmonete* (red mullet). The last, grilled and served with butter and lemon, is a real gourmet's delight in even the more modest restaurant. Then there is always the Portuguese *caldeirada*, or full-brown fish stew, containing a wide variety of fish and spiced and flavoured with herbs and wine. Perhaps this and the *bacalhau* are truly the most Portuguese of dishes.

The meat dishes are never so typical of Portugal, at least for me. But there are a few exceptions. One is the oven baked kid, (*cabrito assado no forno*), and another is the dark pork meat (so different from English pork), grilled, or stewed with clams in the famous *ameijoas* dish frequently called *carne de porco Alentejana*. Certain ways of cooking game, chicken, liver and kidneys are also quite special—the liver in wine; the chicken, traditionally, with a hot piri piri sauce brushed over it as it grills, and the game stewed in spices and garlic. The salads that accompany these dishes have a flavour that is very evocative of the countryside—the hint of coriander or marjoram.

All these run-of-the-mill Portuguese dishes, and some I have not mentioned (like *dobrada*—tripe with beans and chicken and pork; or the *cozido á Portuguesa*, a great dish of boiled cabbage and beef with sausage and ham and morcela, a Portuguese boudin, added in), are the usual fare in the simple category of restaurant. Any Lisbon street contains many such houses. A friendly host and a gang of active boys assure a cheerful and efficient service. The standard is not very variable; such sweets as the ubiquitous *pudim flan* will be everywhere. But there will be fruit and good cheese and coffee. It is never (at the time of writing) necessary to spend more than about forty escudos to eat a very satisfying meal. In fact, in most places, it would be hard to spend more.

EATING IN LISBON

My second category is that of the really 'special', truly interesting restaurant: something on its own, not cheap but extremely good value. There are many of these, and the cost—while fifty or one hundred per cent above that of the kind I have been discussing—nearly always represents incredible value for money.

Memory plays its part in any judgement, but above all where food is concerned. The place and the time and the company can never be dissociated from the menu. When I think of eating in Lisbon, the first thing that comes to my mind is a summer afternoon in the picturesque garden of the Gondola on the Avenida de Berna. Here, with the sun dappling the white tablecloth through the thick foliage of the ancient bougainvillaea and glancing on those enchanting little panels of azulejos set in the walls, I seem to be in an older Portugal. The day seems to prolong itself; conversation in this atmosphere is gentle and leisurely. It is a garden transplanted into the city from some quiet country setting. The strong healthy girls in their crisp aprons, who serve with such good will, increase the impression. It may be early in summer and we are eating fresh figs and Chaves ham; strawberries will be on the menu, a vast cheese board, and a demoralising trolley of cakes and fancy puddings that will undermine any diet.

Or I think of a cool autumn evening at the Cortador. Its long narrow room is crowded. The waiters in their butcher's aprons are serving large plates of clams with pork meat as starters. Huge steaks, superb T-bone or entrecôte, with a Dão Terras Altas wine make us feel so mellow that the somewhat theatrical act of the beaming, fat and jolly proprietor seems the perfection of a hospitable host. He is bald and redfaced, full of jokes and strong opinions. It is said he learned his trade in the Feira Popular. If it is your first visit you will have the privilege of his company at table for the dessert. A bottle of vintage port (and what port!) is plonked down and we drink on the house. In return, a first visitor is expected to give some currency of his own country to the house (the walls are plastered from floor to ceiling with notes from all nations). The reason for the transaction is that you are to receive a small pocket knife, the knife of the cortador (the meat cutter at the slaughter-house); a knife must not pass hands without some payment, even if only token payment. This little restaurant is laden with photos and mementos from customers from all over the world who have enjoyed the crowded atmosphere and the superb steaks. From the ceiling hang myriad hams, sausages, and all the paraphernalia of the cattle farm . . . bells, straps, and the traditional costume of the cowherds.

Recalling a more elegant sort of episode, I think of Tavares. Here the attraction is the decor, the charm of red silk and velvet, chandeliers and gilded ornamental frames on great mirrored walls; an atmosphere that evokes Proust. It is one of the most elegant of Lisbon's restaurants. While I have had splendid evenings there I have also had moderate food—though never less than enjoyable. One goes for the setting as much as the food. And the company is important too—people of the old school, of the Portuguese aristocracy. Civilised, witty, and gay, their company throws into relief a side of the character of the race that is only obliquely observable in the usual encounters with the lisboeta of the middle class.

Lisbon reveals its wit on two levels—the workaday lower classes who have a sardonic sense of humour that cuts through all sham and nonsense, and the upper classes (even in Portugal a threatened and vanishing race) whose love of good conversation and whose sense of the ridiculous enlightens any scene. These people also have a sense of the grand gesture, both spiritually and practically. I do not think the sort of hospitality they are prone to offer can easily be matched elsewhere. When I think of what is valuable in the conservative spirit, I think of the quality of life some of the old school of Lisbon gentry have managed to preserve in a world that for them is falling apart.

On the other hand, the burguesia, the middle-class man of affairs, can have a solemn, serious, exaggerated sense of his importance that can fill even the casual visitor with gloom.

All this is only partially related to the subject of food, but it does matter who it is that makes up the clientèle of a restaurant. And in spite of my remark about the solemn self-importance of the Lisbon middle-class man of affairs, I have to take back much of the derogatory implications when I think of the Martinho da Arcada. Here is a restaurant where the upper civil servant and managerial types (at least that's our guess) eat their lunch. It is one of the very best restaurants in the city. An old panelled room in a pure Pombaline corner of the Praça do Comércio, it has not changed in two hundred years.

An odd aspect of the case, as far as I am concerned, is that it existed mythically for me before David Wright discovered it in actuality, as he has related in our book *The Minho and North Portugal*. In the novels of Eça de Quieroz (once again I go back to the master, but without apology), it is portrayed as a centre of literary and political gossip. For example, when the hapless Artur, in *A Capital,* dreams of literary success in the great city, he sees himself entering the Martinho amid a ripple of excited interest among the gossipy literati. It is there he goes on the night when a review of his slim volume finally appears in *O Século* . . . 'That evening he entered the Martinho, very moved. For certain the volume, made popular by the notice in *O Século,* had already been read. In the hum of conversation it seemed to him he heard his name, bits of the book being quoted; for certain they must be watching him, examining him; and he studied his movements, his way of sitting in the chair, of passing his hands through his hair, in order to make a more favourable impression, to give a public revelation of his intimate genius . . .' It is, of course, a pathetic delusion; nobody is talking about poor Artur.

The Martinho is still a popular place. There is certainly no less buzz of conversation and general noise; but it no longer merits the title it was given even as late as the twenties, when one old guide-book described it as the centre of Lisbon gossip. It has original eighteenth-century azulejos of peculiar charm in the entrance by the kitchen, well worth looking at. The food is nothing less than superb. The solid burguesa atmosphere makes it seem even better. The waiters give the impression of being the same that served Eça de Quieroz; and a couple of little uniformed boys will run out and get you anything you want, from cigarettes to newspapers.

The Leão d'Ouro in the Rua 1° de Dezembro, off Rossio, is another of these solid middle-class places which at one time had a distinguished clientèle and still preserve much of their old atmosphere. Here, there is a bar where one can eat at a high counter: ideal for those who like shellfish or snacks served with a cool white wine or a draught beer. The restaurant in the room next to the bar is large, spacious and solemn; the food itself is solid and solemn—and, of course, excellent. It is something of an institution.

Perhaps the best of the burguesa restaurants is the Porto de Abrigo. Again, it is immensely popular with the well-off managerial type—the equivalent of the upper-bracket London city worker. Always crowded by people who clearly love food, it has the drawback of not being a very leisurely place. It is somewhat like a speeded-up gentleman's club. In the district where it is situated, by the Cais do Sodré in the Rua dos Remolares, there are many alternative places almost as good. This district caters for business people lunching in town. The standard is generally high—the food purely Portuguese.

In the streets behind the National Theatre, down the Rua Santo Antão, there is a group of restaurants that must have special mention. The chief of them is Bomjardim. For some reason there are quite a few similar restaurants clustered in the same area. Bomjardim, and others nearby, cater specially for the lover of chicken grilled on the spit. It is a popular place and has, besides the speciality of the house, an extensive menu. Here, the chicken is always hot and fresh and spicy. It is served with a large mixed salad in an atmosphere that tries to suggest a farmhouse, with lots of azulejos and plain wood, but which for all that is very much that of a popular lisboeta city restaurant.

Most of the solid good-class restaurants I have mentioned so far are lunch places first and foremost. Also, not many have a view. I should mention therefore one sightly 'tourist' place with a magnificent outlook. Good, though not exceptional, for food, its great attraction is a view across the Baixa towards the Castelo de S. Jorge. For once, whoever built the restaurant put the windows in the right place. The evening light as it changes on the pastel colours of the houses climbing up the hill to the old walls of the fortress creates a visionary dream-picture, a Kubla Khan fantasy, moving and beautiful like a Venetian painting. This restaurant is called the Quinta, and it is at the top of the extraordinary street-lift in Baixa that takes you up to the Carmo from Santa Justa.

Good eating-places of this order, having a special character and strong personality, are still very numerous in Lisbon. They deserve a treatise of some length. One could not hope to do justice to them in a brief outline. Nor could one ever realise how rich a vein this element represents in the life of the city by merely paying the odd visit here and there to those that one might happen to come upon. It is usually by returning to the same place over a long period that its true quality becomes apparent. From the restaurant's point of view, the regular client is the focus of the whole operation; thus the catering is more considered than a casual visitor would imagine. However, I pass on to my third category, equally deserving of attention and not less peculiar to Lisbon: the cervejaria, the beerhouse-cum-shellfish emporium.

The cervejaria constitutes a hallowed and popular institution. Frequently it will be a huge hall, with a great counter running for twenty metres down one side; all tiled, as often as not, with some hideous wall decoration in garish azulejos or mosaic. Most of these places appear to be of recent construction. A typical example is the Sagres Cervejaria on the Avenida da Liberdade.

Sagres is the national beer—the only beer. (I once met a German tycoon who deplored the fact that he and his friends were unable to open up a brewery to make real German lager in Portugal. Long may he be frustrated, I say.) The draught Sagres beer is superb. Known as 'imperial' (one simply asks for an *imperial* and gets a draught beer straight away) or *cerveja a copo,* beer by the glass, it is served ice cold. To be sure of getting it always in prime condition it must be drunk where there is a continual rapid consumption so that it is always fresh.

There will be the inevitable mountains of shellfish on display. Large parties of lisboetas will be seen tackling with gusto, and without inhibition, gargantuan platefuls of crayfish (much preferred to lobster), langoustine, prawns, shrimps, spider crabs and rock crabs, cockles, clams, and that peculiarity of the city, *perceves,* or *percebes* (called goose barnacle in English, I believe—though I have never myself seen it outside Portugal).

The atmosphere of the cervejaria is busy, noisy and unsolemn. There is at least one cervejaria that is a gem of architecture and decor; a historical curiosity, one might say. This is the Cervejaria da Trindade, in the Rua Nova da Trindade. It has been famous for many years. Its principal feature is a series of large nineteenth-century polychrome azulejo panels of unusual charm and quality. They are the work of Luis Ferreira (known as Luis das Taboletas). These panels are set in walls running the entire length of the establishment, in what is traditionally said to have been the refectory of the old Convento da Trindade. This was an ancient convent dating from the thirteenth century. Having passed through various vicissitudes, it was finally destroyed by the 1755 earthquake and then rebuilt, only to be knocked down for the opening up of the Rua Nova de Trindade in 1836.

Many of the houses along this street, where once the convent occupied the space, still preserve original features from the old institution, including azulejos. But the azulejos in the pub do not come from the convent, for they represent the symbology of the nineteenth-century freemasons whose meeting hall it was. These panels must be seen by anyone who loves azulejos. Besides a naiveté of drawing and a delicacy of colour that makes them of great interest, they also have the fascination of their subject-matter. The cervejaria has been restored in recent years, but the architects have shown unusual imagination in not changing anything. In places where the old azulejos have been of necessity replaced, excellent antique style substitutes have been used. Only the expert eye will notice any discordant note. As for the originals, they show fulsome allegorical ladies representing the elements, the seasons, truth, commerce, etc. There are some fine colourful birds and strange sun figures, and marvellous detail.

At the Trindade, apart from an infinite variety of shellfish, there is a menu which includes excellent meat and fish balls, and the classic pub steak in the Portuguese manner. This is common to a lot of beer halls. The steak is a thin and usually tough slice of rump beef that comes to table sizzling in half an inch of spicy sauce in an earthenware pan. It is accompanied by fried chip potatoes and a salad. With a large litre caneca of the freezing fresh draught beer, I have lunched at the Trindade on such fare with the greatest pleasure. I would add one caution: if you want to look at the azulejos and enjoy them in peace, don't go on a weekend. On Saturdays and Sundays the Trindade is like a madhouse, with riotous eating and drinking on a vast scale. The best time is a weekday morning, when there is a positively convent-like quiet about the place.

My last category of Lisbon eating-house would also need a special and prolonged discourse in order to do it even moderate justice. I would entitle such a discourse 'The Lisbon Taberna as a Cultural Institution'. For truly there is a whole social world and a complete cultural background behind the endless variety and innumerable oddities that make up the level of the city occupied by the taberna. They are individualists and eccentrics to a man, the taberna owners. They gather round them groups which include more individualists and more eccentrics. These groups become clubs. One of the features of any taberna will be pictures of the Club, framed in bizarre and often genuinely surrealistic fashion. Frequently, these pictures of the club take the form of a small stage—for all the world like a puppet stage—with a set of cardboard cut-out figures representing members of the club. Usually, the club will have some sort of ironic or comic title like 'The Pilgrimage of the Badly-Dressed' seen by Wright in the Alfama. Its function is simply and solely to organise eating and drinking parties, (though one taberna owner told me that they sometimes do charitable work). David Wright and I, on one of our trips to Arrábida, came across one of these clubs out for an excursion—a food and drink jamboree. We boggled at the quantities we saw them put away as dish followed dish. For example, the *caldeirada*, or fish stew, was brought to them, literally, in buckets.

However, in the taberna itself life is not like that. Gossip, a browse over the morning paper, a glass of wine with a *prego* or a *chorçio*, or at lunch time the simple meal of grilled sardines or fried fish, is the usual form. But one cannot make any general rule about the drinking and eating norm in tabernas, for they are all individual, beyond any category. Some of the large tabernas in the Bairro Alto, for example, extend into several sections. They specialise in *petiscos,* often of a quite sophisticated kind. Others are tiny passageways. But always the denizens of these places are 'characters'. Uninhibited, delighted to see a stranger, they will not hesitate to join in conversation or make fun both of themselves and of the visitor.

Evening in the tabernas has a busy after-work atmosphere.

Taberna

Workmen and frequently women and even children, enjoy the hours between work and dinner, exchange gossip and banter.

The character of the taberna has a noticeable difference in the various bairros. Those of the Alfama are unlike those of Bairro Alto or Madragoa. A number, particularly in the Bairro Alto, seem to be owned by Spaniards. This may well be a hangover from the days when the Galicians more or less ran the lower-class catering business and provided the messengers and odd-job men of Lisbon. In the nineteenth century it was customary in Lisbon for these Galegos to stand on corners waiting to be employed. A lot of the waiters in Lisbon are still Galegos.

The reader will be aware already that David and I enjoy the taberna and find its world a source of vast human interest. Rembrandt was criticised for spending so much of his last years in the pubs of Amsterdam among the lower classes. It seems to be probable that the pubs of his time were not unlike the tabernas of Lisbon of today, and in that case there is no mystery about his habits. I can see Rembrandt's old faces of Jews and ageing wrinkled savants in any Lisbon taberna—and how often have Wright and I been brought up sharply by the gravity and dignity of some old josser. An old bespectacled chap in a grubby greatcoat discourses gravely on the question of human communication: the rough company around him does not find it odd. Wright exclaims to me, 'But this fellow has the dignity of James Joyce.'

[Here let me interpolate that Swift and I usually spent our evenings pub-crawling in the Bairro Alto after a simple dinner at a taberna near his pensão. This was called A Bicaense, in the Rua da Bica—a steep cobbled street running up the hill from the riverfront, threaded by a funicular tramway whose single, and singular, vehicle butted its way up or down the precipitous incline about once every ten minutes. A Bicaense consists of a long, high-ceilinged bar with a sawdust floor. Thirty or forty smoked hams from Lamego and Chaves, rust-red haunches suspended with twine from the rafters, overhang a counter backed by the usual battery of formidable wine-barrels. Here we would have our preliminary glasses of wine, with petiscoes of olives or slices of smoked ham, before adjourning to the dining room.

The dining room is a large chamber, in aspect somewhat petit-bourgeois. The rows of tables covered with white napery can, and at lunch time do, seat seventy or eighty persons. At one end is a large serving-hatch; at the other, high up on a corner-bracket, the inevitable telly. Generally we would have steak and chips, a litre of vinho tinto or perhaps a bottle of vinho verde, followed by cheese and coffee and brandy. The bill for the two of us would come to a little more than ten shillings. Always we were served by the same waitress—a daft old body who managed everything one-handed because her left forelimb was permanently employed in holding a transistor radio to her ear. At first I thought it must be a hearing aid, till I discovered that she only moved it when taking an order, when she would shift the little box a couple of inches for a moment or two. This obsessive absorption with the radio in no way diminished her efficiency as a waitress or even, as we found, her capacity for assimilating and retailing gossip.

Not many people would be in the restaurant in the evening— at least, compared with midday, when it would be packed; for the taberna was a favourite lunching-place for office workers. And what lunches, when set against the pie or sandwich that is all the average London white-collar man can, as a rule, afford. Here you could get a square meal and a bottle of wine for about the same cost as a pie and a pint of Guinness in the West End. D. W.]

Going out to eat of an evening in Lisbon is an adventure for anyone with the nose for human diversity and oddity, for culinary curiosities. The city lies waiting with an endless range of the charming, the exotic, the pleasant and the peculiar. From the top to the bottom there is a richness to be enjoyed— who knows but it may be the last of its kind. For standardisation is on the way, and Lisbon like other cities shows a distressing capacity to accomodate the self-service and quick snack bar. These still carry with them saudades* of older and better places. Thus they preserve some shadow of the world they replace. But for how long? Will the day come when we will not be able to find that little place with the fat patrão behind his counter piled high with the fruit of the day, and the cheeses and the puddings and cakes, the dozen tables with solid citizens tackling full plates with considered determination, the floor of scrubbed boards, and azulejos on the wall? Someone tells us that here the anarchists met before they assassinated Dom Carlos. We order a *vinho branco especial* on the leisurely advice of the waiter.

---

* Saudades: a difficult word to translate. A yearning, nostalgia, or longing for what has been or might have been.

A Little History

PATRICK SWIFT

It is the incomparable setting on the banks of the Tagus estuary that gives the city its splendid visionary aspect. The river is one of the mightiest arteries of the Peninsula. It makes its way down from Aragon through a wild mountainous land with fortified and castellated towns on either bank. By the time the Tagus has reached Abrantes, 150 kilometres from Lisbon, it is 180 metres wide. It continues to widen until, between Vila Franca and the city, it reaches 6,000 metres across. Here it is called the Mar da Palha—sea of straw; a vast expanse of water that narrows again where Lisbon rises in terraces from the right bank, like an amphitheatre, some sixteen kilometres from the sea.

Of all the explanations, legendary and mythological, of the origins of the city's name, the quaintest—and very likely the correct one, is that it was a Phoenician colony that called it *alis ubbo*, meaning 'delightful little port'. The Phoenicians had a sense of scale. The various other attempts to find an etymological explanation for the name Lisbon are not so interesting: Ulysses, Lisa and Eliza and so on. There are legends of the wandering Ulysses founding the city at the river mouth. But that there was a Phoenician colony here is a historical certainty, and it seems equally certain that this colony was on the hill where the Castelo de S. Jorge now stands.

With the Romans in 205 B.C. the matter is completely historical. Raised to the dignified category of a Roman municipality with the name Felicitas Julia, Lisbon was subsequently known in Latin as Olissipo, or Ollisipona. The Romans occupied the same area that the Phoenicians had: the south slopes of the hill of the Castelo de S. Jorge. It is known that the port then occupied what is today the Baixa. The Rossio would have been the harbour, in fact. Thus the bank that went up towards the present-day district below S. Jorge would have been the main part of Roman Lisbon.

The contours of the river around the city were similar to those we still see on the other side of the estuary, the outra banda. The city, walled and fortified, rose on the side of such an inlet as that of Seixal and Barreiro. But the river has its prehistory. Up country, where now it spreads its flat margins into long fields of mud, it is joined by its tributary the Muge. Here, excavations have revealed kitchen middens of many metres deep, evidence of a settled community some five thousand years before Christ. There is, too, in archaeology such a thing as the Tagus Culture. This refers to the rock-cut tombs and collective graves: artificial caves found in the Tagus estuary, associated with the most ancient origins of man. At Belém in the archaeological museum, a mass of items collected from the Tagus estuary gives one some idea of this early culture.

Of the historic Roman era, numerous vestiges have turned up from time to time. Not far from the cathedral in the Rua S. Mamede, evidence of a Roman theatre was found in 1798. In the same district, lapidary inscriptions from baths dedicated to Cassios were unearthed. The Carmo museum houses a collection of inscribed stones from various parts of the city showing the passage of time through those pre-Christian centuries when Lisbon was an important Roman city linked by three great Antonine military roads with Emerita Augusta, present-day Merida, in Spain.

After the fall of Rome, the northern barbarians held Lisbon until the beginning of the Visigothic era. From this epoch there exist documents: one relating to the city walls, known as cerca velha, and one relating to the Sé, or cathedral, which was in turn a mosque under the Moors. The Mussulman domination lasted until 1147. Then occurs the great siege of Lisbon in which the crusaders—English, German, and Flemings—joined with D. Afonso Henrique and the Portuguese army to retake it for Christianity. Of this event there remains detailed documentation. The city, at this time called Lissibona, had a population of between twelve and fifteen thousand. In the eyes of the greedy crusaders it was a prize worth fighting for. It had, indeed, been repeatedly attacked and, from time to time, sacked in the preceding centuries: in the early ninth century by Dom Afonso the Chaste, later by the King of Leon, and yet again in 1093 by Afonso VII of Leon. But this final siege under Afonso Henriques was a more serious affair. It marked the end of the Moors in Lisbon.

The document that gives a detailed picture of the event was written by an English crusader, presumed to have been a priest, to a correspondent in Bawdsey, Suffolk.* The manuscript is at Corpus Christi College, Cambridge.

It was a prolonged and desperate siege and by no means easily won. There were times when the besiegers almost gave up; times when they came so near to fatal quarrelling that the venture all but foundered. At a crucial moment a messenger sent from the beleaguered fortress to beg help from the Wazir of Évora was intercepted; and—according to the English version—it was an English tower brought up against the walls on the river side of the city that finally enabled the besiegers to take Lisbon.

King Afonso Henriques' interest in the affair was that of a

---

* For a good rehash of the story, told by the English crusader (known as Osbern, or Osbert, from the incipit Osb. in the ms.), the reader should turn to Rose Macaulay's *They came to Portugal*.

responsible monarch intent on regaining and solidifying a kingdom. The crusaders, on the other hand, were interested simply in the loot. During the parley, Afonso held hostages from the Moors. At one point the situation got so out of hand that he threatened to turn on the crusaders himself and abandon the siege. It is reported that in the end the Germans and Flemings were first into the city. There followed complete disorder and pillage. The siege had taken seventeen weeks. It was the end of the Moors, not merely in Lisbon but in all the surrounding countryside. Even the formidable rock fortress of Palmela was abandoned, as was Sintra and the land on both sides of the Tagus. The Moors were entrenched only at Évora and Alcaçar do Sal.

During the siege of Lisbon the King, with the Portuguese army, had camped in what is now the Largo da Graça. One can get a good idea of the city at the time of the reconquest by walking up from the river, where the Museu de Artilharia now stands, via the Largo de S. Clara to S. Vicente; and from the Largo da Graça back down to the Praça da Figueira. The latter square is where the crusaders camped. There is still enough left of the walls, and of the gates, to give one a very sharp impression of Lisbon at the beginning of its Portuguese era. The maze of streets below the Castelo de S. Jorge and most of the Alfama cannot be much different today from what they were in the twelfth century. This area largely survived the earthquakes that repeatedly wrecked Lisbon.

Speaking of earthquakes and Lisbon, it is usually supposed that the 1755 event was the most disastrous. This is somewhat wide of the truth. The city had suffered repeatedly and one of the worst occasions was in 1531. So much so that we find manuscripts of the sixteenth century mentioning the absence of notable palaces and great buildings. Pombal's radical rebuilding and replanning of the lower part of the town made the 1755 episode of far greater consequence to the general aspect of the city than any of the others.

The city's history as capital of Portugal begins with King Afonso III. It was he who first established a court there. From this time its real development may be dated. By the fifteenth century the population was upwards of 50,000; quite a sizeable town.

But it was the sixteenth century that saw the type of activity which was to mould Lisbon into the place it basically still is today. Then began the Discoveries; a great volume of trade began to flow into the city from all over the known world. The crowds of traders and mariners, the strange, the new, the rich and exotic products of that astonishing upsurge of energy that marked the era of the Navigators, made Lisbon a centre of cosmopolitan activity and one of the great commerical centres of Europe. This was the time of the famous Manuel, whose name attaches to the architecture developed in that period. One of the richest kings of the age, he monopolised by royal edict many of the key items of trade flowing in from the fabulous East. He collected a tribute of thirty per cent, no less, on all spices. Five per cent of this tribute was set aside for the building of the Jerónimos monastery at Belém. To this day, it stands a fitting monument to the wealth and brilliance of the city in Manuel's reign. By the end of the sixteenth century the population was estimated to have numbered one hundred thousand inhabitants. The city was spreading west and north so that a whole new section came into being, with numerous new convents and palaces marking the opulence behind this growth.

The sixteenth century also saw a few unpleasant things in Lisbon, however. There were two earthquakes. The Inquisition caused havoc among the converted Jews and Muslims known as the New Christians. The massacre of the New Christians sheds some light on the life of the metropolis at that time. The municipal council was then dominated by the guilds. They had a representative body known as the House of Twenty-Four. In 1506 riots broke out and hundreds of Jews were killed. The House of Twenty-Four was held responsible by the king and suppressed. The riots had been started by two zealous Dominicans who, the story goes, ran through the streets inciting the mob. An account of this episode survives in verses of Garcia de Resende (1470–1536), and in this version the two monks were later burned for their misdeeds.

The verses are:

Vi que em Lisboa se alcaram
Povo Baixo e vilãos
Contra os Novos Cristãos
Mais de quatro mil mataram
Dos que houveram ás mãos
Uns deles vivos queimaram
Meninos despedaçaram
Fizeram grandes cruezas,
Grandes roubos e vilezas.

I saw that in Lisbon low people and villains launched themselves against the new Christians. More than four thousand they killed of those who were at hand. Some of them they burned alive, children were stoned. They committed great cruelties, great robberies and villainies.

Mas El-Rei mandou sobre ela
Com mui grande brevidade
Muitos foram justiçados
Quantos acharam culpados
Homens baixos e bragantes
E dous frades observantes
Vimos por isso queimados.

But the King took action with great alacrity. Many were tried and many found guilty. Low men and brigands and two observant friars we saw burned for this.

El-Rei teve tanto a mal
A Cidade tal fazer,
Que o título natural
De nobre e sempre leal
Lhe tirou e fez perder.

He took it so badly that the city should do such a thing, that the natural title of the noble and always loyal he took from them and made them lose it.

It is interesting to note that the city had a degree of self-government through the House of Twenty-Four, and also that the Jewish population should have enjoyed the protection of the king against popular anti-semitism. Altogether, some fifty culprits were executed; and the Dominican monastery was suppressed. However, one of the conditions of the marriage of Manuel to Isabel, daughter of Ferdinand and Isabella of Spain, was that the Jewish population should be expelled from Portugal. It gives some idea of the importance of this community when we read that 20,000 congregated at the port for embarkation and that there they were cajoled, tempted and threatened into conversion, though without, apparently, much success.

The Spanish persecutions had driven some 60,000 Jews into Portugal: all rich and educated citizens much valued by the monarch.

Other events included a great plague in 1569. Dom Sebastião set off on his fatal adventure in Africa. The battle of Alcantara was fought in 1581, when the Portuguese crown was annexed by force by Philip II of Spain. This last fact—which meant sixty years of Spanish domination—left its mark on the city. Philip, like a good Spaniard, favoured the Jesuits and the Inquisition. It was he who completed the Jesuit church of S. Roque, originally given to the order by D. João III. The impact of the foreign reign was of a puritanical nature and even the merchants from abroad found themselves harassed on religious grounds.

The Inquisition also found time to persecute the various 'Sebastianists' who began to appear in Lisbon. This strange phenomenon, called 'Sebastianismo', was the product of the myth that grew up from the death in battle of the young D. Sebastião. It was believed that he had miraculously survived and would return to claim his kingdom. It is thought that this messianic myth may have had its roots in the fears of the New Christians, who had so much to lose through introduction of the Inquisition by the Spanish. A number of characters appeared in Lisbon claiming to be the returned king, but they got short shrift. They make an odd collection, these false Sebastiões: one a cobbler, another a handsome country youth from Alcobaça, another a pastry cook with high ideas. Even a Messiah appeared on the scene at about this time.

The sixteenth century must be noted for one other very important event: the Portuguese fleet began to catch cod in the Newfoundland fisheries, and dried cod—the famous bacalhau of Portuguese cuisine—rapidly became a staple of the country's diet. The spring celebrations in Lisbon for the departure of the cod fishing fleet date from this time.

The seventeenth century in Lisbon was a time of expansion and increasing prosperity. It saw the restoration of independence and the installation of Braganças on the throne. The first king, João IV, seems to have been a reluctant monarch.

Looking at his fabulous palace and estates in Vila Viçosa in the Alentejo it is easy to sympathise with his disinclination to risk all this for a political gamble. But his wife was a Medina Sidonia—a resolute and ambitious woman. The actual rebellion, or take-over, was almost without bloodshed. Nevertheless, the scene in the Terreiro do Paço on that morning of 1st December 1640 must have had its dramatic and romantic overtones. Any visitor to Portugal will notice how this date is sacred to the nation; there is not, I suppose, a single town, or even village, in the whole country without some street or square named the First of December. In Lisbon, the new king had his troubles; and it is not at all clear that the whole of the Portuguese aristocracy was as keenly patriotic as it might have been. At an early date in his reign a palace coup was put down, four nobles and a group of commoners being hanged.

The first years of the Bragança reign were, all in all, pretty rough for João IV—a time of intrigue and trouble. Among other things an assassin was bribed to shoot the king as he passed in procession. There were also some tricky relations with England, where the nation had just committed regicide. Prince Rupert sailed into the Tagus with a small fleet; and shortly afterwards the Commonwealth sent out Admiral Blake. Lisbon all but became involved in English internal politics. And the British merchants of the English factory played an important role in the settlement that João finally reached with the Commonwealth. Certain very important concessions for English trade were written into the agreement: for instance, that English merchants in Portugal should never be asked to pay more than twenty-three per cent in custom duties, and were to be consulted about all increases. They were to have religious liberty, their own civil justice, their own burial place. This saw the English ensconced in Lisbon and Portugal in a very special way. It confirmed the resident English in their peculiar relationship with Portugal for the next two hundred years.

All this was clinched permanantly when Portugal entered the Grand Alliance in 1703, joining the Dutch and English against the Bourbons. The aim was to put a Habsburg on the Spanish throne. The political point of the treaty was to give the Allies a base for operations in the Peninsula. For the Portuguese it meant a guarantee of their overseas possessions and trade routes. But it carried grave and unforeseen consequences for the country, and it was to be the key to Portuguese foreign policy right up to modern times. The powerful wine traders gained preferential terms for the entry of Portuguese wines into England. The English got free access for manufactured goods into Portugal: a disaster for the nation's industries, so carefully nurtured by the Count of Ericeira in the latter part of the seventeenth century.

Looking for architectural or artistic evidence of the sixteenth and seventeenth centuries in the city is not a very rewarding business. There is little that is not so greatly modified that it has ceased to look of its time. Here and there a pure detail can be found: a stone corner of a building or a gateway with the original arms carved above an arch, or a niche that has eluded the many alterations and rebuildings that mark the succeeding phases of Lisbon's history. Most of the remaining great houses belong to the fantastic reign of João V. And after João V came Pombal whose effect on the city as a whole was drastic.

The eighteenth century in Lisbon was divided cleanly into two eras by the great earthquake. The first half belongs to the luxurious, devout and utterly indulgent João V. His reign has been referred to as a Divine Opera—a delirium of luxury at the expense of the Brazilian mines. It was a time of peace for Portugal. The only military adventure the king ever risked proved, by chance, to be a glorious one. Portuguese ships sent to assist Venice and the Pope against the Turks saved the day at Cape Matapan. Under the command of the count of Rio Grande, they disobeyed the French order to retreat and were solely responsible for the victory. Lisbon is full of great houses, with huge entrances and over-ornate gateways, that date from this epoch. Few are of artistic merit. As at Máfra, what impresses is the prodigious scale, the unlimited expenditure: the ultimate effect is somehow not moving on the artistic plane.

The king was given to flamboyant gestures, such as importing the Chapel of St. John the Baptist complete from Italy to be installed in the church of S. Roque. It is worth looking at today—a masterpiece of its kind. The king was pious: ministers complained that they were overrun by clerics. One Portuguese writer has described João's private life as a 'nauseating mixture of devotion and sensuality'. But he went to great lengths to foster the arts and sciences, and there remain many important monuments to his efforts. The foundation of the Academy of History, for instance, and the famous 'political testament' of D. Luis da Cunha in which were enumerated the reforms necessary for the nation.

For the execution of this great scheme was named one José de Carvalho e Melo, better known to history as the Marquês de Pombal. One should recall that it was under João that the *Corpus Poetarum Lusitorum* was published, and it was he who had the mass of manuscripts relating to Portugal copied in Rome. He forbade the destruction of antiquities. He built the aqueduct, still one of the most superb monuments in Lisbon, and brought to the people the luxury of abundant water. Most of the handsome street fountains date from his reign. He sent many of the brilliant minds of his generation abroad to study— these men were known as the 'Homens estrangeirados' in Portugal and contributed enormously to the good of the nation.

João died in 1750, exactly in the middle of the century. The remainder of it was overshadowed by Pombal. Pombal's rise and fall were remarkably rapid and the period of his violent and controversial rule saw a complete transformation of Lisbon.

Above all, it is the earthquake of 1755 that the visitor to Lisbon associates with Pombal. The reconstruction of the city following this cataclysm forms his greatest monument. At least, it forms his visible monument. His impact on the life and organisation of Portuguese society was profound on all levels. But the Baixa today means Pombal. It is probably true that the drastic nature of the changes is a fair expression of his personality. The most famous remark attributed to him at the time of the earthquake—'Bury the dead, feed the living and close the ports'—was really made by a different Marquês, Alorna, who used the word 'cuidar' ('care for the living'), incorrectly 'feed' in the popular version.

Alfama

(*Luis Fonseca*)

Street lift to Largo do Carmo

(*Luis Fonseca*)

Cinema, Rossio

(*David Wright*)

Rua da Bica

(*Luis Fonseca*)

Fleamarket still life

(*Peter Neilson*)

Fishmarket varina

(*Peter Neilsen*)

PAO means bread
AMOR means love

(*Peter Neilsen*)

In the Mouraria

(*Luis Fonseca*)

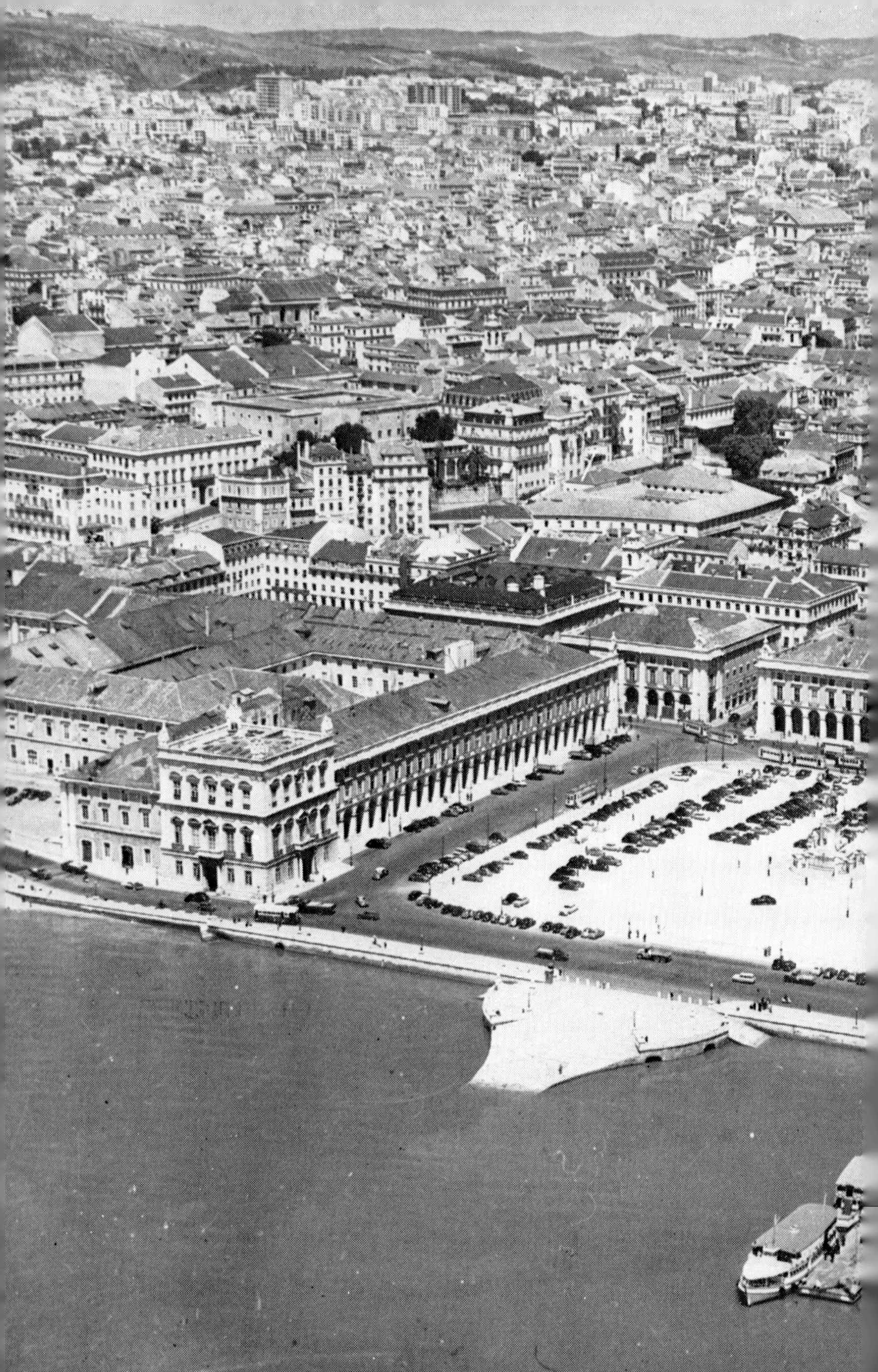

Lisbon (*Luis Fonseca*)

David Telles placing a Bandarilha
(*Peter Neilsen*)

The Forcados

Statue of Eça da Quieroz

(*Patrick Swift*)

Fountain in Rossio

(*Patrick Swift*)

Castelo Branco, Bishop's Gardens

The Bishop's Gardens, Castelo Branco
Right, a fountain (*Phillipa Reid*)
Below, a flight of steps with effigies of the kings

Lunch hour in the flea market

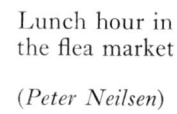

(*Peter Neilsen*)

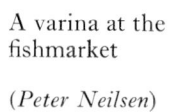

A varina at the fishmarket

(*Peter Neilsen*)

What part Pombal's engineers had in thinking up the form the new city was to take is hard to say. Whether the idea was wholly the Marquês's or whether Manuel da Maia or Eugénio dos Santos de Carvalho, who actually produced the drastic solution for him, exercised any originality history does not record; almost certainly they contributed a lot. Compared to what they set about doing in the Vale de Baixa the damage caused by the earthquake was minor. Theirs was a conscious exercise in city clearance and planning. To achieve their aims, the whole of the ancient section of Lisbon—the heart of the medieval town—was simply knocked down and removed. Before this, the valley had been an irregular area of ups and downs with a haphazard criss-crossing of steep defiles. It was made level. The clean straight lines off the engineers' drawing board were imposed on it. It was a geometric, mathematical solution. It took many years to put into effect. Such a wholehearted transformation is a tribute to the ruthless courage of Pombal. He took extreme advantage of the opportunity to alter the city's character. The rubble of ruins and building materials survived into the nineteenth century. It gave to Lisbon one of the finest squares in Europe. Later, Pombal added a worthy equestrian statue—his master José on the famous black horse.

Other important things happened in Lisbon during Pombal's reign. Industries were founded: the Jesuits, a passionate hate of the Marquês's, were expelled: there was the famous Tavoras conspiracy when the king was shot at. Pombal, in the latter part of his career, conducted a reign of terror such as Portugal had never known or was ever to know again. It was inaugurated at Belém with the brutal public execution of the Tavora conspirators. From then, Pombal's power was supreme.

After Pombal, whose power died instantly with José I, Lisbon's next dramatic epoch came when the French flag flew over the Castle of S. Jorge, and Junot briefly ruled. The ravages of the Peninsular War wreaked havoc all over Portugal. But in the second quarter of the century, the city of Lisbon saw great expansion. It was then that whole new 'bairros' came into existence: Estaphania, Campolide, Campo de Ourique. Great avenues were commenced connecting the old city with the outlying areas of Benfica, Campo Grande and Arieiro—tree-lined open streets that are today full of character and charm.

Many of the nineteenth-century buildings were in their time pastiches or even vulgar imitations of other European types of building. Now, they have the charm that only time can endow. The National Theatre in the Rossio, for instance, seems the perfect façade for the end of the square; and even the imitation Manueline railway station in Restauradores has a charm from its vulgar age. It is a matter of alarm to see some of the follies of the second half of the nineteenth century being pulled down now. Up the Avenida da República I have seen some gems of architectural exuberance making way for the inevitable glass and concrete. Lisbon is rich in these follies but they deserve to be preserved.

The great growth from the point of view of population came in the last fifty years. The number of people living in Lisbon has doubled within this period. Now over a million, the population was less than half a million in the 1920's.

But there is one saving factor in the growth of the city; the old and the new so far have managed to co-exist, quite separately from each other. To travel from one end of the town to the other going northwards is to make a historical journey through eight hundred years of city architecture. Personally, I find something poetic in the tree-lined avenues of the nineteenth century; these and the old Lisbon of pre-earthquake seventeenth-century streets are the most evocative and moving. Pombal's Lisbon is fine, but not charming. In detail it is fascinating for most of it survives quite unchanged. The square is superb—exhilarating even as it is now, full of roaring traffic.

But above all it is the contrasts to be found in a walk in Lisbon that make it such a rewarding town to wander about in. Move from busy street to quiet remote square, from narrow crowded alley of medieval character to broad open avenue full of trees and sunlight. Go, even, into that new concrete jungle of the part of the city that stretches towards the airport. I find it all crammed with interest.

Museum of Ancient Art

I can never be in Lisbon for long without paying a visit to the Janelas Verdes or, to give it its proper title, the Museu de Arte Antiga. It is a place to solace the spirit. As an art gallery it has none of the gimmicky new decor, trick lighting, nor any of the overcleaning and overpresentation of the paintings that has made so many of the great collections of Europe tiring to visit. It is not a great museum in the class of the National Gallery in London, or the Louvre in Paris, or the Prado in Madrid. These stupendous collections are vast and intimidating. To use them one needs to exercise rigorous discipline. Confronted by a plethora of master work, restriction, selection, and intelligent use of one's time become essential. In the Janelas Verdes, on the other hand, the gallery receives you like a quiet old friend who will never tire you. There are masterpieces to be seen, but not too many. There is a unique collection, but it is not necessary to dash from hall to hall to encompass it. And the attendants have an equally quiet and gentle attitude.

And there are some paintings of the first order to be seen. A marvellous Jerónimo Bosch, for one thing; a Dürer; and a Piero della Francesca. There is a section with a fairly comprehensive collection of ceramics, starting with some fine Hispano-Moorish items, and reaching to the nineteenth century. This is not too large a collection to be distracting. It is possible to survey the historical changes and developments as one passes from one glass case to the next without getting the usual museum indigestion.

For those with plenty of time there are numerous odd and beautiful things to be found. Portuguese furniture, tapestries (some of the original Arraiolos carpets), a fascinating section devoted to jewellery and precious gold and silver work, including the famous Custódia de Belém made in 1506 by the jewellers of Gil Vicente with the gold brought back by Vasco da Gama as tribute from the island city of Quiloa off Zanzibar. This section is absorbing and full of treasures assembled from the various great monasteries of Portugal. But for the visitor who is passing through and can spend only an hour or so in the Janelas Verdes there is no doubt at all as to what he should look at: the section devoted to Portuguese primitive art, nearly all dating from the fifteenth and sixteenth centuries.

The centre-piece and keystone of this collection is the famous set of panels by Nuno Gonçalves. Properly called the Panels of São Vicente de Fora, as it was from this church that they originally came, these six panels constitute a masterpiece of painting by any standard. But more than that, they express in a strange monumental way, and with mysterious notes not at once apparent, something about the Portuguese of the era of the Discoveries. Something still very much relevant to the country today. They have been reproduced so often, have been so frequently used for advertising, for tourist brochures and for commercial packages even, that one could be put off from going to see them and submitting to their hypnotic power. Do not be put off. It is one of the most rewarding things in Lisbon. As painting it is of an extraordinary quality. Although ostensibly a pair of triptychs consisting of two groups of portraits with São Vicente at the centre of each, the composition is far from simple. Each face is individual, one might say fiercely individual; but it is a masterly construction—so many finely drawn portraits are assembled as a group, yet without discord. In the treatment of the folds of the costumes all the power and weight of Zurbaran is foreshadowed. Look especially at the monks, particularly the monumental kneeling figure with the black cap. Or look at the boldness of the kneeling beggar in the great brown robe, who incidentally holds a rosary made of fish bones such as can still be found among fishermen of Algarve.

Apart from its masterly quality as painting there is the endlessly absorbing question of the symbolism of the work. On the face of it there is a straightforward story here. But there are also many other possible interpretations. São Vicente is, of course, the patron saint of Portugal. He appears at the centre of the two main panels. In one, the saint holds an open book; in the other, the book is closed. By the open book Dom Afonso V kneels, his bronzed soldier's face contrasting sharply with the pale sickly look of the young prince directly behind him—the future Dom João II. Above this is one of the most vivid faces in the whole panel, that of Henry the Navigator. Representatives from all levels of the kingdom are contained in the work: the premier dukes are here, the archbishop, monks, beggars, fishermen, the head of the Jewish community holding the Talmud and wearing the star of David on his breast. The sacred relic of the saint and the coffin in which his remains were brought to Lisbon are featured. But above all, it is the spiritual quality—that mixture of determined practical faces; faces of men of action, cheek by jowl with others of a profound gentleness, all imbued with a religious dedication—that gives the panels their particular power. The assembly of ship's captains and princes, clerics and saints, beggars and soldiers, all patently enlightened by a passionate sense of mission, says more about the spirit of that astonishing age of Discoveries than any other document in existence. It is the Lusiads in visual terms. Here in this picture is the explanation, if there be an explanation, of the incredible outburst of energy that marked that era.

The rest of the collection of the Portuguese school should be looked at in conjunction with this major work. Taken together, it constitutes an expression of Portugal at its peak hour—the Portugal that played a key role in transforming western man. Some of the paintings are haunting works in their own right. All are fascinating as documents of their age. Look, for instance, on the face of the young Dom Sebastião. This work by Cristovão de Morais says more to explain this strange wayward prince and his grandiose obsessions than any theory about his behaviour can do. For details relating to life of the time one can look at the anonymous *Birth of the Virgin,* an early sixteenth-century work in which domestic utensils as used in country places today are portrayed in detail—the baskets, the charcoal grill and straw fan, the ceramic jugs. Similarly, the pictures showing scenes from the life of S. Tiago have an interest from the historical point of view (apart from being fine paintings). The investiture of a knight is here depicted; the apparition of the Virgin before the battle gives an idea of the religious and warlike character of these men. The picture of Moors engaged in full battle is tremendously expressive of what the reconquest meant in the Peninsula.

There are many paintings here with this especial historic importance, capable of giving the visitor a feeling for the history of Portugal that the reading of volumes might not provide. The arrival of the relics of Santa Auta at Madre de Deus, painted in the early sixteenth century, shows the river and the façade of the convent as it was in its original form. In the paintings of Cristovão de Figueredo there is a pervading gentleness and poetic feeling that is very Portuguese. Even in the gory detail of Christ in the tomb there is this gentleness and tenderness combining with the agonised expressions of suffering.

It would be hard to find a better way to get a general idea of the whole Portuguese mystique than by pottering about among this collection. Yet oddly enough it is only in recent times that these pictures were brought together. The museum was only installed in the Janelas Verdes as late as 1884. The building has, over the years, been adapted and transformed to house the collection. It originally belonged to the Counts of Alvor and was known as the Palace of the Green Windows. It is basically a seventeenth-century building, and at one time it belonged to the Marquês de Pombal.

The present collection came into existence at the time of the suppression of the monasteries. In 1833, when the religious orders were suppressed, an Academy of Fine Arts was created and the bulk of the works af art confiscated from the orders was entrusted into its keeping. It was in fact a combination of academy and art school intended to take the place of the Confraternity of S. Lucas. Later on, it was changed into the Escola de Belas Artes for the teaching section, and a separate institution to take care of national monuments and works of art was set up. It was a long time before the original collection finally inspired the idea of a national art gallery. The 1884 exhibition in the Palacio das Janelas Verdes marked the first ever inventory to be taken of the nation's art treasures.

But the work of making the museum into the institution it is today was chiefly that of one man, José de Figueiredo, an art critic and connoisseur. He took over the museum in 1911 and, together with Professor Luciano Freire, an expert in identification and restoration, he finally established the existence of a school of Portuguese painting and brought together the collection we can now see. Its two great elements are the Portuguese School of painting and the section of precious metal-work and jewellery dating from medieval times.

Figueiredo identified the Nuno Gonçalves panels, which had lain unhonoured in the patriarchial palace of S. Vicente until attention was drawn to them by Joaquim de Vasconcelos. Figueiredo established their authenticity as the work of a Portuguese painter of the mid-fifteenth century, and the name of Nuno Gonçalves was found to be inscribed on the right boot of the king, D. Afonso V, in the painting. Apparently (according to a work by Francisco da Holanda, *Da pintura antiga,* where the first reference to the panels is found) they were painted for an Altar of S. Vicente in the Sé Catedral of Lisbon. Here they were installed and remained up to the beginning of the seventeenth century.

Hard by the palace of Janelas Verdes, a charming square, with an elegant chafariz dating from 1775, is named after José de Figueiredo—and deservedly so.

Sé Catedral

The Cathedral of Lisbon is a cold, venerable block peculiarly devoid of external decoration. A busy tramlined road curves close by the façade. The only point from which it can be quietly viewed is the tiny garden off the road, where old men sit beneath trees, a green haven dwarfed by the austere towers rising above it. The most impressive approach to the cathedral is from below, near the riverside. Here, by the curious Casa dos Picos (a sixteenth-century house of the family of Afonso de Albuquerque), one can ascend through the Arco das Portas do Mar and climb up through a clutter of buildings piled precipitously on the steep incline to the imposing romanesque monument. Its very simplicity creates a strong and solemn aura.

It was once thought that the cathedral pre-dated the Moors and had been used as a mosque. Modern research tends to discount this legend, which probably arose from the finding of one or two stones worked in Byzantine fashion (now in the Carmo museum). It is believed that the original was built by D. Afonso Henrique. Repeated earthquakes (1337, 1344 and 1347) caused heavy damage in early days. Over the centuries the building was altered and added to until it became a gigantic hotch-potch of architectural styles. In the late nineteenth century the work of undoing all the accretions of the years was begun: what we see today is the bare bones of the original structure. There are one or two corners where examples of the baroque encrustations removed from the rest of the cathedral can still be seen: one gloomy chapel from the Spanish domination, and some rich João V decoration. But it is the cold simplicity of the nave, and above all the remains of the old cloister, that are most moving.

To see the cloister you need to find the guide and buy a ticket. He will probably point out the pillar near the entry which is quite off centre owing to the 1755 earthquake. What one sees is mostly early fourteenth century. Beautiful vaultings with some interesting details on the capitals of the fine pillars in the arches. There is a remarkable wrought-iron grid, older than thirteenth century and clearly Moorish influenced. The rose windows, each different, set above the arches are very beautiful.

We found the caretaker full of information and anxious to impart all of it. An odd spiral staircase set in one of the old chapels was explained as being the entrance to his home. He lives on the premises; as all doors lock on the inside, it is only through his romanesque apartment that exit and entrance can be effected when the cathedral is locked up.

While I was looking at this fine old iron spiral staircase, my daughter Katty had found another oddity: a great scraggy old raven, which our friend the caretaker kept in a box behind chicken wire. The symbol of Lisbon, he explained. He was keeping up a tradition now almost extinct. Not long ago it was the custom among the ordinary folk of Lisbon to keep a tame raven (corvo), the bird of the city. The caretaker's bird answered to the name Vicente.

The Church of São Roque

The Church of S. Roque must be one of the most famous of Lisbon tourist attractions—not just of our day but ever since its famous chapel of St. John the Baptist was installed there by João V. This chapel is legendary for the richness of its materials, and it has astonished generations of visitors impressed by the recital of the precious stones and metals used in its construction. It is made of rare marbles, Italian and African alabaster, amethyst, jade, jasper, lapis lazuli, agate, porphyry, diaspore, and ancient breccia—not to mention mere gold and silver. One can easily imagine the romantic nineteenth-century mind being fired by such a list. It sounds like something conjured up by the imagination of John Keats, though in fact the chapel was made in Rome in the middle of the eighteenth century (Dom João V ordered it in 1742). 'The execution of this jewel is of a rare perfection', wrote a French traveller in 1857. 'In France we do not have, and are unlikely ever to have, anything comparable.'

The chapel was completed in Italy and shipped out to be set up in S. Roque, a monument to John the Magnanimous King. Before leaving Rome it was blessed personally by Pope Benedict XIV in the church of S. António of the Portuguese—a small service for which the king paid His Holiness some 100,000 cruzados. Three ships brought this extravagant construction to Lisbon in 1747, and with it the artists who were to mount it. There can be no doubt about the skill of these artists. The obvious example is the great picture of the Baptism of Christ in mosaic. This, with the two lateral pictures in the same genre, is a miracle of patient workmanship. Similarly each object and detail is the work of a skilled and famous Roman craftsman: the entrance arch by Rotoloni, the royal arms by Giovannini in Carrara marble, etc.

Having said all this I must report that for me the Capela de S. João Baptista is a curiosity: it does not move me as art. On the other hand I love the church of S. Roque. I love it for its sixteenth-century azulejos and its mad golden baroque chapels, strong and bold and full of life, not the work of sophisticated mannerists but of simple provincial carvers.

The church is famous for many reasons other than its John the Baptist Chapel. It was here that the great Portuguese orator and writer, the Jesuit Padre António Viera, preached his famous sermon, which took two days to deliver. A remarkable Portuguese-Brazilian (he was born and he died in Brazil), his writing is of a special kind of brilliance and of importance in the development of Portuguese literature.

Madre de Deus

A seventeenth-century print shows Madre de Deus as it should be—overlooking the river on an open square with steps leading down to the quayside where ships lie moored along the front. It is thus too that it is seen in the sixteenth-century painting in the Janelas Verde showing the arrival of the relics of Saint Auta. Now a tramline runs close by the door down a narrow street with a high wall all along one side, making it hard to appreciate the imposing nature of the building.

Madre de Deus is one of the most absorbing monuments in Lisbon, and it is one of the best places to see a wide range of Portuguese art. It was originally a convent founded in 1509 by Queen Leonor, wife of D. João II, on the site of the house and orchards of the widow of Dom Álvaro da Cunha. Its original scale was modest and it was never finished in the lifetime of the foundress. A miraculous image of Nossa Senhora da Madre de Deus, however, attracted the attention of the faithful and the crowds flocked to the little convent. This, in turn, brought it to the attention of the king and the grandes senhores of the court who showered it with offerings and privileges.

What we see today has little to do with the original convent. Of the primitive chapel, only old paintings (one in the sacristry) can give us an idea. The Asilo de Maria Pia, occupying the palace next to the convent, is also of a later date. D. Leonor lived in the Paço de Xabregas on this site, but the present building is the old palace of the Marquêses of Niza. The Paço de Xabregas was outside old Lisbon (the district of Xabregas was only made part of the city proper in the nineteenth century) and had many great historical associations.

Leonor was a remarkable woman who had a tragic life—during the struggles between the monarchy and the nobles she saw her own brother killed by her husband the king. Later her only son, the young prince D. Afonso, died prematurely. Finally, widowed at the age of thirty-seven, she devoted herself to religion and charity. She was a patron of arts and letters and it was here at Xabregas that Gil Vicente* first presented his *Auto da Sybilla Cassandra*. Nor was this the only institution she founded. The Casa de Misericórdia at Lisbon and the Hospital of Caldas da Rainha both owed their existence to her patronage and piety.

Madre de Deus is, however, a special case. For some reason, it gets little attention in guide-books. But it is not to be missed, for it has great historic and artistic interest. It contains painting of the Portuguese school of the first importance. Recently, a museum of azulejos has been installed there by the Gulbenkian Foundation: a fascinating aggregate of odds and ends from all parts of Portugal, giving a good idea of the pre-eighteenth-century azulejo, always more colourful and primitive before the total dominance of blue set in. There are, too, a number of examples of Moorish and Mosarabic tiles. All are beautifully displayed. It is a pleasure to linger among the refreshing colours and gay details: birds, plants, and hunting scenes still as fresh as the day they were painted, and fired with the enchanting irregular glaze of the older tile makers. They are mostly of seventeenth-century Lisbon manufacture. The most important of the panels were rescued from the old Palace of Praia in Belém, the property of the Duke of Cadaval; all in greens, yellows and the purplish browns of manganese oxide. But there are also some enchanting items brought from Évora.

The nave of the church offers an interesting sidelight on the

---

* Gil Vicente (1470–1536) was the father of Portuguese theatre. His work has a caustic and satirical quality and is an endless source of vivid information about the life and customs of Portugal in the fifteenth and sixteenth centuries—it is magnificent theatre.

Madre de Deus

azulejo of the eighteenth century. Here we see a series of panels of vast scale running right round the walls. At a glance they look like typical Portuguese blue azulejos of the eighteenth century. A second look, and they are immediately seen to be quite different in character. They are stiffer, the glaze is drier and the blues are harsher; the drawing lacks the soft fluidity and the curvilinear grace of the true Portuguese azulejo. They were made in Delft in the seventeenth century to Portuguese design—and nothing can emphasise more the unique quality of

Portuguese azulejos than the contrast in style they offer, with the two (not first-class) nineteenth-century side panels of Lisbon manufacture.

As for painting, here is one of best places to see the sixteenth-century Portuguese school. The best paintings relate to the martyrdom of Saint Auta, who was one of the eleven thousand virgin companions of Saint Ursula. The body of Saint Auta was sent to D. Leonor by the Emperor Maximilian and was borne up the Tagus to the door of Madre de Deus on the 12th September 1517. Here it was received with all possible pomp and ceremony, and the queen ordered a retable of the arrival to be painted. The central panel of what was originally a triptych is the painting that can be seen in the Janelas Verde, but the remaining panels, badly cut to fit into frames, are at Madre de Deus. These paintings, known as the work of Mestre de Santa Auta (possibly by Cristovão de Figueiredo or Gregório Lopes), belong to the golden moment of Portuguese art. The delicate tones and fine draughtsmanship, as well as the detail of the pictures (the caravels on the river in the background), speak more eloquently than any words of the spirit of the nation and the epoch. The style reminds one of Memling, but the gentleness pervading the work, and the ingenuous, almost feminine sentiment, is utterly different.

There are numerous things to make a morning well spent in this quiet convent atmosphere: the cloister with the tombstones of the founder and the first abbess; the chapel of Saint Anthony with paintings and azulejos of the eighteenth century; the sumptuous choir with the relics of the martyred saints set in gilded glass cases (and beautiful azulejo-lined window recesses). The relics are mostly unidentified, though the guide pointed out the skull of Justin Martyr to us. The choir dates from the sixteenth century and preserves the original chairs, but the whole is overlaid with baroque decor of the eighteenth century.

One of the interesting features at Madre de Deus is the use throughout of the symbols of the queen and of King João II. Hers is the camaroeiro—the shrimpnet—and his the pelican feeding her young with her own flesh.

Mosteiro dos Jerónimos

A visit to Belém is not simply a good idea; it is an absolute must. One could spend days or weeks with pleasure among its historical buildings and museums. The way to Belém takes you past the Museu dos Coches; once there, the Monastery of Jerónimos, the Archaeological Museum, and the Museu de Arte Popular all merit attention.

But it is the Jerónimos above all that has to be seen. This is unquestionably the greatest monument the city has to offer. It is also the best possible introduction to the Manueline style, that unique Portuguese architectual phenomenon. The device of naming styles after the reigning king of an epoch is frequently a clumsy way of labelling architecture of the past, but in this case there is the exact justification of the great monastery by the river having been built by Manuel I in gratitude, as tradition has it, for the immense achievements of the Discoveries.*

One must recall that Portugal, towards the end of the fifteenth century, was becoming rich in a fantastic way. In the sixteenth century Manuel was, for a time, the most wealthy monarch in Europe. His titles make a splendid list: for example, Lord of the Navigation, Conquest and Commerce of Ethiopia, Arabia, Persia and India. The result of royal monopoly of all the trade flowing from the voyages of discovery made Manuel rich beyond dreams, and the envy of the rest of Europe. It was with money coming from the spice taxes that he built the great monastery. From Belém the caravels departed, and it was at a small chapel here that Vasco da Gama prayed before his voyage to India. Of the tribute of thirty per cent collected by the crown on all spices, five per cent was set aside by the king for the building.

The famous gold monstrance of Belém—known more often by the name of the maker, the poet and dramatist Gil Vicente, who was also master of the mint—was made at the same

* The original intention may not have been this, for the Papal Bull founding the convent at Belém is dated December 1498 and the arrival of the Bérrio with Paulo da Gama bearing news of the Discoveries is July 1499.

Jerónimos

period with the gold paid in tribute by the ruler of Quiloa and brought back by Vasco da Gama.

It is against a background of spectacular richness that Jerónimos must be seen. It can truly be called an expression of the spirit of its time. The style called Manueline spread through the whole of the country. There is hardly a town or village of even modest consequence that cannot show at very least a window or doorway in this manner.

There has always been some discussion as to the exact historical position of Manueline architecture. Was it merely a transitional period between gothic and renaissance, with admittedly special local features? Or can it be considered as a unique style with a beginning and an end of its own? This argument will not concern the casual visitor too much. But any traveller will notice that there is a very distinctive and all-pervading characteristic to be seen everywhere—from Caminha,

Braga and Vila do Conde in the north, through Sintra, Lisbon and Évora, the castles and palaces of the Alentejo and the churches and monasteries of Algarve. This is the gradual and increasing intrusion—until it becomes orgiastic—of Nature; of a naturalism that is not merely ornate but becomes a fulfilment in stone of a spiritual concept.

The Manueline period did not last very long. By 1517, truly renaissance influence brought in by French sculptors had begun to change the scene. Manuel recruited his first architects from Batalha. The master stonemasons from this source—Marcos Pires, Boytac, Anriques, Mateus Fernandes, João Rodriques—working throughout the country, at Coimbra, Guarda, Tomar, Sintra and Belém, developed a strong and unique style in a comparatively short time. At Belém, it was Boytac who created the basic concept in Jerónimos. He had already built the Church of Jesus at Setubal (worth looking at with this fact in mind) and had worked at Batalha and Coimbra. Here the elements that relate the monastery to Batalha and Santa Cruz de Coimbra are his work; he directed the building for fourteen years, and the great south door is basically his masterpiece.

The first stone was laid in 1502. Fairly full accounts exist of the beginnings of the work. One Pero Travassos was in charge of the scheme together with his clerk João Leitão and these two, with the prior of the monks of Saint Jerome, formed the accounts committee (Mesa dos Contos) who received the cash flowing in for the works—chiefly of course the five per cent from the Indian spices. As a matter of historical curiosity, it may be noted that this was paid by the Florentine banker Bartolomeu Marchione.

The work continued over fifty years. As it progressed numerous influences came to be added. After Boytac, João de Castilho, the master of Tomar, took over in 1517. He introduced, among other collaborators, the French sculptor Nicolau Chanterene, who brought the first renaissance elements with touches of Italian taste. His statues on the west door (set in niches by Boytac, it should be noted) of D. Manuel and the queen D. Maria, Saint Jerome and John the Baptist are among his masterworks. But the most important characteristics are the result of the original plans of Boytac and his truly Manueline style; João de Castilho was a major contributor. Under João III, Belém was abandoned in favour of his great projects at Tomar.

Jerónimos is, above all, related to the sea and the Portuguese mariners. Fittingly, it is here, still, in the spring of every year that the cod fleet is blessed in a moving ceremony.

The whole effect of the architecture is of lightness and spaciousness. Although the doorways and pillars are all crusted with decoration, they are light and airy. Inside, the pillars soar aloft to a fine vaulted ceiling. Part of the effect is achieved by the way in which the three naves have been given the same height. The pillars with their mass of carving seem slight and elegant. The whole gives the impression of being one nave, and in this the sense of space is very much accentuated (the actual size is ninety-two metres by twenty-five metres). The spacious feeling might lead one to ignore detail but this would be a loss. There are gems of carving to be found at all levels and in all corners of the building. In general, it is the carving in the exuberant style of João de Castilho—frequently laid over the original work by Boytac, as in the great pillars—that merit attention. Numerous gems by Mestre Nicolau are also found throughout. At the bottom of a great pillar facing the transept can be seen a medallion with a portrait traditionally said to be of Boytac, although some scholars think it more likely to be of João de Castilho, as it dates from his time.

Apart from the church, the thing that must not be missed is the cloister. It is a work that owes its principal features and its basic elegance to Boytac, but it was added to and finished by João de Castilho. By any standard, it is a masterpiece. The thin pillars between the arches supporting the vaulting afford its special grace. They rise and spread out naturally like plants. The ground level is pure Manueline; the upper gallery witnesses the renaissance influence. What shows the genius of João de Castilho as an architect is the upper gallery running round the cloister. It seems so natural, so much a part of the whole, that it is hard to imagine that it was not conceived as such by Boytac in his original plans. There is detail here, too, that can detain one for hours: carving from all the periods during which the building went on, work from the hands of the great sculptors of the day—Felipe Henriques, Pero de Trilho, Fernando da Formosa, Francisco de Benavente and many others.

Ethnological Museum, Belém

The Ethnological Museum adjoins the Jerónimos. The building is a pastiche of the Manueline monastery and dates from 1859. To quote the *Guia de Portugal*: 'The Manueline decoration was not assimilated, neither in spirit nor technique, its artistic value is doubtful, its historic value nil.' The collection itself however is of first importance to the study of the prehistory of the Peninsula. Here are housed many unique items from the western 'Atlantic' sphere and, for the expert and layman alike, a visit to this collection is not to be missed. Much of the material and the background it comes from still awaits systematic analysis. At the moment of writing, there is not even a catalogue or brochure available at the door.

For the casual visitor, the absence of a catalogue is more of a nuisance than a tragedy. The museum is officially divided into three sections—archaeology, anthropology and ethnography; or at least to begin with. Recently it was rearranged. The new presentation has a lot to be said for it from the point of view of the non-expert. Instead of separating prehistory from recent anthropology, each section now shows the progression of different artefacts from prehistoric times to the present day in individual show-cases. On entering, one finds a fascinating display of country artefacts of cane, of straw, of cork—model boats, nets, and other implements of the fisherman, oxen yokes, pottery lamps and bronze lamps. Where possible, these displays start in prehistory and present examples of the objects as they evolved down the ages. This is very complete in the case of the lamps, for instance. Arabic and Visigothic lamps are well represented, and there are some fascinating oddities such as the use of sea shells as lamps—a device which one imagines must be very ancient.

The section devoted to the world of the shepherd is of great interest. There are beautiful examples of carved wooden tools, and crooks, and bags, small shepherd's flutes, and those terrifying collars worn by the dogs of the serra for protection against wolves. The displays of ironwork also start with items from prehistory and go right through to present times. But the main and most important part of the museum is devoted to palaeolithic, neolithic and Iron Age finds in Portugal. There are at least twenty thousand items, some of unique importance.

One should look out for the exquisite examples of engraved schist plaques, totem devices and symbols of authority. Other unique things are the inscribed stones from the Algarve and Alentejo written in the old Iberic script and still undeciphered—the letters are known by their Latin counterparts but the meaning of the words remains a mystery. Besides these, there are stone idols and some fine examples of cut stone from the castros of the north, all of which deserve attention as being peculiar to the Portuguese side of the prehistory of the Peninsula.

But the main central hall contains what I consider makes a visit to the museum absolutely essential even for the casual tourist. Here we find the famous carved granite warrior figures and the great guardian boars from the Celtiberian north. These are astonishing; they make a dramatic impact both as carvings and symbols. They stand like giant totem figures but combine a realism in the carving that adds absorbing historical interest to their meaning. The warriors hold round embossed shields and wear short tunics. They have arm bands and wear torcs round the neck. Their short swords are held rigidly in formal stance at their sides. Of particular interest are the heads—typically Celtic, with the characteristic formalisation of the eyebrows and moustache and the bulging round eyes. The whole adds up to a spiritual and physical projection of the hero of the great Celtic sagas—of the Táin Bó Cuailnge, for instance. There is a superb group of carved boars, seven of them perfect specimens, the scale and power of which leaves one in no doubt as to the character of those mythical beasts—the bulls that fight it out in the Táin, for example, whose strength and prowess are of another order, superior to natural animals.

If one went to Belém only to see these great Celtiberian figures and nothing more, the visit would be worth every minute spent on it. But there still remains the Luso-Roman section, with graves and statues and vast mosaic floors taken from a spacious Roman villa unearthed in the Alentejo. There is also a section on ceramics and a collection of dolls—the latter has spellbinding potential, if I may judge from the amount of time my daughters Katty and Julie spend there.

For myself, I go repeatedly to this collection and find it an endless source of interest. Its scale is reasonable for a one-visit quick survey. Half an hour pottering about here will give a better idea of the Lusitanian background than much reading.

Torre de Belém

The ancient fortress of S. Vicente de Belém, by the water's edge, has an air of being stranded out of its time. It is basically a romanesque gothic structure. The plans were ordered by D. João II and sketched by Garcia de Resende (at least, so the Chronicler himself tells us) but it was built by D. Manuel. Its original function was to cross fire with the Torre Velha, a similar structure on the other bank of the river, a work of João I. It was, when first built, somewhat out in the river; but with the passage of time the area between the fort and the bank silted up and it now stands jutting into the water like a vast prow.

The master builder was Francisco de Arruda and the faintly eastern air (Byzantine cupolas adorning the lookout posts, etc.) comes from the influence of some years spent by the builder working in Morocco as a fortress constructor. Because Arruda's influences are Portuguese, Manueline, and Moroccan, entirely free from Italian or Spanish ideas, many take this to be the expression par excellence of the spirit of the nation, the reverence for tradition and the dream of expansion.

Basically, the tower is a simple quadrangle with a broad polygonal platform in front surrounded by battlements. Most of the superb Manueline carving and decoration is on the outside. The usual symbols abound, the escutcheon of the king, the cross and the sphere of the Order of Christ, and so on. There are verandas with slim pillars and arches that have a slightly incongruous look on the austere walls. On each corner of the fortress, the lookout towers seem to hang off the wall proper on an upturned cone that, in every case but one, is supported by a dragon. The exception is that of the northwest, where the supporting animal is a rhinoceros. This is almost certainly the earliest sculpture of a rhinoceros in Europe.

Inside, the tower is austere and little ornamented. The so-called royal room (sala regia), a square, vaulted chamber of impressive proportions, is worth visiting. A good time to see the Torre de Belém is at sundown, when it can be very moving to watch the golden light of the evening fall across these ancient stones. It is in some ways a grim interior too. The thought that it once served as a state prison provokes gloomy reflections: many distinguished prisoners were held here; in 1641 the Duke of Caminha, the Marquês of Vila Real, the Archbishop of Braga, and the Count of Vale de Reis were all locked up in its dungeons. Here too, for his support of the Prior of Crato,* D. Pedro da Cunha, the father of the Archbishop of Porto, was imprisoned and died.

The tower is a unique symbol, recalling the era of expansion and Manueline glory more evocatively than many greater monuments.

---

* Prior of Crato: pretender to the throne after the death of D. Sebastião. The aged Cardinal King Henry proclaimed penalties for all who sheltered the prior.

Feira de Arte Popular, Belém

Arte Popular means handicraft and folklore. I have become an unashamed addict of popular art in Portugal. In Ireland, years ago, I was never one of the arty-crafty folk-enthusiasts. But then it was the people and not the folklore or the crafts that put me off. Now I am an addict.

There survives in Portugal a whole world of hand-made objects, still being made and still being used. But it is almost uniquely the world of the peasant. This world is doomed. However much we may like the mule and the ox, nothing will stop the tractor from taking over. In truth, the process is much further advanced than one might judge from a superficial look about the countryside. An old oxen cart, an ancient chillon cart with thousands of years of history behind it, trundling along a main road, strikes a note one remembers. The tractor and the modern farm equipment that are taking over are not so striking. But today, at every fair in any Portuguese country town, there will be a stall with tractors and modern implements on show. Their use is more and more widespread every year, as I should know, having once been in business with a gypsy dealing in mules; the market was collapsing even then, five years ago. But that is another story.

The Fair is held every year in spring and early summer in the Museu de Arte Popular. The museum was founded by António Quadros' father at a time when there was still no difficulty in obtaining folk objects, when the culture of peasant art and artefact was in full flower in Portugal. It is one of the great collections of its kind: it is doubtful if there is a better one anywhere in Europe. The Fair, however, is not the same thing at all. It is what it says it is—a fair. Country craftsmen from all over Portugal come here, set up their stalls, and show and sell their produce. Some of this ware is from small factories. Even some of the large factories show their products. But so do the individual makers of all classes of country objects: leather, iron, tin, pottery, straw and cane work, glass. Mostly the standard is high, little is corrupt or vulgarised.

The Fair includes a theatre; this is the more professional and arty side of the occasion. Here they show films—and this, I think, does put me off a bit; films about crafts, in my experience, are the kiss of death. No doubt there will be a place for them in the documentation of a lost era. But if I cannot get my handicraft by wandering through the fairs, taking a drink here and there as I go, then I fear it's not for me. When we arrived at the theatre (this theatre, I should say, forms part of the museum), a puppet show was in progress. It was a show brought up from a village in remote Alto Alentejo. It seemed worth while looking in. We were rewarded.

It was dark and cool in the theatre, and the little puppet stage was set for a barber's shop scene. This was fun; the main interest, for me, lay in the dolls and their costumes. There was also music, mouth-music and hand-clapping, which had a strange other-world quality. The language was beyond me, but it was mostly beyond the comprehension of my companions also. It was an archaic form of speech—perhaps specially so for the purposes of the theatre. Even the running commentary was unintelligible to the educated Portuguese ear. There were shouts back and forward to the audience, also rather obscure—it appeared later that the man who was responsible for bringing the puppet show to the fair was standing in for their traditional country audience and engaging in the sort of banter that was a normal part of the show. This became clear when it was found that Rosa Ramalho, the famous folk-sculptor, had come in. The puppeteers immediately included a number of jokes for Rosa in their shouting and buffoonery. The barber story was not much out of the ordinary tradition of the puppet show. It revolved about the usual sort of slapstick that makes up the puppet theatre: a country man refuses to pay the barber, the barber attacks him, and, successively, his friends, the priest, the police, the local dignitaries, come to try to deal with the barber until the army is called in—and even they cannot get the better of the fearful chap; and all ends with terrible buffeting and shouting. It was great fun, but it was what followed that made this a memorable evening.

This was nothing less than the History of the World. It is hard to describe how a tiny puppet stage, with these small figures in curious antique costume, mesmerised us and completely held our attention for half an hour or more. The music off stage was part of the hypnotic effect. It was sung by the group in slow measured plain chant. Strange, sad, long notes telling the story of the beginning of the world. The voice of God would speak out, 'Let there be light', and on the dark little stage a gold disc rose. Ditto for moon and stars. Later, the Garden of Eden and the naming of the animals. There were some divergences but in general it followed the Bible. God when He appeared did so with great drama. A clap, a cloud of smoke—and suddenly there He was. He was authoritarian and rather cross, dressed in red and looking like a cardinal. He tended to be fussy; quite out of patience with Adam when Adam asked for a mate. This was comedy. And part of the effect was the alternation between the unearthly music and the slapstick. The chant provided the continuous story, the background; individual singers and speakers provided the dramatic moments. The singing and the visual impact of the puppets and their costumes, added up to a moving performance.

This show was a family affair, as we learned during the interval from a large, bearded young man—the one who had been doing all the shouting during the barber-shop piece (the History of the World was far too solemn for any interruptions of that nature). The family had always been the performers, makers and presenters of the puppet show as far back as anyone knew. It was the opinion of the young man that both the text and music, as well as many of the dolls, were medieval. Even the costumes were of unknown age, far older than any member of the family could recall.

It is true of all Alentejo music that it sounds, as this did, like church music. Very close to plain chant. It has been said that this is due to the fact that the Alentejo was the domain of the great religious orders. This might also apply to the puppet show which had many overtones of monastic culture in both music and costume. The costumes and all the paraphernalia had been passed down through the generations. It was obvious that the dolls had been replaced from time to time; some looked much less archaic than others. Also, there was a peculiar disregard for scale; some were small and some large, without any apparent method or order.

Museu dos Coches

The museum of coaches was established by Queen D. Amélia and opened in the year 1905. It is today a unique institution that outdoes many such competitors—that of Madrid or Versailles for instance. The collection is housed in the old picadeiro (riding school) of the Palace of Belém. Under the splendid painted roof of Francisco de Setubal and Nicola della Rive, in the former ring surrounded by a vast gallery, about one hundred items are assembled.

The building in itself is a curious example of the Louis XVI style applied to domestic architecture. It was built by the Italian Jacomo Azzolini by order of D. José. Here, as one guide-book puts it, 'so many elegances paraded to assist in the jousts and tournaments of the court, and the most illustrious aristocratic horsemen of the day showed their finesse, the Marialves, the Alornas, the Angejas, the Lavradios; and here Junot taught equitation to the little blonde countess of Ega, his mistress'.

The richness and profusion of carving, painting, gilding, of inlay and mosaic, of brocades and velvets, of rare Bohemian glass, and of exquisite and expensive decor is truly staggering. There are litters and dogcarts, Berlins and landaus, and unbelievable extravagances of the great coaches from the time of João V. The royal coach of João V is sumptuous to a degree. Some of the travelling coaches are even fitted with toilets. But the most way-out and extraordinary objects in the collection are undoubtedly the coaches made for the ambassador to Pope Clement XI. These are baroque sculptures on wheels, of most elaborate workmanship. They were made in Rome and used by the Marquês de Fontes who designed them. As goes with the character of João V they outdid in luxury anything seen on wheels up to that time. They are full-scale carvings of symbolic subjects in the baroque vein of the day. What is fascinating is the sculptural part of the coaches. Figures of Minerva, Silenus, allegorical figures of Navigation and War and Hope are grouped on the front and back of the coach. Even Adamastor is represented, as is Apollo and a host of other figures designed to show João V as a great maritime power and a great promoter of the arts.

Other things worth looking for are the coach that brought Philip II to Lisbon: a solid and workmanlike job without the usual extravagant royal decoration, but a rare example of its kind (probably the only one in existence), and the crown coach made in France to the order of D. Pedro II for the marriage of the future king João V to Maria Anna of Austria, a masterpiece of the Louis IV period.

The array of harnesses and equipment on show together with examples of court costume, are also of absorbing interest.

Museu da Cidade

Incongruously situated now, among warehouses at the far end of the Lisbon docks, stands the elegant Palacio da Mitra. It is a seventeenth-century building, refurbished in the eighteenth and again in the nineteenth century. It retains all of its dignity and solemnity—is in fact majestic, princely and opulent in aspect. As the name—mitra meaning mitre—recalls, it was the bishop's palace. The docks here are known as Poço do Bispo (Bishop's Well), emphasising the point. At present it houses the Museu da Cidade, the City Museum of Lisbon.

This is a curious corner of the city, not usually visited by the tourist. The museum is a restful undemanding collection of prints, documents and objects with historical associations for the city of Lisbon. The prints are interesting, showing the way in which the city has changed—slowly in the early centuries, and incredibly rapidly since the mid-eighteen hundreds. There is a section of paintings and drawings—nearly all from recent years —some of real quality but mostly interesting for their illustrative aspects: what the old squares looked like, what the street sellers were selling, and so on. There is a large picture entitled 'Fado', referred to as the masterpiece of the painter Malhoa: it is dated 1910 and shows what the popular view of the fadista was in those days—low class and disreputable.

There are some showcases with good examples of work from the various ceramic factories of Lisbon, principally the famous Rato (the factory that was re-established by Pombal after the 1755 earthquake in an effort to rationalise the ceramic industry). There are a number of maquettes for the equestrian statue of Dom José (of Black Horse Square) and some fascinating paintings of what the statue and the square looked like when first finished: elaborate flights of steps led down to the water's edge in ornamental style.

All of these things make a visit worth while—though probably only if one has caught the magic of Lisbon and is already curious about its past and its development from medieval town to modern city. But what makes the trip down to Sugar Street (Rua do Açucar, the street where the Palacio da Mitra stands) truly rewarding is the building itself and the azulejos that line its walls. It must be one of the most perfectly preserved examples—of those available to the public—of a noble house where azulejos have been used throughout and are almost one hundred per cent intact. These are all of the eighteenth century. All blue, though here and there yellow has been introduced to point up a baroque frame at the corners. It is a joy to walk through the great house and savour the cool impact of these unrepetitive flowing blue and white designs. In the dining room (or what I guess to have been the dining room) there are lighthearted hunting scenes. Long French windows open on to a small rose garden (the guide picked a rose for my youngest daughter) and the place exudes an elegant remote charm. All the windows have window seats and azulejos lining the recesses. To see a house with the truly Portuguese domestic use of the azulejo in full flower, I recommend this quiet museum. On the day we last visited it, only three other people had signed the visitors' book. Not a soul came or went during the couple of hours we spent pottering about the cool interior.

Gulbenkian Foundation

At the corner of the Avenida Berna, set back among newly made gardens, the Gulbenkian Foundation has its headquarters and the museum which houses the famous collection. It is an uncompromising, typically contemporary solution to what was a delicate problem. For across the Praça de Espanha on the opposite corner is one of the most beautiful of Lisbon's old palaces, now the Spanish Embassy and impeccably kept up. In the event, Lisbon has been lucky; this massive block with plain low-slung bands of concrete, dark wood, and large plate-glass windows set in severe lines has a discreet air about it and does not at all obtrude on the older building. Some people regret the failure to attempt any specifically national type of design or finish. For instance, the traditional materials of Lisbon—azulejos, wrought iron and calçada portuguesea (the typical cobbling)—have not been utilised. But if one puts this aside (and I think there is some genuine cause for regret there) the building must be accounted a success by the standards of modern architecture. Above all, the immense care and fine workmanship lavished on the stone and wood finishes throughout make it a pleasure to visit the place.

For the visitor, it is the contents of the museum that are the attraction. It is a great collection of paintings, containing many unique masterpieces—and even among the minor items, each piece is a perfect example of its kind. The presentation is worthy of the high quality, and it must be—with its finely judged lighting for each item, and its air-conditioned glass cases—the most advanced and luxurious of its kind in Europe. The lighting is particularly interesting. There is a light beamed from ceiling level on to every piece. This light passes through a lens and is calculated so that it fits the exact area of the picture or object, and not an indiscriminate part of the wall as well. On the few occasions when I visited the gallery, this delicately balanced focus had not been perfectly achieved in all cases. When this happens there is an unreal effect of a square of light not quite fitting over the rectangle of the picture, as if

A LITTLE HISTORY

the glass of a frame had slipped and hung suspended, mysteriously tilted in space.

The architect responsible once took me over the building and drew attention to the main problems and the consideration that went into solving them. Perhaps there is one arrangement about which there will be two opinions. Some of the small oils, the Corots for instance, have been mounted into the wall with a canvas surround and no frame. This seems to affect the scale of the pictures, reduces them to miniatures. On the other hand, it isolates them and focusses attention on them—an obsession with mounters of exhibitions. From that point of view, it is a success. But the hanging of the paintings in general is first rate. Each is given a good space but not so separated as to eliminate the sensation that one is viewing a collection made by one man: this is important in this case.

Gulbenkian—Calouste Sarkis Gulbenkian to give him his full name—was an extraordinary man by any standard. The complete collection (here presented as a whole) expresses something of his powerful personality. An Armenian, born in Turkey, he made his fortune in Iraq. He was Anglophile by culture, but obsessed, as the collection shows, by Eastern and French art. He became Portuguese in his last years and lived on a whole floor of the old Avis Hotel in the centre of Lisbon. The importance of this for Portugal is hard to over-estimate. What the Gulbenkian Foundation has established is not merely a fabulous gallery, with a collection that rivals in many ways the Wallace or the Freer, but a great cultural centre that will in time have a revolutionary effect on the artistic and literary life of the nation. Apart from obvious amenities for the common man (the circulating library, the excellent series of pamphlets on aspects of Portuguese civilisation, the bourses, grants and scholarships) the effect it is having in bringing first-class music, ballet and art to the city in a continuous series of important exhibitions and concerts is already evident.

Certainly the visitor to Lisbon will be well advised to find out what is going on at the Gulbenkian Foundation. He is quite likely to find some exceptional lecture, ballet, concert, or exhibition taking place during his stay. But even if not the permanent collection remains a 'must'. In the soothing atmosphere created by the plain wood, the rough concrete, the granite walls and the soft brown marble floors there is a world of absorbing interest, of magnificent art seen in a near perfect setting.

On entering there is the large green pátio—seen through glass—with Rodin's Burgher of Calais (acquired by Gulbenkian directly from Rodin) and the beautiful Apollo of Houdon. These two pieces are set in diagonally opposite corners of the gardened pátio and manage to create a feeling of mystery and unearthly space in a strictly modern ambience. The pátio occupies most of one side of the foyer.

The collection proper starts to the right of the foyer with the earliest pieces—Greek, Roman, Egyptian and Assyrian. One proceeds in more or less historical progression through the marvellous oriental and Islamic ceramics, carpets and perfect examples of wall tiles with the characteristic flower arabesques in those incandescent turquoise and dark blue glazes. The Far Eastern gallery, really the Japanese–Chinese section, contains ceramics, sculpture, prints, lacquers, tapestry and embroidery. Throughout the collection, items are grouped by place and time, the different genres being presented together. This makes for pleasantly varying interest and emphasises the fact that it is an individual's far-ranging choice. Sculpture and jewellery, for instance, are quite as important as painting here, and there are splendid examples of period furniture and great tapestries.

The catalogues are clear and full though perhaps one could wish for fuller illustration. The first catalogue is devoted to Far Eastern and ancient art and the second to European art up to 1900—though including nothing that might be called 'modern'.

Without doubt the pivot of the painting section is the room containing the two major Rembrandts and the Rubens portrait of Helena Fourment. There are three other superb small paintings by Rubens. These great paintings are seen to perfection here. The soft muted colours of the surroundings and

A LITTLE HISTORY

the discreet lighting make it a joy to contemplate the work of these masters—nor do the pictures seem to have been messed about as in London, where I find it difficult to look at the Rembrandts since they were cleaned and harshly lit.

It would be a pointless labour to enumerate the things worth looking at. Almost every piece has some importance. The large group of René Lalique jewellery (very well displayed in its own gallery with some well chosen wall decoration of the period and rather theatrical lighting) makes a fascinating historical moment live—Art Nouveau, with all its decadence and magic.

Near the English Cemetery

Preface to a Journey

PATRICK SWIFT

It seemed a good idea to contact the gynaecologist before going on our trip to the Beira Baixa. One morning I got our friend and guardian Senhor Menelli to put through a call to Helle, Lima's wife. Helle is a tall blonde Scandinavian who moves through Lisbon like a visigothic vision and whose knowledge of the city is formidable. She had offered to introduce us to her doctor. When I got her on the phone, however, she broke the news that the man had dropped dead a short time before.

This set me back a little, provoking a certain angst regarding the frailty and the fallibility of the human creature. Women, thank God, are less prone to this paralysing reaction to elemental situations. Helle had already arranged for us to see the doctor who had taken over the practice.

This took us up to the top of the Avenida in the district beyond the Marquês de Pombal roundabout. Here in a block of modern offices we found very businesslike and relatively luxurious doctor's consulting rooms. The waiting room was not designed to soothe my awakened nervous system. Apart from a couple of striking Iberian ladies in fashionable gear, there was nobody about. On the wall, however, was a big blackboard and on the blackboard were some well drawn large illustrations, done in chalk of different colours, showing the birth process in some detail. It transpired that it is the custom here to give weekly lectures to the expectant mothers, the gynaecologist taking on the role of mentor and guide as well as performing the more run-of-the-mill medical functions. There were also nice soothing modern lithographs and etchings; but somehow the large chalk drawings on the blackboard had a compelling power with which the etchings miserably failed to compete.

Not exactly reassured by this mixture of lecture hall and waiting room I reclined in a vast armchair and hid my feelings in a fancy magazine. But it turned out that waiting was not to be my role. I was to see the doctor too. Helle, who was in charge of the episode, further added to my fears by telling us how Lima had not only assisted at the birth but had also photographed the whole proceedings. Nor was this unusual. It was more or less expected that husbands would join in the affair from start to finish. At this stage, I recalled my failing spirit and refused to see the doctor. I am Irish and old-fashioned, and although well up on modern developments—the Dicky Read system, and the rest (Oonagh had already been through this with our first two daughters)—I had never been able to overcome the melancholy results of brainwashing received at the hands of the Irish Christian Brothers . . . at least, not enough to be able to take an active part in having a baby. Moral support and complete enthusiasm for the modern psychological approach I can offer and proclaim. I found Lima's photographs beautiful and moving. But I had grievous doubts as to my capacity to go through the proceeding myself.

At tea, after the doctor had declared Oonagh fit and in order, we pondered the medical opinion that the baby might arrive in about ten days' time if not sooner. This was considerably earlier than our original estimates. We were sitting in one of those new faceless tea-rooms, posh and full of gimmicks, with numerous overfed and over-dressed ladies stuffing fancy cakes into bland city faces. Somehow, the very atmosphere decided us to go ahead and get a few days at least of the country before the big event curtailed all further movement. Oonagh's enthusiasm for the trip overcame the lurking fears I did not care to mention.

Where I had refused to see the doctor Oonagh now refused to inspect the nursing home. I had to set off alone and make the necessary arrangements.

The place was on the Avenida da República and turned out to be an interesting institution. To begin with, it was an architectural fantasy; one of those mad creations of the late nineteenth century, and turn of the century, that flourish in that district. These constructions are frequently cocktails of strange details brought together with total disregard for the functional demands of the building. Thus one finds incorporated into the single space French, Italian, German, and maybe Spanish or country Portuguese items; arches, verandas, pillars, capitals and carved putti, fin-de-siècle flowers and birds, elaborate gates, heavy ironwork and great railings enclosing overgrown gardens. Italian mosaic will rub shoulders with German Gothic carvings, classical pillars will hold up mosarabic verandas, in an orgy of copying from a host of sources.

Now they appear rare flowerings of a peculiar period. In their time the vulgarity and grossness of the concept made them the butt of many an intelligent attack from responsible architectural writers. They were taken to be the perfect demonstration of the lamentable results that can follow from the

Oonagh Swift

absence of an overall planning control. The Lisbon municipality had no overall scheme for the development of these newer parts of the city, then growing so fast. Each house was considered as an isolated case and the folly of the method became apparent only when all the houses were up.

The wheel has now come full circle, however. These creations are seen to have a charm, an exotic period flavour, that places them in a category all their own. They now enter the phase of historical and artistic curiosity and, more than that, even achieve an aesthetic quality. They should be made national monuments before the last of them tumbles to make way for the seven-storey block. There are still, I am glad to report, a number of good specimens to be seen. Just to look at them will repay a walk down the Avenida da República.

Old Market by Praça Duque de Saldanha

A Journey by the Tagus

DAVID WRIGHT

In 1962, on my first visit to Algarve, Swift had shown me the south of Portugal. We had discovered the north, independently and together, when we explored the Minho and Trás-os-Montes in 1966. Now that we were together again in Lisbon, it seemed logical to extend our investigations to the middle parts of Portugal and complete our survey of the country.

There were two objectives to the idea. One was that we had been commissioned to write about Lisbon—and here we were contemplating a trip to the Beira Baixa and the frontier of Spain. Men of our ingenuity, we knew, would have no difficulty in negotiating so frivolous a consideration.

The other impediment to our plan was more substantial. Oonagh was due to have her baby. A room had been booked for her in a Lisbon nursing home, and the gynaecologist was of the opinion that the infant might pop out at any moment. If we travelled too far from the capital there was the risk that the baby might insist on making his or her appearance before Swift could drive Oonagh back to the nursing home. You could not blame a mother-to-be for not fancying the idea of a happy event occurring in some remote country inn or rural hospital—or even while en route. As a matter of fact, it was Swift and I who were least sanguine about the hazards. Our wives, with the cheerful hardihood that women assume when it suits them, seemed unperturbed. Oonagh—after all, the person principally concerned—was eager to make the trip. Swift and I decided to ignore our misgivings and be guided by our womenfolk. Or that's how we saw it.

Thus there was the element of a gamble about the project, which perhaps lent it spice.

'If the baby *is* born on the trip, it'll be copy for the book,' I pointed out. Oonagh said she'd look at it in that light.

On an uncertain, shine-and-shower October morning we set out. Our destination, we decided, would be Abrantes, a town on the Tagus, not much more than a modest but safe 140 kilometres from the capital.

'Let's go by the south bank of the river,' said Swift. 'Otherwise we'll have to go by way of Santarém, the same road we took when we went to the Minho.'

To reach the south bank of the Tagus we took the motorway to Vila Franca de Xira, whose famous bridge used to be the first to cross the river until the new suspension bridge at Lisbon was opened in 1966. We bowled along the raw new motorway, passing the big Sagres brewery on our right, and soon reached the bull-mad horsebreeding town of Vila Franca. Over the bridge, which is nearly a mile long, we found ourselves in the great flat alluvial savannah on whose pastures are reared the horses and fighting-bulls. I pointed out to Pip the Estalagem Gado Bravo, isolated on the houseless and treeless cattle plains. Here I had stayed with the Swifts before beginning our journey to the Minho. It is a famous hang-out of bullbreeders and toureiros and even has its own private bullring. Some kilometres beyond the Gado Bravo we turned left, taking a secondary road that promised to return us to the Tagus.

While we were on the main roads I had again been impressed by the noticeable increase in motor traffic since I had last been in these parts three years before. Most of the cars—perhaps ominously—were decorated with stickers proclaiming Discipline, Courtesy, Prudence. There seemed to be correspondingly fewer carts and carriages, and even these were mostly equipped with pneumatic tyres. Now we were passing through ricefields where—another sign of progress—the working girls wore transparent plastic waterproofs. One we saw riding along the road on muleback, swathed in this billowing see-through material, like a bride attired in an ectoplasmic wedding-dress. We rejoined the Tagus at Muge—a somewhat melancholy collection of cubic, yellow-white, and low-slung buildings, like many of the villages in these parts.

'The oldest remains of human life in the Peninsula were discovered here,' remarked Swift.

In prehistoric times Muge was an inlet of a great maritime gulf on whose banks shellfish-gatherers settled. Excavations here by Ribeiro and Paula e Oliveira and, more recently, Abbé Roche, have yielded the most useful group of human skeletons on which to base the anthropological history of the Peninsula. More than two hundred burials were unearthed. For a long time it was held that late Mesolithic culture came to the Peninsula from Africa: the inhabitants of this region were known as *Homo Afer Taganus*. The excavations at Muge proved that Tagus Man was, in fact, descended from European Upper Palaeolithic stock. Here a few families over some hundreds of years built up great mounds of shells and sand, with traces of charcoal. Facing south-east, these mounds formed windbreaks against the north and west winds. They were no fools, these people: as anyone who lives in Portugal knows, this is the only orientation for a building. In time, the inlet on which they lived silted up and gradually formed the rich alluvial bed characteristic of the Ribatejo.

At any rate, we were getting into deep country. No longer did we pass farm wagons wheeled by Michelin or Dunlop. Near Alpiarça, we stopped at the Casa dos Patudos, a large house standing by itself, miles from anywhere. It reminded me of one of those New England old colonial mansions celebrated by Orson Welles in *The Magnificent Ambersons*. An odd touch: the rafters in the verandas carried rows of spikes to guard against birds. The house is now a museum; and it wore that posthumous expression that seems to settle over all dwelling-places that were once lived in but now exist only to be looked at. Unluckily it was a Monday—the day on which most museums and showplaces in Portugal are shut. So we could not get in, and missed seeing its collection of furniture, ceramics, azulejos, and paintings (one of them a Reynolds!). After a short halt we drove on, through Chamusca, famous for its water-melons (piles of these to be seen beside the road) and its wine, till about two in the afternoon we came in sight of the sandy reaches of the Tagus.

These great stretches of yellow sand blended with the autumnal colours of the leaves of the vines. Across the river we could see Abrantes perched on a greenly terraced hill whose slopes were dotted with olive trees. A small post-office tower dominated its cluster of white walls and red roofs.

It had been a long morning's drive and we wanted a good lunch. In Portugal you can turn up at a restaurant or taberna at almost any time of day and be offered something substantial as a matter of course. We were less worried about the lateness of the hour than the difficulty of spotting the best place to eat: for these can be elusive. It is not always the most garish and contemporary-decor'd café that offers the better fare. Oftener than not, it is some unassuming and old-fashioned establishment down a side-street, so well known to the locals and so well patronised by them that it sees no need to advertise itself. In the small rural towns one can spend days before finding— perhaps just before one leaves—some temple of gastronomy where no one would have thought of looking for it. Therefore, after parking the car in the middle of Abrantes and while the others had an aperitif in the nearest taberna, I did a quick scout round for a likely place. But I drew a blank.

'There doesn't seem to be anything else for it but that big modern café in the main street,' I reported.

This was an establishment called O Pelicano, done up in that rather lowering glaze-and-glass style one associates with hamburger-bars and espresso-cafés in England. Thither we repaired, however; and were presently and pleasantly surprised by being served a quite outstanding mixed grill on a spit, aided by a bottle of the locally famous Chamusca wine. The restaurant, despite its somewhat off-putting (for us at least) modernistic decor, was obviously *the* place to eat at Abrantes, and a centre of local social life. Evidently the establishment was far older than the building that housed it. Appearances, in Portugal, can be doubly deceptive.

Abrantes

We were now ready to see the town. It was bad luck that it should be a Monday. For this reason we were unable to get into the fine sixteenth-century Misericórdia near the top of the hill. But here it was that we were picked up by a little man in a neat black suit and pork-pie hat. As a local resident, he felt it devolved upon him to compensate for the Misericórdia being closed and to constitute himself our guide to Abrantes for the rest of the afternoon. It is quite astonishing to what an extent the Portuguese will put themselves out to assist a stranger or a visitor.

First he took us up to the old castle on the summit of the hill on whose slopes Abrantes stands. A tablet in the gateway tells that the spot was fortified by the Consul Decius Junius Brutus, the Roman conquistador of Lusitania, in 135 B.C. But the castle, or its remains, that one sees today was built more than a thousand years later by Dom Diniz. He was one of the great constructive rulers of Portugal, called variously the Farmer King or the Poet King. Very likely the hill of Abrantes has been fortified since the dawn of history: for, strategically speaking, it is one of the keys to the central plain of Portugal. Napoleon recognised this when he created Marshal Junot Duke of Abrantes as a reward for capturing it in 1807 (thereby paving the way to the French occupation of Lisbon and, so Napoleon thought, the addition of Portugal to the French Empire). But the most exciting period in the history of the castle seems to have been in the twelfth century, when it withstood a fierce onslaught by the Moors in 1148. Within the wide circuit of its curtain walls, little remains beyond the ruins of a donjon near a thirteenth-century church now converted into a museum. Through the keyhole of the latter we glimpsed a scattering of headless effigies—relics of the Roman occupation—and a few broken pots and sherds. The ground of the inner bailey had recently been flattened. Our guide explained that until lately there had been a barracks which had been knocked down in order to excavate the old parts of the castle. These excavations had not yet commenced. So the level area enclosed by the curtain walls was covered with a carpet of herbs, conspicuous among which were bushes of deadly nightshade hung with black-purple berries.

From the battlements, or better still from the fairly rickety upper stages of the tower, one may enjoy a memorable view. That afternoon, we were offered a panorama of flat plains bounded by distant hills, of serried olive groves, of white townships and villages gleaming through dark greenery, while huge and billowing cumuli emphasised the vastness of the sky. Indeed, a sense of vastness was a dominant and peculiar quality of the view around us; one that is not often obtained from similar vantage points in England, perhaps because of the thickness of the atmosphere.

Our guide now led us to the sixteenth-century church that stands adjacent to the castle—the Igreja S. Vicente. There was a pleasant bareness about its interior. While we were looking at it, the priest came out of the sacristy and introduced himself.

'This church was originally a mosque,' he told us. 'Then it was dedicated to Our Lady of the Conception. But when they brought the body of St. Vincent to Lisbon it was re-dedicated. Look.'

He pointed to some fine azulejo panels depicting the fleet of carracks that convoyed the body of the saint to the capital. And with pride he showed us what was, for him, the principal treasure of the church: a painted stone figure, the effigy of one of St. Francis's disciples, whose remains were buried nearby.

After we had said goodbye to the kind priest, Pork-pie (as we had tacitly christened our friendly guide) led us down the hill to the lower part of the town by a series of pretty and whitewashed lanes set off by some odd but charming little houses—one had the wall of its gable decorated with painted bas-relief swallows—till we came to the Praça Raymundo Soares. This small square is a jewel, though it has no really notable buildings. But there is a house faced with green azulejo tiles and distinguished by curious oval windows. And round the corner of the square are some odd little shops—for example a chemist's whose window displays a stuffed owl wearing a pair of spectacles and smoking a pipe. Altogether a very taking quarter of the town.

Our guide now led us up the hill, back to the Misericórdia where we had first encountered him, in order to see the church of S. João that stands opposite. It is one of the showpieces of Abrantes, though I preferred the simpler and barer Igreja S. Vicente. Here the Master of Avis is said to have heard Mass before marching to fight the battle of Ajubarrota, which freed Portugal from the domination of Castile. There is a fine high altar, and interesting altar-pieces in the nave—one of them the original pre-baroque sixteenth-century work; but for me the best thing was the great carved organ with outflaring trumpets. Though the sacristy—as nearly always in Portuguese churches —should not be missed. It is nobly but simply furnished with black carved oak cupboards and a long table flanked by an imposing set of brass-studded leather-covered chairs. And there is one of those formidable grandfather clocks with which almost every other sacristy in the length and breadth of Portugal seems to be equipped. The present church, we were told—for its priest had joined us; it was at his invitation that we had seen the sacristy—had been begun in the sixteenth century on the site of a thirteenth-century church founded by St. Elizabeth.

Outside the Igreja S. João we said goodbye to the priest. We thanked and bade farewell to our friend in the pork-pie hat who had sacrificed his afternoon to a parcel of complete strangers.

Abrantes has an excellent hotel—the Turismo do Abrantes— besides one or two much cheaper pensões. Eager as I was to see something of the Beira Baixa, I would have been quite content to stay in this pleasant little town, within easy reach of Lisbon and the maternity home. But it was the intrepid Oonagh who insisted on going on.

'Let's get as far from Lisbon as possible on the first day,' she said. 'Then we can start coming back in our own time—or the baby's.'

It was coming on to five in the afternoon when we set out from Abrantes in the direction of Castelo Branco, which stands more or less on the Spanish frontier. We kept to the south bank of the Tagus. As we drove further east, the vegetation became more tropical. Wedges of prickly pear bounded each side of the road; for the rest, the stony brown soil carried a crop of heather and green scrub interspersed with olive groves.

Then darkness fell. We made a dramatic crossing of the Tagus at Porte do Tejo, near the village of Rodão: the black waters of the river glittered in reflected light far below. The bridge that leaps the gorges is the last bridge over the Tagus before the frontier—the next crossing of the river is at Alcantara in Spain, fifty miles to the east. We did not reach Castelo Branco, which stands some thirty kilometres north of the Tagus, till eight-thirty that night.

Castelo Branco

As it was so late, and dark, we did not hunt round for a cheap pensão but put up at the first place that offered itself—the rather grand Hotel do Turismo in the broad main square of the town. Here the Swifts took a suite while we made do with a room with bath, for 135 and 105 escudos respectively. We do not normally travel in quite this style, but these were the only rooms available in the hotel that night. The Swifts elected to dine in the hotel, but Pip and I felt we would prefer a change from its tourist splendours and see if we could rustle up something in one of the small tabernas somewhere in the town.

The square in which the hotel stood lay at the base of the hill on whose slopes the older quarter of Castelo Branco climbs up to the inevitable—but at that hour invisible—castle. A quick scoot round, or rather up and down, the steep little lanes of the old quarter revealed a notable absence of pubs. Only one was open; perhaps the others had closed because it was so late. However, we had a drink; which introduced us to the extraordinary custom that obtains at Castelo Branco cafés and tabernas of serving wine in white china coffee-cups with saucers. Many rural townships of Portugal have their own peculiar idiosyncrasies—this is Castelo Branco's

Eventually, we repaired to the Almeda Salazar, the main avenue of the town, and there found a big old-fashioned café-restaurant with a typically heavy Edwardian mahogany-and-mirror decor. In a sort of raised mezzanine room or wide gallery behind and above the bar, away from the drinkers and coffee-sippers in the main room, we were served an excellent meal of grilled cuttlefish, Amarante wine, fruit and a superb local cheese, for just over ten shillings a head.

Pip went to bed early; I stayed on to have a nightcap—a glass of bagaço at the bar.

Castelo Branco is the capital of the province of Beira Baixa. Overlooking it is a ruined castle built by Dom Diniz, who erected most of the strongholds in this area. Like Kilroy, Marshal Junot was here too; he sacked the place both coming and going. The tourist brochure, which Swift picked up in the hotel lobby, offered additional local information: 'Fine olive-oil, cheese and honey are among the best productions, not to mention cork and pork sausages.'

We were breakfasting, though not on cork sausages, in the Edwardian restaurant-café: at least, Swift was having breakfast and I was sitting over a coffee-cup of vinho tinto.

'There's an odd statue in the square opposite the town hall,' Swift remarked. 'It's to one Amado Lusitano, who seems to have been a sixteenth-century Jew on the run from the Spanish Inquisition. And it's a modern statue. Why pick on a sixteenth-century Jew? It seems he was a doctor from Salamanca, and famous for writing clinical treatises. I'll have to find out about him.'

Later Swift discovered that he was João Rodrigues, known as Amato Lusitano, a Jewish doctor of medicine (1511–68) who was famous throughout Europe in his day for his clinical methods. He was proceeded against by the Inquisition. We afterwards found that in this part of Portugal, so near to the Spanish frontier, there is a quite strong Jewish strain in the population even today. If we had travelled another fifty kilometres north-east of Castelo Branco we would have seen Monsanto—a picturesque and remarkable hill-town squeezed among huge granite boulders, some of whose houses have rooms cut out of the living rock. The inhabitants of this village are reputed to be extraordinarily handsome, with aquiline features. Some say they are descendants of the Sephardi Jews who fled to this more or less inaccessible refuge at the end of the fifteenth century. In 1917 Samuel Schwarz investigated these Jewish communities, Cristãos Novos ('New Christians') of the Beira Baixa. He started at the village of Belmonte (birthplace of Pedro Álvares Cabral, the discoverer of Brazil) in the north. As he gained the confidence of these people, he managed to penetrate into other communities in Castelo Branco, Monsanto, Penamacor, Idanha, etc. Schwarz found that a whole ritual still survives, with its own peculiar prayers and customs. Chiefly it was the old women who had by heart the orations and rites, and who presided at the religious reunions. The old women were completely unaware of any other Judaic community existing in the world, or of any other Hebraic orthodoxy. Schwarz had great difficulty in convincing them that he was a Jew. One of these old women in Belmonte said to him, 'Seeing that you pretend to know of other Judaic prayers different from ours, repeat to us at least one that you know in this Hebraic language which you say is the language of the Jews.' Schwarz obeyed, and recited the prayer 'Yisroäl', although he could see that the woman knew nothing at all of Hebrew. As soon as she heard the word 'Adonai', she cried to those around: 'Yes, he must really be a Jew, because he can say the name "Adonai".' After this, Schwarz was admitted to many religious meetings in the New Christian community and was allowed to assist with their prayers. He collected a large number of curious old orations, full of poetry and historic interest. He found that the entry of Saturday was celebrated, as well as many old Hebraic feasts. (See *Archaeology and History,* vol. iv 1925: *New Christians in Portugal in the 20th Century.*)

'What was the dinner like at the hotel?' I asked. 'We did pretty well at this café.'

'The food was O.K.,' he replied. 'But the service wasn't. They shut down at ten o'clock on the dot. Snatched our plates away, wouldn't even give us coffee.'

'It seems to me the more you pay the worse you fare,' I observed. 'When we ate here it was much later than that, but they served us as a matter of course—and some more diners came in before we left.'

At this point we were joined by our wives. We gave them coffee, had a brandy ourselves, and were ready to start the day.

Apart from its general charm, Castelo Branco has one major attraction to offer the sightseer. This is a unique jewel, one of the best things of its kind in Portugal: the gardens of the old episcopal palace. They were begun in the eighteenth century by one Dom João de Mendonça, Bishop of Castelo Branco, and completed by another bishop, Dom Vicente Ferrar da Rocha. At the time of our visit the old palace was being converted into a museum of popular art, so we could not get in; but the gardens —far more wonderful in their way than any building—were open.

They are formal topiary gardens: a controlled riot of box-hedged parterres, clipped trees, stone pools, fountains, staircases and effigies, of flowing scrolls and arabesques imposed upon or created from water, leaves, and stone. I rank them—along with the great stairway leading to Bom Jesus at Braga, the Vila Mateus in Alto Douro, and the Forest of Bussaco near Coimbra—among the more satisfying visual and spiritual experiences I have been afforded in Portugal. The most striking, though not necessarily most beautiful, feature is the staircase whose stone balustrades are sentinelled by lichened effigies of Portuguese kings—something like a score

*Bishop's Garden
Castelo Branco*

of them, each engraved with name and connotative: 'the Farmer', 'the African', 'the Judger', 'the Brave', 'the Eloquent', 'the Handsome', and so forth. At the foot of the staircase stand two very small statues—one is of Dom Filipe I, 'O prudente'. Apparently the Bishop who created the gardens disliked this couple of characters vehemently enough to insist on the diminishment of their effigied portrayals.

Less eye-catching, though more remarkable, is the oblong pool decorated with artificial islands of stone. These islands have been given formal foliate shapes and are planted with flowers. On an upper terrace, flanking the palace, is a water-tank with steps leading down to it—as it might be a bathing pool?—the wall facing it ornamented with exquisitely beautiful and crumbling stucco bas-reliefs. The gardens and their pools are on several levels. The lowest comprises the main area. Embroidered with hedges of box clipped in formal shapes, it is blazoned with pools and fountains, effigies of saints, evangelists (though St. Luke has been given St. Mark's lion), and such personified abstractions as Death—a carved skeleton bearing the traditional scythe. When we were there some visitor—or more probably one of the gardeners—had stuck a half-smoked fag-end between the grinning teeth of the stone skull. This somehow gave it a last touch of the macabre. Or so it seemed to us on that showery morning, when at intervals a thin mizzle of rain shook across the heraldic abstractions of the eighteenth-century gardens.

High above, on its hill, the ruined castle of Dom Diniz looked down, swirled about with trails of vapour.

We had no cut-and-dried itinerary. There was no point in planning one when Oonagh's baby might at any moment send us scuttling back to the Lisbon maternity home. But it had been agreed that, if we could, we would try to visit Marvão, a remote walled town like Monsanto on the top of a mountain near the Spanish frontier. Both Lima and António Quadros had urged us to see it when we discussed our trip with them in Lisbon. Marvão was on the south side of the Tagus, which meant that we would have to retrace our route to the bridge at Rodão. This would give us a chance to see some of the countryside that we had passed through in darkness the night before.

As we approached the Tagus after leaving Castelo Branco, the road skirted square fields divided by drystone walls. Olive groves covered the hills: the soil beneath each olive tree defended from erosion by a curtain wall of drystone, as if it were a gun-emplacement. A little past noon we crossed the bridge slung between the canyons through which the yellow Tagus picks its way some hundreds of feet beneath. Here we stopped at a roadside taberna overlooking the gorge. Outside its door hung a huge freshwater fish, bigger than any salmon I have set eyes on. A flowerpot made of old tyre-covers, painted green, stood by the threshold. In the bar-room, which like most rural tabernas was a general store as well, we had a vinho tinto. While Swift asked the landlady about the fish, I wandered outside to admire the dramatic gorge backed by mountains terraced with olive groves and crowned with rocks. In the distance I saw dun undulating hills; the river wound through them like a scar. Swift came out of the pub.

'She says it's a barbo,' he announced. 'They caught it only this morning. Weighs four kilos.'

Nisa

We went on; seventeen kilometres brought us to Nisa, a small town in the high Alentejo. As it was now around one o'clock, lunch was indicated. We stopped the car in the pretty main square of the town—dominated by an odd rustic-looking clock in a kind of open ironwork box—and soon found our way to the unpretentious bar of the principal taberna. Here we had one of our travelling lunches. Instead of trying for some substantial, but time-consuming, meal we simply asked for a 'prego', a sandwich. This, all over Portugal, takes the form of a bread-roll split in half and filled with pieces of freshly grilled slices of pork or roast sucking-pig. These pregos, washed down with either vinho tinto or vinho branco, are sustaining, inexpensive, and delicious.

The mantelpieces, shelves, and wall-brackets in our pub were lined with examples of local pottery: red clay bowls, jugs, and urns decorated with a swirling pattern of white dotted lines. These, naturally, attracted Swift's professional attention. After examining one of them, he exclaimed with surprise.

'These decorations are quite out of the ordinary. Usually it's slipware done with dots of white clay on red. In this case the dots are chips of marble.'

He turned to the patrão and began questioning him about the provenance of the pots. Within a few minutes he had obtained the name and address of the potter, and elaborate directions.

The pottery was on the outskirts of the town: a small house at the end of a by-lane, backing on open country. Broken potsherds outside a doorway showed that we had reached our destination. Two girls were on the premises when we called. One of them went to fetch the potter. It was a one-man establishment. The pottery consisted, in fact, of a single room with a kiln at the back; a bicycle hung suspended from an adjacent wall. On another wall were stuck great blobs of wet clay, ready-to-hand to be turned on the wheel which stood near the doorway. Broken, spoiled, and discarded pots piled higgledy-piggledy on the floor, where lay a conical heap of marble cobbles, waiting to be broken up into chips for decorating the pots (the chips were kept in a cork bowl).

Soon enough the potter appeared: a dark-haired, handsome young man. Swift and he were soon deep in a technical conversation. Presently Swift asked the young man to throw us a pot—which he did, first washing his hands in the clayey water of a bowl. He scooped a lump of wet clay from the wall and placed it on the wheel, which he worked by treadle. As he shaped the spinning clay he talked, barely attending to the form he was creating: his work seemed to be done entirely by touch.

'He says he's not really a potter,' Swift reported. 'That is, he doesn't come from a family of potters—which is unusual. An old potter who lives not far from here taught him the trade. He only makes pots in summer—in winter he farms.'

First the potter made for us a bowl to the traditional local pattern: then, obeying Swift's specifications, he made two candlesticks. For Swift was thinking of using this man's work for his new pottery in Algarve.

'Those lines and patterns of marble chips are always done by the girls, it seems.' Swift told us. 'By tradition, it's their job.'

Having exchanged addresses with the potter, and bought three or four of his pieces, Swift was ready to resume our meandering journey. Marvão was still some forty kilometres distant. But before we reached Marvão, we had a brief look at Castelo de Vide, whose white and glittering walls and houses, high among the hills, we discerned while still far away.

Castelo de Vide

Castelo de Vide lies 1500 feet up in the serra, a brilliant pastiche of a Spanish town: and why not? The border is a bare twenty kilometres to the east. There is a castle occupying the summit of the hill on which it is built—but let the brochure which we obtained from the Turismo speak for itself: 'Beyond the profusion of reasons of historical and architectonic interest, Castelo de Vide has some points from where it is possible to enjoy panoramas of unforgettable beauty as, for instance, those that are presented to who mounts to the Donjon, or detains himself at the Monteiro or stoops in the churchyard of the hermitage of N.S. da Penha. Endowed with hotel installations that satisfy the most exigent tastes, the purety of the air and amenity of the climate, the tranquillity of its life and the excellence of its food, constitute a true balsam for the spirit and a powerful tonic for the body.' But enough. I endorse this praise, though we did not test the hotel installations (the town has two hotels—probably simple but probably good—to accommodate visitors to the big fairs held there in January and August).

Castelo de Vide is one of those rare places whose perfection is animate: not an embalmed, reconditioned beauty, as in the case, say, of such showpieces as S. Gimagnano in Tuscany, or the walled city of Obidos (which Swift has described more sympathetically than I could in our book on the Minho), or the corpselike immaculacy of dead villages like Amberley in Sussex or Troutbeck in Westmorland. At any rate, the point about Castelo de Vide is that it is not only 'unspoiled'— Ann Bridge, in her *Selective Traveller in Portugal* remarks that some of its streets and squares have been untouched since the fifteenth and sixteenth centuries—but functioning and alive.

We admired its magnificent granite fountain, the narrow white lanes of old houses with Gothic and Manueline doorways, and the sober flourish of ironwork grilles guarding their windows. There was a particularly beautiful street of cottages in the penumbra of the old castle. In the main square we found a taberna whose entrance was almost obliterated by tall and tangled yellow daisies growing in tubs outside the door. Within, apples suspended on strings from the ceiling, arranged to compose a sort of inverted umbrella, constituted a decorative artefact which could win any teenage pop-sculptor an exhibition at any fashionable avant-garde gallery. . . . Yet this contemporary-seeming composition was unsophisticated, autochthonous, genuine popular art.

Castelo de Vide remains in my memory as one of the most placid, taking, and picturesque—in the best sense of that now pejorative adjective—little town that I have yet encountered. The pig's ear sandwiches that we sampled at the taberna appeared to confirm the 'excellence of its food' promised by the tourist brochure. We learned from the patrão of this place that the town takes its name from the grape vine—'videira'—that produces its remarkably good local wine. I might add that the town is also a small spa (its bottled mineral water is sold all over Portugal). If ever I have a nervous breakdown, I think Castelo de Vide is a place where I would choose to recuperate.

Marvão

The fortified hill-town of Marvão stands ten kilometres from Castelo de Vide, on the road to Spain. As the car spun down the spool of grey tarmac stretched out along the valley floor, we saw the silhouette of its towers and battlements grimly perched on the skyline of a tall mountain. A sharp turning to the left, and we began winding and looping up to a seemingly inaccessible citadel standing nearly 3000 feet above sea-level. The Romans were here: they called it Hermínio Minor. We entered by an exiguous medieval gateway piercing the thick walls that entirely surround this almost impregnable fortress-town. Narrow lanes of whitewashed cottages with fine granite doorways led us to an open space on the battlements, where we were able to park the car.

Marvão is an austere place, and has a deserted, though far from derelict, look about it—an air of having more houses than people. There is a good small estalagem—the Ninhos de Águias—a shop or two, and the inevitable taberna. You can make the circuit of the walls—an experience not to be missed—in ten minutes or so. The parapets will lead you to the ruined fortalezza, which was built, like that of Castelo de Vide, by Dom Diniz. It stands on a jagged crag of granite, all Portugal swimming below—as magnificent, not to say alarming, a view as you are ever likely to see, and one that makes patent the strategic importance of the place. For Marvão and its fort stand on an isolated peak. To the east, the distant mountains of Spain look like castles. Directly below the steeply sloping curtain walls—on whose towers and battlements one or two rusting cannon yet remain—grow pine trees and firs, brilliantly viridian, burning like green torches. Kestrels hover and swoop; billows of cumuli, riding higher above the castle than its broken tower overtops the plain below, brood over the immense

Marvão

scene. It is claimed that on a clear day you can see up to seventy miles.

Picturesque is not really the adjective for Marvão. Without being grim, it has a hardness and bareness—one might say a practicality—which will not sit with the soft romantic associations of the word.

Portalegre

Evening was drawing on; we should have to find somewhere for the night. We were only nine kilometres from Spain, and not noticeably nearer the Lisbon maternity home than we had been at Castelo Branco.

'There's a pousada at Portalegre,' Swift inadvertently alliterated. 'I think that's the best bet. Oonagh ought to stay somewhere really comfortable.'

We arrived at the pousada—high on a hill overlooking Portalegre, with a castle to one side and to the other a large double-towered cathedral standing on the edge of a steep slope. Oonagh elected to dine at the pousada and have an early night, but Pip and I were curious to see the night-life of Portalegre and try out its restaurants. So Swift said he would drive us in as soon as Oonagh had eaten and gone to bed.

In the time of the Romans, Portalegre was known as Amoea. It is now a small and apparently thriving industrial metropolis. We parked the car somewhere in the middle of it, in one of the many tiny but finely proportioned squares which we discovered to be a feature of the town. The first thing we did was to go to the nearest taberna for a glass of wine and a petisco (snack). After a couple of rounds, we moved on to the next place; by which time it had become clear to all three of us that the restaurants of Portalegre were going to have to forgo our custom that night—we were on an old-fashioned pub-crawl...

But as it is the custom to eat when drinking in Portuguese tabernas, we must in fact have consumed a square if variegated meal in the form of the cold grilled fish, like carapau or sardines, and the various cheeses and savoury sausages that were available in the different establishments we patronised. Some of them often announce anything special that may be available by hanging up a small handwritten placard—'Há porco' ('We have pork'), 'Há leitão' ('sucking-pig'), and so on. One of our pubs had a mysterious placard, 'Há —' followed by a coloured drawing of some kind of fungus. This was too much for our curiosity: we ordered a dish of it, despite the close resemblance of the drawing to Fly Agaric (one of the poisonous species). When we had eaten it (roughly stewed and of no particular delicacy), Swift got into conversation with the patrão. He learnt, not wholly to our gratification, that what we had eaten were Amanitas of some sort (not only Fly Agaric but the Death Cap belongs to this category). The local name for this particular mushroom, the patrão explained, was different from the usual Portuguese word for it. So to prevent or forestall argument, he simply drew a picture of the fungi and let people call them what they liked.*

---

* Swift eventually identified it as Amanita Rubescens (The Blusher.) He remarked that the only other place he knew of where mushroom is served with hot sauce in the tabernas is Cordoba in Spain.

We ended our evening in a sort of underground taberna—a series of cellars like alcoves opening one into the other—with a furious dispute (never really resolved) about the relative density of the bird populations of England and Portugal . . .

The principal industries of Portalegre revolve about cork and wool. Swift was at that time designing a tapestry to be executed at the famous tapestry factory of Portalegre. The next morning, when we had all breakfasted and packed, the first thing we did was to visit it.

The factory occupies a fine old building in the middle of the town—a former Jesuit convent, the Collegiade de S. Francisco. The entrance—a stone-pillared azulejo-faced porch leading to a light, tall, airy, whitewashed staircase—is not what one would associate with a factory. We were shown into the visitors' waiting-room on an upper floor—a room furnished with ancient dyeing-vats, antique carved chests, and hung with tapestries done in abstract contemporary designs. A nice plump girl soon appeared to escort us round the factory.

First we were shown a long, low, raftered workshop occupied by two rows of looms, fifty feet long, running the length of the workroom and lit from above by fluorescent lighting tubes. At each loom, groups of three or four girls were working on individual tapestries, following a plotted design in which each colour had been given a number corresponding to different-coloured threads dangling from the numbered spools overhead. They worked fast, their fingers moving like harp-players plucking the strings.

Next we were taken to the upper workshop, where we saw an even longer row of looms—their length may have been as much as a hundred feet. One tapestry, I noticed, bore the signature 'F. Leger'. Our guide told us that it had been ordered by his widow, who lives in Switzerland. We then saw a huge abstract tapestry that was being made for the Gulbenkian Foundation at Lisbon, designed by the architect João Abel Manda. After that we were shown another room where girls were at work on the highly skilled task of plotting tapestries from the original paintings, transferring the artists' design on to squared paper with numbers for the relevant colours.

'Orders for paintings to be made into tapestries come to us from all over the world,' the plump girl told us.

The factory, she said, took great pride in its connection with Jean Lurçat, the artist who revived the famous Aubusson tapestries in France. It began when Lurçat gave the director of the Portalegre factory one of his own tapestries to copy. The factory took on the job. When it was completed, Lurçat came to see how the work had been done—to find he could not tell the difference between his original tapestry and the copy. Thereafter, the girl told us, he had all his tapestries made at Portalegre. One point of superiority, she explained, is the fact that, while Aubusson tapestries are made of separate sections sewn together, the Portalegre tapestries are made in one piece.

'Now judge for yourselves.' She pointed triumphantly at a wall on which hung two tapestries of a cockerel rampant: the Aubusson on one side, the Portalegre copy on the other, and in the middle a portrait of Jean Lurçat, the frame embroidered with all the different coloured wools used in the copy of his tapestry.

'We won the international prize for tapestry at Lausanne this year,' she added.

Next she took us to a vast storeroom where the paintings that had been copied for tapestries were preserved. With pleasure Swift and I recognised the original painting for a huge tapestry of Decius Brutus and his Roman legions crossing the Rio Lima. The tapestry itself we had seen at Viana do Castelo three years before, on our tour of the Minho.

We could not leave Portalegre without looking at its cathedral, even if we missed the convent of Conceição with its azulejos and the baroque portal of Estremoz marble. Owing to its site as much as its size the cathedral is the most prominent building in the town. Inside it is stately with great painted altars. Its very grand priest—tall, whitehaired, looking exactly like Robert Graves—established himself as our cicerone. Had it not been for him, we might not have seen the painted busts of the artist responsible for the altars and of the architect who built the cathedral; these are set high up in the west wall. Certainly we would not have known whom they represented.

The priest also led us to the sacristy. One wall afforded a robust and energetic depiction of the Flight to Egypt in azulejo tiles. On the other side stood great carved oak chests with enormous drawers for clerical vestments, mounting ancient cataracted mirrors. A pair of tall and imposing marble tables occupied the centre space. As often in Portugal, the sacristy was as interesting as the church itself.

Next door to the Sé Catedral is the Museu, which ought not to be overlooked. We stepped inside for a brief glance, but found ourselves still there almost an hour later. The most attractive exhibits, for us, were the selection of first-rate eighteenth-century Portuguese faience porcelain, and an exquisite carved ivory virgin of the seventeenth century. Worth mentioning are a number of specimens of barbers' bowls, used for cupping blood, and a somewhat bizzare gathering of wooden pestles and mortars collected by one José Régio, a poet.*

Elvas

It was time to resume our travels. We took the road to Elvas, passing the concrete skeleton of a large new regional hospital that was being constructed by the Portuguese equivalent of the Ministry of Works. Our road led through endless plains of olives, sometimes accompanied by the Rio Gaia. We were running more or less parallel to the Spanish frontier some fifteen kilometres to the east. It was well past the lunch hour when we came in sight of a church-tower peering over a hill. In a minute or two we stopped on the outskirts of the small town or village of Arronches. A little church—not the one whose tower we had seen—stood hard by: washing was hanging out to dry in its porch, while white fantail pigeons strolled about the dusty precinct, occasionally giving its dry earth a perfunctory peck. A capless garda leading two horses came over to speak to us. Swift asked if there was anywhere

* But see Swift's remarks on p. 237.

we could eat. He directed us to the town café in the main square.

Here, we had some excellent pregos of fried pork with first-rate vinho tinto. The café was full of locals, some sitting over cups of coffee, some reading the newspaper, some just sitting. We were now in the south—or if not quite in the south, next door to it. Not far away, in view of our café, stood the church whose tower we had seen when approaching. It was, according to the Blue Guide, thirteenth-century gothic, and it looked interesting. But as it was past noon, the church was locked, and we did not have the energy to enquire for the key. We satisfied ourselves with admiring the fine doorway over whose left and right sides had been inscribed the minatory legend: *Paraiso para sempre. Inferno para sempre.* ('Heaven is for ever. Hell is for ever.')

The road that took us out of Arronches took us right round the town, which sat on its hill and looked at us. Elvas lay fifty kilometres to the south. On either hand, the level plains dotted with dry grey-green olive trees and broken with outcrops of boulders of grey granite recalled the strangely exhilarating monotony of the bushveld—at least, to me. We passed through only one large village—S. Eulália—whose Algarve-type perforated chimneys reinforced the 'southern' atmosphere we had felt at Arronches. A long avenue of stripped cork oaks—there is nothing stranger than the rust-brown colour of the trunks when denuded of the cork bark—prefaced our arrival at Elvas. The town is set on a swelling hill in the midst of a wide plain. Its presence is announced by a huge stone aqueduct with three tiers of arches—a construction that was completed in 1622 and is said to have taken more than a century to build.

'Elvas is rather sinister,' say Ann Bridge and Susan Lowndes in their invaluable *Selective Traveller in Portugal*. 'Light and fanciful,' contradicts Sacheverell Sitwell in his now out-of-print *Portugal and Madeira,* though he says he did not himself visit it but was only going by report. Elvas is a garrison-town and the place where the sugar-plums come from (the surrounding plain is a garden of oranges, plums and medlars). We found it rather businesslike, with a main street choked by prosperous

Elvas

traffic, and some fairly sophisticated shops. In one of them Pip found a wide range of the painted clay Estremoz figurines which so enchanted her, selling at thirty escudos apiece—or about half the price asked for in Lisbon.

Badajoz, the frontier-town of Spain, is scarcely twenty kilometres away. There is a thirteenth-century castle—for Elvas, as one would expect, is a fortified city—and a Manueline Sé Catedral; a regional museum of note, with Roman mosaics and a collection of Estremoz pottery. But the only thing we properly examined was the extraordinary sixteenth-century

Igreja das Freiras de São Domingos near the top of the hill behind the cathedral. It is an octagonal church: quite small, like one of those round churches of the Templars. Inside, it is entirely lined with blue and orange azulejo tiles dating from 1659. There are three altars—two gilded and one plain—with marvellous carvings; eight painted pillars support the cupola, which again is lined with azulejos. The interior is dominated by a superb pulpit consisting of a remarkable ironwork railing set into a pedestal of painted stone. The gloom and glitter of this strange little church has something oriental about it.

Outside, in the bare and dusty praça, stands a tall stone pillory with iron dragon-heads for the ropes to which criminals used to be tethered. No one who visits Elvas should miss this church.

On our way out of Elvas we stopped for a moment to look at the odd, but beautiful, fountain built in 1622 to receive the water brought by the great aqueduct—six marble pillars support a cupola on which stands a dumpy effigy of Dom Sancho II on horseback.

We were not quite sure where we would spend the night, but decided to try Vila Viçosa, where there is a great Bragança palace and a famous little pensão, the Lisboeta. Our route took us westwards, past Vila Boim with its Algarve-type pepperpot chimneys. The stuccoed estate-walls endlessly lining the road were distinguished by a marginal blue painted ribbon running their entire lengths.

At Borba we intended to take the left turn for Viçosa, but stopped instead, fascinated by the aspect of a village that seemed almost entirely built of marble. Marble doorways, marble window-jambs and lintels—even the very cobbles were of marble. Swift and I left Pip and Oonagh in the car and took a brief stroll up the main street—there seemed to be quite a number of antique shops—before coming to rest in a small taberna. Embroidered headstalls in brilliantly coloured wools hung from the walls of the bar. Near its counter was suspended a bunch of tightly-clustered, dark purple grapes with the bloom still on them. We were joined by a long-haired youth with a folder of water-colour paintings—he was about as near as you can get to a hippy in Portugal—who said he was from Sagres, hitch-hiking to Lisbon. The grapes, he informed us, were the local grapes—'uva Moreto'—from which the wine was made. And magnificent wine it was too. We tried both the red and the white—impossible to say which was the better. Swift was filled with enthusiasm.

'Marvellous stuff!' he exclaimed as we returned to the car. 'This place stinks of wine!'

'So do you two,' our wives pointed out.

Before leaving Borba we looked at a small seventeenth-century church, the Igreja Matriz, built of marble: the interior is remarkable not only for its azulejos but also for the ribbed roof. Its geometrical purity and the white marble contrive to give the visitor the impression that he is standing in the middle of an abstract sculpture.

'All this is Elvas marble,' Swift told me. 'It's the most famous in Portugal. And it was in the marble quarried round here that they found the prehistoric cave-paintings.'

On the road to Vila Viçosa we passed long lines of blue-jeaned cyclists riding in single file—quarrymen who had knocked off work for the day and were returning to their homes. Soon we came upon the marble quarries themselves. They are, so to speak, open-cast quarries, and the gleaming pyramids of marble blocks look like skin eruptions on the dark brown soil.

Vila Viçosa, when we reached it in the gathering dusk, seemed a neat, elegant, somehow haut-bourgeois township. The ducal palace, which was begun in the first decade of the sixteenth century and took almost exactly a hundred years to complete, is the main feature of the place—though there is a castle (one of Dom Diniz's, naturally) and several churches of interest. Large and imposing, though severely reticent, the palace fronts an enormous square where, at one time, bull-fights were held. An equestrian statue of Dom João IV stands in the middle, for it was from this palace that he, as Duke of Bragança, set out to assume the throne of Portugal when the sixty years of Spanish dominion came to an end in 1640. And it was here, too, that the penultimate Bragança king, Dom Carlos I, spent the night before his assassination at Lisbon in 1908.

It was far too late for us to see the palace; in any case, what we were looking for was the Pensão Lisboeta. It is so famous in Portugal that it dispenses with any kind of signboard or nameplate, and thus caused us strangers much searching. And when we did find the house, there was no accommodation. The date was October 16th—in other words, the eve of the commencement of the hunting season. The pensão, like almost every other country hotel and pensão in the length and breadth of Portugal, had been taken over by Tartarins from the city, who were only waiting for the first blink of dawn next morning to sally forth with shotguns and rifles to shoot down every living thing in fur or feathers.

'We can't be more than twenty kilometres from Estremoz,' said Swift. 'It's quite a big place, we're bound to find somewhere to stay there. And it's on the road to Lisbon.'

So we turned west again, humming by the marble quarries with their huge squared-off blocks of undressed carbonate of lime. It was well past dusk when we reached Estremoz and pulled up in the Rossio, its vast tree-lined main square. At the opposite side of it we could see the lights of a large building, which looked as if it might be a hotel.

Estremoz

It was the Hotel Alentejano. From the outside we guessed that we must have discovered a real old-fashioned Portuguese hostelry—than which there are none better. When we entered we found ourselves in a lofty and spacious hall dominated by a splendid staircase of white marble, grandly carved in a nineteenth-century style. Had they rooms? We were lucky. One of those diminutive uniformed page-boys which are so charming a feature of Portuguese inns led us up the imperial staircase. The Swifts were going to take a room-with-bath; Pip and I, not being expectant parents, were content to have a double-room tout-court.

The page led us first to the room allocated to the Swifts. It turned out to be an immense panelled chamber thirty feet in length and proportionally wide, high-ceilinged, the windows dim with lace and draped velvet curtains. The 'bathroom' was part of this boudoir: an arrangement of screens, tented with gauzy white mosquito-netting, the bath itself dimly visible—a see-through bathroom, as it were. The Swifts were delighted.

Our humbler room was at another wing of the rambling old house, reached by means of a balcony and overlooking a courtyard where—bucolic touch!—a large Massey-Ferguson farm tractor stood parked. The way to our room led past the kitchens—which were on the first floor—and I had a glimpse of enormous cauldrons, huge stoves, a gigantic kitchen-table, copper pots and pans. After one look at that battery I made a mental note not to waste time looking for a restaurant that evening but to eat in the hotel. When we had been shown and approved our double-room, two elderly men in aprons came in and made the bed for us with clean linen and blankets.

I left Pip to unpack and found my way to the great entrance-hall, where I discovered Swift talking to a little old lady, straight-backed and silver-haired, whom he introduced to me as Dona Maria Natália Baraona Lima de Magalhães.

'This lady is the owner of the hotel,' he explained. 'She is going to tell us something about the place.'

The old lady, very much a grande dame if ever there was one, invited us upstairs to her office, a tiny room filled with silver-framed photographs, vases, calendars, knick-knacks and bric-à-brac. The house, she said, was built in 1898 as the private residence of a big landowner whose property included many of the famous marble quarries of the district. (The great palace of the Escorial near Madrid was built with marble from Estremoz, by the way.) This explained the abundance of marble in the house—and the grand staircase, which was carved by a sculptor called Sousa Leita. Dona Maria was the daughter of the original owner of the hotel, who had bought the house fifty years ago and converted it into a hostelry.

'It is still the only hotel in the south of Portugal,' she told us, dismissing as beneath notice all those jumped-up skyscraper doss-houses at Lagos, Portimão, Albufeira and Montegordo—or perhaps denying them the honour of inclusion in the same category as her own establishment. The old lady was obviously and properly proud. The hotel had distinguished guests. 'Count de Castro of Guimarães, Baron Linho, President Salazar, President Carmona, the Queen of Italy, Dom Manuel de Bragança . . .' Many another name she gave us, as if intoning from some ancient *Almanach de Gotha.* But what she was proudest of was a brass lampshade presented to her by the College of Jesuits, who had fled from Spain during the Civil War and stayed at the Hotel Alentejano.

Swift and I returned to the splendid vestibule to find Pip and Oonagh waiting for us. There was still half an hour to be got through before dinner would be served, so we ordered a bottle of white Borba wine as an aperitif. It was not quite as good as the wine drawn from the cask that we had sampled at the little taberna. While we were discussing this, a man came in bearing several brace of partridges. Swift leapt into action. The partridges had been shot that day by the bearer; Swift saw to it that the hotel purchased a brace and a half for our dinner . . .

This was eaten in the dingily magnificent dining room on the first floor. A sumptuous, bucolic meal it turned out to be. Soup and fish prefaced the partridge, which was followed by great bowls of fruit; seven or eight jugs of white and red wine came to our table—wine of Borba, but this time drawn from the cask and distinctly better than the bottled stuff we had been drinking earlier. (As this is not usual I think it worth noting.) We wound up with coffee and brandy, at which we were joined by an Englishman who was staying at the hotel. So far we had met none but Portuguese on our travels—one of the charms of Portugal is that it is so easy to get off the beaten track of tourists. And our Englishman was not even a tourist—he was an agricultural drainage expert and consultant who was engaged in a survey in the neighbourhood with a team of young Cambridge engineers.

The next morning we saw something of Estremoz. From the open balcony near our bedroom, where a cage with a yellow canary hung suspended, I had a view of the vast pomegranate-lined Rossio. To the right of it rose a hill, plated like an armadillo with the close-set rooftops of the old quarter of the town. Some of these roofs had distinctive patterned tiles. The hill was crowned by a tall, imposing keep and a palace—both, as usual, to do with the indefatigable Dom Diniz.

Soon after breakfast Pip and I strolled round the square— a respectable morning's exercise, it is so big—admiring the lamp-posts hung with iron baskets holding earthenware pots of growing plants, and the small permanent market on the eastern side. This market consists of vegetable and fruit stalls, and tiny wooden booths like newsagents' kiosks. The latter are butcher's booths, though they hardly offer elbow-room for the raising of a meat-axe. One side of the square is lined with shops and cafés; the other with seventeenth-century palaces and convents.

When the Swifts joined us, we looked over the old convent facing the square. It is now a hospital. We entered through the marble cloister—the carved grotesque capitals of its columns were notable—to see its small azulejo-panelled chapel, where the pièce-de-resistance is a remarkable crib by Machado de Castro. As cribs go it is a very small one—far smaller than those by the same master which can be seen at the Estrêla Church and the Sé Catedral in Lisbon, but superior in quality if not size. Besides the central drama of the birth in the stable, there are dozens of little figures busily engaged doing all sorts of things—a sense of excitement emanates from the work.

Not far from the convent, we stumbled upon the Rural Museum, which occupies a single large room. One of its features is an exhibition of cork carvings, miniature farm implements and vehicles, besides models of entire farms. These cork artefacts are not as kitsch as they sound, being on the one hand genuine folk art and on the other a record and an exposition of traditional agricultural methods which even in Portugal are fast disappearing under the impact of technology.

But the great point of interest of this museum is its collection of Estremoz figurines—the little painted clay effigies that fascinated Pip. Those in the Rural Museum were seventeenth- and eighteenth-century examples of complete sets. We were able to understand the function of individual figures that had hitherto puzzled us. For the principal set of these figurines, consisting of perhaps forty or fifty pieces, was of a religious procession—the effigy of the Virgin being carried through the town, followed and preceded by torchbearers, the town band with different instruments, uniformed horsemen, acolytes, the priest or bishop walking under a canopy. Another set was of figures for the Christmas crib; this included individual figures illustrating features of daily life—spinning, pig-killing, sausage-making, ironing, scrubbing clothes, and so forth. All these are still made in the same designs and colours, though the older ones (such as those in this museum, or at the Ethnological Museum adjacent to the Monastery of Jerónimos at Lisbon, where there is a singularly fine collection of Estremoz figurines) have a patina, a je-ne-sais-quoi of execution, which renders them aesthetically superior. No one knows much about them, though their ancestry is thought to be Roman or even Etruscan —and they do certainly evoke that pastoral, essentially pagan and hedonistic aura which one associates with the calm and smiling clay effigies on Etruscan tombs.

Naturally, we visited the inevitable castle. The old town, through which one passes on the way up to the stronghold, is very pleasant. The houses are whitewashed—of course!—but decorated with painted grey pilasters. Near the top of the hill the older houses exhibit curious marble doorsteps that jut upon the pavement like shelves. On the flat summit of the hill stands an isolated keep, nearly a hundred feet tall, not far from the palace of Dom Diniz. There was, as usual, a remarkable view. Immediately beneath spreads the town, flights of pigeons intermittenly wheeling above its roofs. The vast Alentejo plains stretch all around, with the serras of the Spanish frontier to the east: we could even pick out the fortifications of Marvão, blue and transparent with the distance.

The palace was barred to visitors while we were there, for it was in the process of being converted into a pousada (earlier, it had been used as a school). However, the curator of the new and as yet unopened museum nearby took us over the palace. Thus we were able to see a little thirteenth-century azulejo'd chapel dedicated to Santa Isabel, the widowed queen of Dom Diniz. This chapel was, in fact, the room where she died—so the azulejos instructed us—on 4th July 1336.

Our man also took us to see the new museum, which was still in the early stages of assembly and arrangement. There was a collection of modern specimens of Estremoz figurines and, in the courtyard, odd carved stones which might have been boundary markers but which the curator called 'estelas funerarios'—tombstones of some kind. The stripped and seasoned trunk of a tree, balanced on four protruding branches like legs, stood in the middle of the courtyard. The bole, projecting upwards, had the shape and carriage of a horse's head—the whole thing, in fact, was an accidental sculpture in living timber of a gigantic Picassoesque horse. The Portuguese, with their eye for such objets trouvés, had removed it to make an exhibit for the new museum.

Estremoz marked the end of our trip. It was time to get back to Lisbon, or at least its environs, lest Oonagh's infant should decide that the moment had now come to make his or her entrance upon the stage. So after a snack lunch of pregos in one of the the big cafés of the main square, Swift aimed the bonnet of the car westwards and we set off.

And got lost. Getting out of Estremoz, we took a wrong turning. Some fifteen or twenty kilometres later, after driving through open plains and forests of stripped cork oaks whose redbrown denuded trunks seemed to smoulder like dying embers, we found ourselves bumping over the cobbled streets of a little town called Veiros. In one of its narrow lanes three huntsmen—gaitered and becapped, their avocation could not be mistaken—strolled towards us arm in arm, singing. They were tight as ticks. One of them carried an earthenware jug which indubitably contained, or had contained, a beverage that cheers and inebriates. We remembered that today was the official opening of the shooting season. A moment or two later we came upon the huntsmen's car, parked outside a doorway.

We knew it was theirs, for the roof was heaped with slaughtered partridges.

Veiros, the map told us, was a town to the north of Estremoz —and we should have been heading west. There was nothing for it but to retrace our wheeltracks.

Returning to Estremoz to pick up our road again, we passed car after car hung with trophies of the chase—decorated and festooned with them, for each vehicle had been turned into a mobile advertisement of the occupants' prowess. Game of all kinds—hares, partridges, pheasants—piled on the roofs, dangling over the radiators, or jammed against the mudguards. At first we found these displays picturesque, even (for man is a hunting animal) exhilarating; but there were too many of them, too many cars overloaded with the slaughter of wild creatures. It became sickening.

'I heard at the hotel that five people got shot yesterday,' remarked Swift. 'Today there are two million of them out shooting.'

We found our turning for the west, and drove towards Setubal through the late afternoon, stopping once at Arraiolos. Setubal we reached as the light began to thicken. The town announced itself when we passed the white pyramids of salt, like the canvas tents of some army, that mark its famous saltfarms. We drove through the town and up the hill to its castle, just before sunset. From the battlements we were accorded another of the extra-special panoramas that seem endemic to Portugal—a view of not only the town of Setubal, but also its harbour, builders' yards, quays and shipping; of its landlocked bay, where the sunken Roman city of Troia can sometimes be seen through the clear water; of the green mountains of Arrábida.

This castle is now an estalagem (inn). We had some thought of stopping there. It is furnished with impeccable taste, and with many magnificent and priceless antiques; it is the last word in comfort. But it is not—by Portuguese standards—exactly an economical place to stay at; and when Swift, who had set his heart on having for his dinner the oysters for which Setubal is famous, discovered that there were none in the kitchens of the castle, he decided that we would try somewhere else for a bed for the night.

But first he would have his oysters. Descending from the castle to Setubal—birthplace of the poet Bocage and (as we were reminded by the names of innumerable streets and squares) of the singer Luisa Todi—we found ourselves passing, in a lugubriously modern and expensive-looking residential suburb of the town, a restaurant with a determinedly contemporary façade. Its name indicated that oysters were a speciality of the house. We stopped.

'This is where we eat,' announced Swift with decision. It was late, we were hungry, and the place had oysters . . .

Apparently we were the only clients—which should have warned us. First of all, while the chef got his kitchen-engines warmed up, we had to wait awhile over aperitifs in the restaurant bar. This was situated down in the cellars, rebarbatively lit with dim, crimson-shaded electric lamps. The atmosphere was exactly that of one of the sadder and more expensive afternoon drinking-clubs of London. Gloom fell irresistibly upon us—gloom that was not really dissipated when we were summoned to the upstairs regions where, in a severely cubic little dining room whose decor can only be described as expense-account modern, we were shown a vacant table in a desert of vacant tables. As always at such restaurants—England, if not Portugal, is full of them—there was an excruciating, long-drawn out wait for the food, not to mention the drink. It was not the kind of place where you can cheerfully order, and be cheerfully served, a jug of vinho to pass the time while the food is prepared. When, at last, it came—prefaced by our hard-earned shellfish—it was adequate but unexhilarating. What lift the wine gave us was immediately dispelled by a bill for four hundred escudos—between six and seven pounds—reasonable by London standards but in Portugal wildly expensive. As we had only had one bottle of wine between us we could not help feeling ill-used.

'We're out of luck this evening,' was Swift's verdict. 'But I've thought of a good place to stay at—a little palace on the road to Lisbon. It belongs to a count who converted the place into an estalagem so that the family could go on living in the ancestral home. It's something quite out of the ordinary.'

When we emerged from the restaurant, it was black night, and raining. So in total darkness we found our way out of Setubal and sped up the N.10—the main highway to Lisbon. About a dozen kilometres from Setubal, we slowed down and swung left up a gravelled drive to halt outside the portico of a big country mansion.

This was the Quinta das Torres—so called, as I realised the next morning, from the towers at each corner of the house, which is built round a courtyard. Pretty maids in caps and aprons took our suitcases to a pair of rooms on one side of the courtyard. These rooms were grandly furnished—the pieces were mostly fine antiques, probably belonging to the family. Ours had a couple of four-poster beds. In shelves and recesses were displayed yet more of the painted clay figurines of Estremoz. Pip, who had bought a couple of dozen of them at Estremoz that morning, simply remarked:

'If I see another of those things I think I shall scream.'

It was now fairly late. Pip and Oonagh wanted to go to bed, but Swift and I needed a drink. Rain was pelting down and the nearest village was a mile away, so there was no question of dodging out to look for a taberna.

'We'll be able to get a drink in the lounge,' said Swift, and led me to the main entrance of the house at the north-west corner of its courtyard. Through the vestibule, past a chintzy sitting room where two or three crisply silver-haired old ladies and gentlemen were fingering the Portuguese equivalent of *Country Life*, we finally reached what must have been the smoking room of the mansion when it was a private residence. This room contained a great open fireplace with a chin-high mantelpiece. An atmosphere of heavily masculine luxury was lent by its deep wing-chairs, solid, heavy and massive ornaments and lampstands.

'Stay here while I see if I can get a drink.' Swift disappeared in the direction of the vestibule. Five minutes later he returned.

'It was a bit of a job, but I managed to get some brandy.'

Sure enough, in a moment or two one of the little page-boys

appeared bearing a silver salver with two large glasses of brandy. These we accepted gratefully. It was splendid stuff too.

We settled down to a long conversation, watched fascinatedly by the page-boy, who, though he spoke only a word or two of English, seemed unable to drag himself away from the spectacle that we presented.

'Most of this side of the house is reserved for the Count and his family,' Swift told me.

'Are they here now?' I asked.

'Gone to bed probably,' he replied.

The time came when our glasses needed refilling. We gave them to the buttons and sent him on the errand. It was some time before he came back. When he returned, it was with one of the pretty maidservants. She seemed to have come to see what we were up to, for she simply looked disapprovingly at us and vanished.

We had hardly sipped our replenishments before she came back. Addressing Swift, she said, 'Your wives want you.'

He translated for me.

'What does she mean? Our wives. It must be Oonagh—the baby's coming!'

So we gulped back that beautiful brandy and sped out of the smoking room, through the vestibule, out into the drive, and ran across the courtyard to the side of the house where our rooms were. I found Pip in her dressing-gown, ready for bed and much surprised at my sudden reappearance.

'What's happened?' I asked. 'We had a message to say that you wanted us.'

It turned out that Pip, meaning to switch on the reading-lamp over the bed, had pressed the wrong button and rung the bell for service (probably the most inevitable of accidents; all hotels seem to delight in this ambiguity of bell and switch). The maid had come; Pip had explained her mistake and apologised.

'I don't know why she fetched you—she can't have misunderstood me, her English is very good,' Pip said.

'It must have been Oonagh,' I suggested. 'I'll go and find out.'

I went out to find Swift emerging from his room.

'A complete mystery,' he said. 'Oonagh's perfectly all right, she sent no message.'

I told him about Pip's accident with the bell.

'I suppose it must have been that,' Swift decided. 'But the maid did make it sound pretty urgent. However, let's go back and finish the evening—we need another brandy after that fright.'

Once more we braved the rain and darkness, marched across the courtyard and round to the main entrance, happy to regain our comfortable smoking room and those balloon-glasses of best cognac. But all that remained a dream. We found the vestibule in darkness, the door shut and bolted, no lights in the windows—the establishment firmly closed down for the night. Only then did we fully understand the stratagem of the pretty maid, how painlessly she had evicted us, how finally and implacably separated we now were from our brandy . . .

Next day we were able to see a bit more of Quinta das

Torres. After breakfast Pip and I wandered in its country-house kitchen gardens, very English in aspect (though the illusion may have been helped by a grey louring morning sky) except for its rows of custard-apples and orchard of figs. We saw something of the formal gardens at the front of the house—heavily shaded with hedges of yew and cedars. There was a large piscina; but of that we had no more than a glimpse, for we were promptly shooed off by its owner, a belligerent white swan with no time for intruders.

Quinta das Torres is the most luxurious, comfortable, and beautifully-furnished hostelry I have stayed at—not that I am a connoisseur of luxury hotels. It was more expensive, of course, than any of the hotels and pensões we had so far sampled in Portugal, yet by English standards incredibly cheap. The bill for bed-and-breakfast for Pip and myself (including that famous brandy) came to two hundred escudos, or a little more than £3—the price of a single room in a dingy second-class hotel in England.

Our trip was nearly over; but we did not return direct to Lisbon. Instead, we drove to Sesimbra—a small fishing village near the extremity of the peninsula south of Lisbon and on the edge of the Arrábida range. Only thirty kilometres from Lisbon, this little village might be a hundred miles distant from the capital. Like the fishing hamlet of Arrábida, which is on the same coast but nearer Setubal, it is remarkably untouched by the grosser forms of tourism. How fortunate the Lisbonese are to have such perfect seaside villages—still unspoiled, yet within less than an hour's drive!

We noticed what seemed to be a very good hotel at Sesimbra —the Hotel do Mar. Instead of being a single building, one of those concrete blocks that do so much to ruin the places whose picturesqueness they exploit and destroy, the hotel consisted of a series of terraced flats on the slope overlooking the village and the sea, the roof of each flat serving as a garden.

We lunched at a simple little restaurant on the seafront, surrounded by the authentic bustle and squalor of a marine village—rusting anchors, tangled cables, nets, and floats. The skies wept, and great Atlantic breakers exploded over the seafront; but miserable as the day may have been, we fell for the charm of Sesimbra. Swift was able to get another plateful of oysters here with no trouble at all, while the rest of us were regaled with a splendid caldeirada do peixe. Then we got into the car for the last time, and in half an hour or so were in sight of Lisbon, spinning over the splendid new suspension bridge. The broad tawny Tagus drifted underneath our wheels as, tinged with sunset, the white houses, basilicas, and churches, fretted with trees and gardens, made a patchwork of the hills on which the city stood.

Postscript to a Journey

PATRICK SWIFT

When we came to the decision to make a tour of the Beira Baixa and the Alto Alentejo, none of us really knew this area. I was pretty well acquainted with the whole of the Alentejo and the Ribatejo, but this corner of Portugal, with its centre more or less at Castelo Branco, was still a closed book to me.

The divisions that mark off this district from the Ribatejo on the one hand and the Alto Alentejo on the other are somewhat arbitrary. The Beira is, in a manner of speaking, the part of the country between the Douro and the Tagus (Entre Douro e Tejo). This is made up of the Beira littoral, the Beira Baixa, and Beira Alta. Yet the designations Baixa (low) and Alta (high) do not indicate any sort of physical difference but merely a difference in latitude. It is rather artificial.

Between the two great rivers there is a vast mountain ridge running diagonally across the country. Up around Guarda, one passes over high mountains and all is rock: houses seem to form a rocky outcrop of the mountain itself. And Guarda is a cold, walled town of medieval purity with a forbidding cathedral (superb vaulting, a magnificent Manueline door, and a roof structure like Lincoln Cathedral) standing bang in the middle of the original walled city. It is the third cathedral of Portugal—a gothic pile coming only after Batalha and Alcobaça in importance. It breathes a tough spirit; this severity of feeling is characteristic of the Beiras. Essentially a frontier fortress from time immemorial it strikes the note that is to be found right through the Entre Douro e Tejo. And when one passes down from Castelo Branco into the Alto Alentejo, this world persists while the mountains last. Places like Castelo de Vide or Marvão have this mountain-fortress atmosphere but are not in any way related to the Alentejo in spirit. The true Alentejo begins where the mountains fall away and the hot rolling plain, with its cork groves and flat white-washed villages set in isolation one from the other, creates a completely new world.

This natural division is recognised by the people to whom the mountains are known as the Terra Fria—the cold land. The mountain lands are of granite and schist—mostly denuded of forest. There are vast areas where only the mountain sheep and goats provide a source of livelihood. These flocks, rebanhos in Portuguese, and the life that goes with them, form one of the kernels of the culture of this part of Portugal. They move seasonally from the high ground to the low as the weather dictates.

But the casual visitor seeing one of these enormous herds scattered across a barren rocky hilltop among the picturesque outcrops would not guess what social organisation and what traditional regulations and orders enable these great flocks to wander across the landscape in this apparently free manner. For they belong not to individual owners but to whole communities. The rebanho transumante, as it is called, is organised by a shepherd-in-chief known as the maioral. It is he who fixes when and where the migration will begin and where the animals are to assemble. He is also responsible for sending out word of the day of the return of the herds.

Traditionally—indeed from time immemorial—the day of departure will be somewhere between the feasts of Saint John and Saint Peter (24th and 29th June). It is then that the weather is considered good enough for the trek upwards to the high grazing grounds to begin. The feast of St. John is consecrated by custom as the ideal day for the departures of the large flocks. The herd, as it moves on its way, will receive further additions from various townlands. These join it at appointed places on set dates. A big herd will have as many as seven shepherds and perhaps up to a dozen dogs in charge. The dogs are vital for a number of reasons: not least because the wolf is still commonplace in the Beiras. These dogs, usually of the famous Serra da Estrela breed—very large, brown, heavy-coated handsome dogs with big sad eyes and sloppy jowls—wear a collar made of leather, with sharp protruding nails as a protection.

The larger flocks, by the time they reach the grazing grounds, can number several thousand head. There will usually be a specially contracted commissariat-man who will come with mule and cart to follow the flocks. His job is to carry the kitchen equipment needed for feeding the shepherds. On the journey he will go ahead and be ready with the shepherds' evening meal at an agreed place. The route and the stopping places have not changed in hundreds (who knows, perhaps thousands) of years. These ancient shepherd paths are called canadas, and the places where they pernoitar (pass the night) and rosear (pass the hottest hours of the day) are all settled by custom.

The shepherds have a culture, too, whose origins cannot easily be counted in years. They have traditionally whiled away the time carving implements from wood. We were lucky enough while in Portalegre to come by chance on the museum of José Régio the poet who made a collection of these carved wooden items, some of great beauty. In Estremoz friends of ours had made a praiseworthy if rather self-conscious and artificial effort to preserve some of this culture—they had organised a few local enthusiasts, who bought the carvings from the shepherds when they came back with the flocks. The designs on these items—which ranged from cups and drinking glasses to forks and knives of various types and other domestic utensils—were of a geometric order, hatching and criss-crossing in patterns, sometimes reminiscent of the schist plaques similarly decorated from pre-historic times. The small, intricate work was the speciality of the shepherds. A tradition of larger wooden utensils also exists—even ploughs and hayforks being made entirely of wood.

The hills of the Beira Baixa in and about Castelo Branco are richer than the highlands. Here we find olive and cork trees with grain planted between. The olive trees are planted with great difficulty and need small retaining walls to hold the earth. The olive oil of Castelo Branco is legendary for its fine quality.

This is a transitional region where the harshness of charneca over to the west is beginning to give way to a more Mediterranean type vegetation and kinder climate. The charneca is the poor small-farmer's region: a land where a meagre living is eked out by a sturdy independent folk on small impoverished holdings. Like the now-vanished 'estatesmen' of Cumberland these are a people of kindliness and dignity, each owning his farmstead, living in a region where the great landlord is unknown. Going south from Castelo Branco, one begins to find the vast estates, often owned by absentee landlords. It is to these that the poor folk of the hills come at harvest time to work the seasonal stint when required. They also come to the olive groves for the olive picking in the area known as O Campo (roughly the lower parts of the countryside between the Guardunha mountains and the Ponsul river).

These poor migrant workers are known in the Alto Alentejo as the ratinhos. When I first heard people speaking of the pratos de ratinhos as being worth collecting in the Beira Baixa and Alto Alentejo, I presumed they meant plates made by a factory called the Ratinho (or even from the Rato ceramic factory in Lisbon which had a famous tradition). It was in Portalegre that I discovered that this type of antique plate was called after the humble migrant worker who brought it with him on his seasonal working period in the Alentejo and in the Campo of the Castelo Branco district. The man who gave me this information was an antique restorer whom I found working in the late evening in a back street. He claimed that he knew of a case where twenty contos (twenty thousand escudos) had been paid for one eighteenth-century ratinho plate. Allowing for exaggeration, it seemed too good to be true. It is, and has been always, a custom in the cottages of the Beira Baixa to make a show of the crockery of the house. Anyone who strays into the countryside and calls on a peasant dwelling will see beautiful interiors with fine displays of plates.

In the Campo area, the houses will be more prosperous and usually whitewashed inside. But in the charneca, the barren slopes of the Guardunha, the interiors are dark, smoky and poor. As one drives down from the mountains and goes south of Castelo Branco whitewash becomes gradually more common. A little at first. A line round the door. Later, all the windows and doors will have a good band of clean white lime circumscribing them, and even a whole wall may be painted. Then, as one progresses into the Alentejo, the entire house is plastered and completely whitewashed and sports a chimney. It is a mystery why in the hills, where the weather is so very much colder and wetter, and where the use of a fire is essential, the chimney is rarely if ever found; and the house fills with smoke. While in the south the chimney assumes a more or less cultural significance, growing bigger and more elaborate until in the Algarve it becomes a fantasy of artistic indulgence—a plaything to show off the skill and imagination of the builder, and the owner's capacity to pay for it. It is in the Alto Alentejo that the custom of putting some decoration on the flat surface of these huge chimneys begins. The date of construction, together with some floral or symbolic pattern in stucco, is the first sign of this cult of the chimney, which reaches its apogee in Algarve.

The immense variety that exists in style and in character of farm and town as well as landscape makes even a short trip through any part of Portugal an adventure. The excursion we had planned was very modest in terms of distance. Anyone spending a few weeks' holiday in Lisbon could easily undertake it without any strain. But it took us over an area of the country that comprised many sharply contrasting cultural manifestations, ways of life, landscape and living. The very richness of the passing scenery can be too much if one tries to investigate everything out of the ordinary that one sees. On the other hand, with an eye in tune to the occasion, it is possible to take a great deal of enjoyment in the kaleidoscopic and rapidly changing scene and still not get visual and cultural indigestion.

An End and a Beginning

PATRICK SWIFT

Autumn turned golden. Down the Rua Dr. Luis de Almeida e Albuquerque the vision of Estrêla shimmered in a mist of colour. The smell of chestnuts roasting on the street corner drifted up through the falling leaves of the trees hanging over the gateposts of the *Jornal do Comércio*. Wright was leaving us and we were to lunch at the Martinho together for the last time. Helle was to join us and Oonagh—still awaiting the emergence of the reluctant baby—was determined not to let this small matter keep her at home. The pensão was by now home from home, Senhor Menelli and his wife our friends and guardians.

At the Martinho we found Wright already finishing his main course although we were not more than twenty minutes late. Airport nerves were already affecting his behaviour. The old waiters were hovering about with special solicitude. The poet and professor (with this dignity they had endowed him) had become a distinguished regular, it was clear. Obviously, he had been well served. A plateful of bones was the remnants of a superb cabrito assado no forno. As we sat and started our lunch the poet—having settled our bill for us—flapped out with papers and bags into the noisy, sunny Praça do Comércio and was gone. The waiter appeared disconsolate.

Our days became a long vigil. From the pensão we took to driving out each day to Estoril and Cascais. There, in the warmth of a mellow season, we would continue our endless discussion: what would we call the baby? If it were a boy there was no problem; it was to be James. But as I was certain that it would be a girl, the problem remained. David Wright had settled on Nora before departing. I had a hankering after the solemn medieval Portuguese Leonor. Thus preoccupied, our lunches on the pavement at cafés in Cascais marked the slow passage of the autumn days with enormous pleasure. The motorway runs beside the sea and all the way is air and sky and water. Some old villas of the earlier part of the century lend grace in a ragged way to the view. Yachts and boats give a romantic touch to the scene. For some unknown reason this marvellous drive—it grew more pleasing every time we did it—is known to the lisboeta as o passeio dos tristes, 'the jaunt of the sad'; perhaps because it is a favourite with the weekend motorist. For us, it assumed a character of ritual—and this seemed to make it more pleasurable.

We tried some of the big popular café-restaurants that face the sea, but found them disappointing in spite of the view. Surprisingly, the little restaurants tucked away in Cascais were full of charm and not expensive. But Cascais in the quiet of those autumn afternoons—with the occasional nanny pushing a pram along the street, an old horse and cart performing some municipal function, smart cars gliding by, children returning from school, boutiques with nice clothes for babies—had an enchantment about it.

One day Oonagh announced that the baby's name would be Stella Patricia. So that was that. Next evening, she felt that perhaps the dilatory infant had at last decided to emerge. I suggested we drive over to the Avenida da República for dinner. Anyway I thought Oonagh should have at least one look at the nursing home before going in. So we dropped in at the nursing home (it had the cunning name Promater) and there it was agreed that at last Stella Patricia, as I now called the awaited creature, could well have decided to come out. We dined next door in the Galeto, sitting at the counter. After a good meal it transpired that the baby had definitely decided to get born. Shortly before midnight, Stella Patricia finally made her appearance. The Portuguese doctor—a pretty young woman with an efficient air—did not forgive me for absenting myself from the occasion.

Envoi

For two weeks my wife stayed in the nursing home with the baby. I continued at the Pensão Santa Catarina and daily made the journey across town, becoming gradually an old hand at the hazardous business of driving in Lisbon traffic (though I have to acknowledge that I never could achieve the panache of my friend Lima). I learned some things about traffic too, and on more than one occasion during the dense evening exodus found it wiser to turn into a side-street and abandon the car. With my settled routine of coming from and going to the Avenida da República, I appreciated the problems of the lisboeta who drives back and forward to work. The city seems to be slowly choking itself with cars.

All our neighbours asked about the baby, and I realised we had become quite well known in the Bairro of Santa Catarina. I raised the question with Senhor Menelli and his wife of whether or not Oonagh might return to the pensão for a few days before returning to the Algarve. Sheer delight filled their countenances; even the maids were excited. So we decided to stay on a while in that glorious autumnal Lisbon. For one thing, I had to register the baby's birth—a job I had been told was not really simple.

One day Oonagh returned to the Rua Dr. Luis de Almeida e Albuquerque bearing Stella Patricia in a brand new carry-cot. The whole staff of the little pensão turned out to welcome her. We found the room full of flowers. During the following days, they could not do enough to help or to please. Senhora Menelli insisted that Oonagh should go out occasionally, that she would take responsibility for the baby.

I went to the notary's office where I was given an appointment for a day the following week on which to do the act of registration. The office was a gloomy little place in an old building hard by the Praça do Duque de Saldanha. It was more countrified than our local notary's office in the Algarve. The notary, as so frequently is the case in Portugal, turned out to be woman. She warned me that if I were to give the child a foreign name, i.e. a non-Portuguese name, I would have to have certificates from my embassy and so forth. By a stroke of good fortune Oonagh had settled for two names that were both on the register of acceptable cognomens. We were merely required to spell them in the Portuguese way, which meant changing Stella to Estella. This done, I received a small black book—the birth certificate. Not only did it record the birth but it also provided on a number of following pages for marriage, children born, divorce, gaol, release from gaol and, finally, death. So everything was in order; our purpose in Lisbon, for the moment at least, was fulfilled.

On a summerlike November morning we loaded up the car. Amazed at what we had accumulated it seemed touch and go whether we would get out of Lisbon with our load. But we did, with the energetic help of the proprietors and staff of the pensão. At last, with the baby installed in the cot, the bags piled up, and every cubic inch crammed with objects, we bade goodbye to Senhor Menelli and his wife and the maids. It was the end of an episode that, we instinctively grasped as we stood on the pavement outside the Santa Catarina, bound us more deeply to Portugal, to the people, and to Lisbon.

The Portuguese Enigma

PATRICK SWIFT

Rossio flower sellers

I brought back from my Lisbon trip two valuable acquisitions—both gifts from António Quadros: his essay, 'O Enigma de Lisboa', and a curious old guide to the city which spoke of things like the 'stony abandoned land' beyond the top of the Avenida da Liberdade (now the Ritz). The first contained several enlightenments, the second a mass of fascinating details.

The essay revealed itself to be a work of ideas, and a type of writing not easily rendered into English. Essentially a reflective philosophical exercise of the mind. A stylish performance. Modern English usage does not accommodate the gentle, slightly romantic, nature of this sort of writing. For instance,

'The variety of form and the variety of colour situates man before the reality of nature. They lend to wandering man, to epic man, to man with a mission, a support which is indispensable and irreplaceable. This is one of the great lessons of Lisbon, a city where nature reveals herself and is systematically symbolised, as though deriving by syllogism from an open concept of being and of being human.' What seems beautiful and meaningful in Portuguese loses in translation. Nevertheless, I found it rewarding to consider this little philosophy or psychology of the city.

The premise is that the development of a city is not accidental: that inevitably it expresses the very soul of a people. Quadros draws attention to the common misuse of the term 'Manueline' in reference to the architecture of the fifteenth and early sixteenth centuries in Portugal—this he calls Atlantic Baroque. A consideration of the meaning of the Manueline style is central to the essay. In the aesthetics of the city's structure there subsists, for him, an intentional element. Through this we can diagnose the psychological Lisbon through the psychographic evidence.

Lisbon is generally agreed to be naturally beautiful by virtue of its position. Rising on hills from the great expanse of the Tagus, it is, as Quadros puts it, beautiful 'a priori'. But, he adds, the significant thing is that in the structure of the town we find a form of urban landscape that instead of shutting man off from nature attempts to reconcile him to it. This trait is so persistent that it cannot be called accidental. It forms a psychological line that cuts across all those diverse elements that have gone to create the conglomerate we call the lisboeta, the Lisbonese, of today: the Luso-Latin, the Luso-Arab, the Luso-Semite, the Luso-Atlantic, the Portuguese. This long line of mixed cultures, races, civilisations and religions, that has resulted in the Portuguese of today had a persistent original element: a special relationship to nature. Something which came to be logically theorised in the work of the Portuguese, Espinoza.

Lisbon is a city impregnated by nature. Quadros sees in the cities founded by Portuguese in far-off Brazil, India, Africa,

China—in Rio de Janeiro, Luanda, Macau—a re-creation of this spirit; a nostalgia for Lisbon. There is no other Lisbon in Europe, and similarly there is no other Rio in South America, no other Luanda in Africa. A characteristic of all these is the survival of nature in the urban context: nature living in the midst of the city. Lisbon is, for him, archetypal, symbolic, mythical.

This point of view is in itself so expressive of something central to the Portuguese character that it throws light on the enigma: to me, it is clear that the Portuguese are—in a way impossible to define—unique and individual. They are apart from the European main stream yet closely involved in Europe at various points of history. To say the nation is 'Atlantic' does express something.

Any visitor travelling by road or rail into Portugal will have been struck by the vivid and startling difference immediately noticeable on crossing the frontier. This applies to any point of the compass, whether from Galicia, Estramadura or Andalusia. There is at once apparent in the air—the ambience—a radical change. H. N. Savory in his prehistory of the Iberian Peninsula, goes into the reason for writing of Spain and Portugal as one whole. In doing so he succeeds in emphasising the point I am now trying to make. He draws attention to the climatic boundary that separates 'wet' Spain from 'dry'. The temperate northern coastal strip with its heavy rainfall and its natural forest cover of oak, elm, and ash extends as far as the Tagus. Its eastern limits roughly coincide with the edge of the Meseta —the inland plateau of the Peninsula. This climate forms the raison d'être of modern Portugal. The western coastal strip has mild wet winters and sufficient summer drought to enable Mediterranean type flora to flourish even as far north as Galicia. This mingling of two diverse climatic conditions—the hot and dry and the mild and wet—is most apparent in the area between the Tagus and the Douro. In other words, in the very heart of Portugal. The whole of this strip, with its particularly heavy and luxuriant vegetation, turns its back on the harsh interior and looks out to the sea. As Savory puts it, looking to sea-ways, leading in early days to the Mediterranean and northern Europe, and more recently to all parts of the world. It was the basis in prehistoric times for an 'Atlantic' cultural sphere (and this has particular interest for French and British prehistory).

All of this is very relevant to understanding the essence of Portugal. Quadros' essay extends this Atlantic idea to an understanding of the personality of the people. It seems reasonable to suppose that it was the settled and civilised farming communities of the seaboard who, persisting as such basic communities do, throughout changing phases of history and prehistory, lent the deepest notes to the personality of the nation. They had a genius for absorbing and transforming foreign influences from the very earliest times (Eastern influence, Greek influence, Celtic influence). Thus the notion that the recurrent dominations—Latin, Visigoth, Arab—and the great impact of the Jews (and Negroes?) could all have been absorbed, transformed and given a coherent character is not by any means fanciful.

Quadros calls the vital element in this sort of absorption and transformation a 'cult of nature'. He sees in it a key to the cultural and religious character of the Portuguese.

Your true Portuguese is deeply religious. Lisbon can be seen, if looked at from this point of view, as a town composed of temples to the cult of nature. The innumerable miradouros, and belvederes, each with its garden (a tiny bit of nature humanised), lodged on the edge of steep hills looking over those unsurpassable views, are temples of an esoteric cult. These places are nearly all legendary and sacred in some way. Even a short list is impressive—Castelo de S. Jorge, the fortress turned into a quiet garden where the peacock struts on the lawns; Senhora da Monte, like a little village square; Santa Luzia, gazing over the rooftops of the Alfama down to the river (a view unchanged since the caravels of the Order of Christ anchored off below); S. Pedro de Alcantara looking across at the Castelo de S. Jorge over the dense life of the city beneath; the Alto de Santa Catarina, a strange little platform set perfectly for watching the ships pass up and down the river; Janelas Verdes, a rich profusion of greenery presiding over the rumble of activity along the docks. Lisbon in modern times again gives expression to this cult of nature: the magnificent park of Monsanto, incontestably one of the finest stretches of woodland within a city that exists, crowned by a hilltop that offers over immeasurable tracts of the Estremadura with the river rolling seawards.

There is an interesting point about the vegetation of Lisbon. When Lisbon offers us a park, it is not merely a rich growth of European trees and flowers—it is a feast of the exotic and strange, a botanic fantasy. Flowering trees and shrubs from the remote and luxuriant corners of India, Guinea, and Brazil fill the parks of Campo Grande, Ajuda, Estrêla, Estufa Fria and the Jardim Botânico. And where in Europe is there a zoological garden which is so much a *garden* as that of Lisbon? The city is full of remote corners shaded in exotic foliage, little shrines to nature, mysterious retreats where couples linger amid the blessings of a beneficent earth goddess.

António Quadros carries this line of thought a step further. Maybe too far. Yet when one thinks of the city, and the streets that climb the numerous hills to little squares looking out on the river, it is difficult not to be convinced. The lisboeta is not satisfied merely with his parks and his gardened miradouros, he brings this cult into the intimacy of his daily life—his window becomes his gardened miradouro, his shrine to nature. Here he conducts this intimate dialogue between man and his primordial environment. Throughout old Lisbon, it is rare to find a house un-bedecked with a variety of pots, cases and boxes bursting forth with a host of different plants and flowers, some trailing many feet down towards the street. The cheering sight of a morning is the ladies of Lisbon watering and caring for their little window gardens; one of the joys of the capital.

The visual aspect of the city supports Quadros' thesis. There is an inherent impulse to grow in harmony with nature, with natural laws. The streets have their own logic in space and time. They follow the contours and do not attempt to contradict the natural lie of the city's position on the hills by the river. In the pictures of the Portuguese painters Carlos Botelho and Maria Helene Vieira da Silva we see confirmation of this feeling; and it can be seen from any of the miradouros, where the cityscape rises before one like a watercolour in faded wash. A gentle blending from yellow to green to blue and pink, with ever-present foliage breaking the lines. The configuration of Lisbon is essentially irregular—a natural form of growth. No great monuments strike across the accumulations of haphazard shape clinging to the steep hills; what monuments there are seem inevitable—pinnacles to a natural mountain of houses and streets.

Architecture reflects in turn harmony and devotion to nature. The applied arts—ironwork, azulejo, precious metal—show a tendency for the fluent and natural form. The spiral, the curve, the elliptical flowing line of the wrought iron of the innumerable balconies of old Lisbon show this. The jewellery, the filigrana, though admittedly pretty degraded in popular reproductions for tourism, is an ancient lisboeta art. In its way it too shows the same tendency. But above all the emergence of the Manueline style, Atlantic Baroque, shows this marriage of the natural with the artefact in full flower. This is a triumph of Atlantic man. It emerges with the same burst of genius and energy that saw the discoveries and the rise of a type of Portuguese—the man with a sense of mission.

Quadros' essay had made me reflect on the phenomenon that is Lisbon. It *is* true that nature is present in and throughout the city. Where else in Europe is there a great central avenue with two complete and very natural gardens plonk in the middle? While the traffic roars up and down the Avenida da Liberdade one can meander by the flowing waters of these little gardens. It is almost possible to be unaware of the flood of poisonous machinery on both side of these oases. But what Quadros is saying is that there is a 'Portuguese' *truth*. A Portuguese truth and, at a certain historical moment a Portuguese *mission*, a national destiny.

It was between the times of D. Diniz and the great Manuel I that Portugal fulfilled its historic role, its great mission. This is not merely, as an English reader might suppose, a conceit of modern Portuguese reflection on more glorious times. The notion of a mission, of a nation with a high destiny was prevalent in the times of the Navigator. In Camões it is given expression on the epic scale (and Camões is one of the great poets of Europe). Other poets such as Guerra Junqueiro, Teixeira de Pascoais, and, more recently, Fernando Pessoa have been obsessed with the idea, have devoted a considerable amount of time and talent to the attempt to understand the national identity—a mission. Pessoa, whose talent belongs to the Parnassian level beyond national considerations, believed that the Portuguese epic cycle that closed with the era of the Discoveries had entered another phase and again awaited completion—that the nation had before it a destiny to fulfil.

Ideas of this order can only be interesting when expressed in forms that are convincing. What is important is that the idea informs literature of a high order, that the concept of 'man with a mission' haunts the Portuguese imagination.

Quadros sees in the Jerónimos at Belém the visible monument to this national mission accomplished through the Navigators. In discovering new continents, new seas, they were discovering a truth of Portugal—in other words, man's relation to nature. The spirit of man oscillates between transcendentalism and humanism, but there is the third dimension of nature herself. Through the dialogue between man and nature lies a way to God.

Unless one can grasp that notions of this order are the stock in trade of the Portuguese mind, one can never hope to understand Portugal. It is for this reason, I think, that so many modern visitors are fascinated and baffled by the mystery of the Portuguese character. To the rational, logical mind it is romantic madness; to the closed political mind it is nationalism. To such people, a passage like this from Quadros' essay, referring to the Jerónimos, cannot mean much:

> I am going to say what a secular and ancestral voice says to all who penetrate the cathedral of Santa Maria at Belém, a cathedral of Portuguese religious feeling, consecrated to the Virgin, protectress of Portugal and whose patrons, significantly, are the Three Magi: 'Thus do you enter the kingdom of God through the gates of

nature. It is in nature, in the world of generation and corruption, in the world of birth and death, that human life unfolds. Do not aspire, egoistic man, for a unique and exclusive salvation for your soul. Meditate on what is inscribed here on this doorway: these are the roots of the earth and the waves of the sea, they are the creatures of the clay and the coral of the ocean, they are the continents and countries, the human race. Behold, man, your destiny: go round the world and ascend with it, if you wish for the triumph of redemption!'

This attempt to relay some of Quadros' ideas is very crude. But it may give a hint of this side of the Portuguese personality. There is in Portugal a continuous form of dialogue carried on from generation to generation, and indeed between generations, and it hinges on the obsession with identity.

In the poetry of Camões where it is epic, it is in full flower of accomplishment. Despite the dark fates that haunt Camões (and find their most beautiful expression in his sonnets), his is a poetry of confidence. Camões, though in life a tragic figure, belonged to an age of optimism and achievement. His is a large and complex world, encompassing the full gamut of human agony and of human glory. It is when we come to Fernando Pessoa that the obsession in its more intimate and human scale is apparent. Pessoa belongs to the company of W. B. Yeats and Ezra Pound. He is one of the great poets of this century. Like Camões, he frequently comes across in his writing as a tragic figure. His poetry ranges from the epic to the lyric. But for the purposes of these remarks about the Portuguese character it is his extreme self-consciousness that is interesting. He was intensely aware of himself as a *Portuguese*. This was an extension of his fundamental introspection. His creation of a theory of poetry called 'sensationism' is very much in tune with the psychology Quadros tries to define in his reflections on Lisbon. In 'sensationism', Pessoa denied the possibility or validity of any form of 'objective' reality. To be open to the world in an affirmative way, to accept and to merge with experience, with life, was central to his aesthetic (though of course he would deny having an aesthetic). He used to quote Espinoza: a philosophy is right in what it affirms, wrong in what it denies. This is close to the idea of being at one with nature. It is worth while quoting Pessoa, for he is both witty and enlightening on being *Portuguese*:

> We cannot admit a man writing in his native language unless he has something to say which only a man speaking that language could say. The great point about Shakespeare is that he could not but be English. That is why he wrote in English and was born in England. A thing that can just as well be said in one language as in another had better not be said at all.
>
> The Portuguese Sensationists are original and interesting because, being strictly Portuguese, they are cosmopolitan and universal. The Portuguese temperament is universal; that is its magnificent superiority. The one great act of Portuguese history—that long cautious, scientific period of the Discoveries—is the one great cosmopolitan act in history. The whole people stamp themselves there. An original typically Portuguese literature cannot be Portuguese, because the typical Portuguese are never Portuguese. There is something American, with the noise left out and the quotidian omitted, in the intellectual temper of this people. No people seize so readily on novelties. No people depersonalise so magnificently. That weakness is its great strength. That temperamental non-regionalism is its unused might. That indefiniteness of soul is what makes them definite.

I am tempted to go on quoting this paradoxical mind. I must at least give one more sample both contrary and enlightening.

> They [the Portuguese] have no stable elements as the French have, who only make revolutions for export. The Portuguese are always making revolutions. When a Portuguese goes to bed he makes a revolution because the Portuguese who wakes up the next day is quite different.

> He is precisely a day older. Other people wake up every morning yesterday. Tomorrow is always several years away. Not so this quite strange people. They go so quick that they leave everything undone, including going quick. Nothing is less idle than a Portuguese. The only idle part of the nation is the working part of it. Hence their lack of evident progress.

Considerable intimacy over a period of eight years has not lessened the mystery of this people for me. I can say this, too: Portugal is a closed book to any but the imaginative and generous spirit; it is no country for

> A levelling, rancorous, rational sort of mind
> That never looked out of the eye of a saint
> Or out of a drunkard's eye.

I would go further. It seems to me that a country so radically different in spiritual temper from the rest of Europe, a country where the religious instinct of man is alive, cannot but have a contribution to make in a world daily going more rapidly down the path of boredom and despair, of technocratic dreariness, the arid desert of modern civilised life.

Here are the last words of António Quadros' essay:

> We must take cognisance of what we are and of what others are and what they represent. If we wish to fulfil our vocation we must discover and realise our individuality, the character of our relationship with our end and our beginnings.
>
> Lisbon is a unique city which has not yet taken account of what she is and what her value is. This is the key, I readily confess, to this essay which I offer on the place where I was born, where I live and where I will die.

at Alcantara

Advice to Travellers

PATRICK SWIFT

Air Travel to Lisbon

Both BEA and TAP operate flights between London and Lisbon. BEA's daily Trident and jetliner flights offer a wide choice of departure dates. Inclusive holidays with travel by BEA scheduled flights are available in Lisbon and many Portuguese resorts. Those arriving by air may contract for car hire in Lisbon, either for short periods of one to six days at a daily rate of between £2 and £4 plus a charge of between 2p and 4p per kilometre, according to the car. On bookings for seven days and over, the daily charge is between £3 and £4 with unlimited mileage.

As the traveller crosses the short space that separates the plane from the arrivals building in Lisbon airport, he senses an element of strangeness in the air. It is something faintly exotic, perhaps a lingering trace of spices and discoveries from another age. David Wright has called it a whiff of Africa, and the South African painter Hardy Brownstein has told me the same thing. This subtle flavour of something remote and curious, from another world, can be lost as mysteriously as it is captured. It exists between the lines. It is an element of the spaces between that concrete jungle growing around the city and the tall trees that fill the new squares; between the wide shimmer of water that waits at the end of each long street that goes down to the Tagus and the spectacularly blue sky that spreads above.

There is, in truth, something inherently exciting in this city, but something that can be discovered only in the detail of a personal experience. For this reason it is not easy to advise the traveller arriving in Lisbon for the first time how and where he will find the true strange heart of the city.

Certainly those who stay in the new hotels, nearly all clustered in or about the top of the Avenida da Liberdade, will have to go out and explore in order to find the Lisbon 'cidade triste e alegre' of the poet, Pessoa, or the Lisbon 'cum mar profundo de varia navegação' of the sixteenth-century André Falcão de Resende. The poetic Lisbon, 'sad and gay' of Pessoa—the 'deep sea of varied navigation' of Resende—still exists. In it, a magic persists that will repay the trouble or the patience required to seek it out. With this in mind, the following notes have been put together: a few hints on how the traveller might go about finding this enchanting city of poetry, of nostalgia, of dreams and visions joyful and heartbreaking.

Where to Stay

The choice breaks down to two radically opposed possibilities: comfort and luxury amid the parks and wide avenues of modern Lisbon, or less comfort but more fun in the heart of the town. It should be remembered that Lisbon is a noisy city, and the hotels in the older parts have the disadvantage of receiving the full blast of the daily life of the metropolis. There are one or two hotels in the centre that can be classed as very comfortable—the Avenida Palace is one, situated by the Praça dos Restauradores near the Rossio; the Mundial in the Rua Dom Duarte is another, very much in the heart of the city and offering modern-style comfort at very reasonable prices (two to three pounds a night).

But, in general, the luxury hotels are to be found in new Lisbon. First comes the Ritz, said to be one of the best in Europe. It dominates the area at the top of the Avenida da Liberdade, looks over the Park of Edward the Seventh and commands splendid views. From the Ritz, which alone is five-star in the official grading, we descend at once to four-star hotels. These, however, are luxurious and usually keep a very high standard of cuisine. There are nine hotels listed by the Portuguese Tourist office as four-star A and a further seven classed four-star B—among the latter, by the way, is the Rex: described in rather lush terms in this book in another context, it is small and comfortable, facing the park near the Ritz. Any of the hotels in these top categories can be completely relied on. Places like the Fenix or the Tivoli offer a standard of service and amenities that can compare with anywhere in the world.

But those who, like myself, are prepared to balance comfort against character in order to have the fun of staying more *in* the city, of sharing something of the busy Lisbon of the Portuguese themselves, can still do well in the older downtown hostelries.

The Borges in the Chiado is situated at the heart of things and is popular with lots of resident English who live outside Lisbon and use it when they come to town. For shopping, it could not be more more conveniently placed. This is a three-star hotel, and there are a few more like it. It is not in the luxury class at all, but it is very comfortable and offers all the usual services. The Metropole in the Rossio is another such: a cut above the old Francfort (described by David Wright) which is in the two-star category, as is the Bragança—hotels with great charm, but the bathrooms are down the corridor and so on.

An odd point that should be remembered is that many small pensões of the first class offer private bathrooms and greater comfort than some of the third-class hotels. Some, like York House—an antique atmosphere of old Portugal in excellent taste, in the Rua Janelas Verdes—are famous and so popular that it is necessary to book well in advance. For friendly atmosphere, for the pleasure of a feeling of personal contact with the management who invariably take a benign, amiable interest in their guests (not at all the tough 'concierge' attitude one associates with boarding houses), a small Lisbon pensão has a lot to be said for it. There are so many of these establishments that it would be impossible to single out even a few for special mention; but the Santa Catarina, described earlier, is fairly typical. The list of places to stay, published by the Portuguese Tourism Office, constitutes a fairly hefty little pamphlet: but provided that one takes the trouble to locate on a map the situation of the hotel or pensão one chooses—remembering that main avenues are noisy and small streets less so—and having some idea of the sort of orientation in relation to what one intends to do, this is the best and most reliable way to pick a place to stay. It is issued regularly and prices will be up to date. Fortunately inflation is not galloping in Portugal yet. Almost certainly a price range of from plus or minus five pounds a night for luxury, down to one pound a night for modest comfort, can be taken as correct for the foreseeable future.

If I had to make a choice and pick out a few from the long list of excellent places to stay I would probably opt for the Tivoli, Fenix or Florida in the luxury class, at the top of the Avenida da Liberdade, and the Avenida Palace in the Baixa—the last particularly because of its central position and 'old world charm'. Among exceptional pensões, almost in the class of the best hotels, I would pick York House and (quite different, but unusual and first rate) Estalagem do Cavalo Branco. For a good inexpensive hotel in the centre, I would take the Borges. There is something very pleasant about stepping right out into the busy shopping district of the Chiado. Although I would opt for the older central part of Lisbon.

Where To Eat

Having settled for an hotel, it is probably a bad policy to eat all one's meals there. The food in hotels, though variable, is usually good. But there are two disadvantages. The set meal will normally be too big, and the opportunity to see more of the city by eating out in various parts of town is missed. I have already tried to give a general idea of the range and scope of the multifarious eating-houses of Lisbon. But if asked to reduce the matter to a few recommendations I would (apart from the supreme Avis) venture the following: for charm and character the Tavares, dating from the eighteenth century and preserving a lot of that epoch: the Gôndola for outdoor lunch, or dinner on a balmy summer evening; the Cortador for a big steak and fun; Restaurante A Quinta for country-style truly Portuguese food—though it has Russian specialities too—and a splendid view of the Castelo de S. Jorge and all the tumble of houses that climb the hill up to its ramparts: a superb sunset panorama; and lastly the Parreirinha, up high in the Alfama, for a very special adventurous evening out in really old-world Lisbon.

I would add two notes to this advice, try a cervejaria (bar) for the fresh draught beer and seafood or perhaps a 'bife a portuguesa'—a thin slice of rump steak served stewing in a hot sauce and accompanied by fresh chip potatoes; and try any of the multitude of frango churrasco (grilled chicken) houses, for they have an elemental Portuguese quality not found anywhere else.

What to See

Everything depends on how much time one can devote to the town. Ideally, it is a city that should be walked about in. On every hand small details of life and art will await the curious traveller. Such things will be missed by those who dash around in car or taxi.

Lisbon is not a great museum city. There are a number of fine monuments and museums that are required visiting, but it would be a very half-baked and unbalanced idea of the city that emerged from a tour of only its major monuments and museums. Life in all its complex city manifestations, all going on in the street, as it were—fills Lisbon with an intense fascination for anyone with an eye and an ear for the rich texture of city culture. To walk up through the narrow streets of the Bairro Alto in the late morning is to enter a world of immense activity, of noise and movement, of an innumerable variety of human activities all taking place left and right as one passes along: here is the fishwife calling her prices to the women who lean out and bargain from the windows; here at an open door, a craftsman pursues some patient task; at the doors of the tabernas, groups can be seen taking a morning refreshment. All is noisy but very friendly, the mood is one of enjoyment and indulgence in the essential energy of life at its fullest. It is like the London of Charles Dickens.

As one passes along one notes the distinguished façades of these old seventeenth- and eighteenth-century houses. There are details of odd carved stones; hallways with walls lined with dimly glowing blue azulejos. Occasionally, in the thick of the city street, a gate gives into a crowded green garden—a small island of nature amid a dense concentration of human activity. To succumb to the temptation to partake oneself of a morning pre-prandial glass is to join the world of busy humanity here. Drop into a taberna, and within seconds you can be deep in some pointless but absorbing conversation with the seemingly nefarious characters who come and go or settle themselves down to take a slow glass. In this way, the flavour of the town can be caught—as it can in a different manner by sitting at one of the street cafés and listening to the endless turmoil of conversation with which Lisbon preoccupies itself. Or again, to linger under the heavy trees in any one of the innumerable little gardens and parks is to enter into another level of the life of the lisboeta. Nothing can replace this sort of contact with what constitutes the kernel of a town. No amount of sightseeing can make up for what one misses if this aspect of the city remains a closed book, as, alas, it does for most visitors.

One of the major curiosities of Lisbon is something very frequently missed by the tourist. It is an institution typically Portuguese, typically lisboeta: the Feira Popular. Here, on an extensive site in the Avenida da República is a full-scale fair ground where, all through the summer, a thorough-going Portuguese fair is to be found in full swing. Here are all the trappings and trimmings of a country fair ground brought into the city. The air is filled with the pungent exhalations of grilling sardines, and chickens turning over charcoal. There are tabernas with draught beer, and roundabouts and stalls of all kinds. And if one wants to know what a Portuguese dinner of the country is like, go there and dine at one of the large popular restaurants on the typical fare of the day. It is noisy and busy and crowded, but great fun for those who can take it.

Another Lisbon institution to which I am very much attracted is the annual Book Fair. This takes place from mid-May to mid-June. Under the trees all along the Avenida da Liberdade, the booksellers and the publishers of Lisbon set up their stalls. Up and down this long serried column of bookstalls the crowds drift in leisurely pursuit of book bargains. Every day during this period the newspapers carry innumerable advertisements for books at knock-down prices. But I have to admit that when I tried to find something I really wanted to buy, I found the reductions were very moderate indeed. Though cheap books abound, somehow they rarely turn out to be what one wants. They are all Portuguese books (though a large amount of translation of foreign classics and current literature is there too, of course), but even if the language is beyond you it may still be an eye-opener to see how well the book production is handled here. The standard of design and presentation is high. Above all, a most pleasant atmosphere is created along the Avenida during the time the Fair lasts.

On the subject of fairs the visitor must not fail to note the great religious feasts that mark the early summer in Lisbon. These are Saint Anthony, Saint John and Saint Peter, the 13th, 24th and 29th of June. The eve of the feast of Santo António is probably the biggest occasion: it is the time for the 'marchas'. Groups from every quarter of the city march down the Avenida da Liberdade singing songs of their own composition. They are all in costume. That night the city is em festa. Every quarter is decorated and people dance in the streets. Above all, the Alfama is the scene for open air entertainment. No one goes to bed. Sardines are grilled on the pavement. Impromptu fado performances are given.

The feasts of São Pedro and São João are similarly honoured. If the visitor happens to find himself in Lisbon at this time of the year, they should not be missed. All through June, life is transformed by these summer celebrations in honour of the traditional saints.

Finally, there is one place in Lisbon for which I have a special affection and which I feel cannot be left out of an account of the 'real' and basic character of the town: this is the famous Ribeira—the stretch of river front where the fish catch is landed. To put it mildly, the fish market by the river is 'colourful'. In truth, it defies description. The senses are assailed by every conceivable exotic sensation: noise, smell, movement, and the stunning visual impact of the sail boats and trawlers, the boxes, baskets and crates, the fishwives and tough fishermen all in a conglomerate of fierce activity. Strange people—different in speech, different in dress from anything you will find in other parts of the city. Along the riverside these markets (there is the fruit market, too) offer a spectacle that has nothing to do with modern Lisbon. But once one has been there and seen and felt and absorbed this special world, one has a new view of the 'varina' when seen striding like a foreign creature

Docks and Fishermen

through the streets of the city selling her fish: she carries with her an echo of this riverside universe. It is all to be found at the Cais do Sodré—a mere few hundred metres from the Praça do Comércio.

And what of Lisbon by night? There is no shortage of discothèques and night clubs. Some are posh and you pay about fifteen shillings a drink (of course you drink whisky—the drink of the sophisticated lisboeta). The Ad Lib is one such, the Carrousel, in the same block as the Ritz (but with its own entrance), is another. Maxime, in the Praça da Alegria, is more a proper night club—though not at all sophisticated in the London or Paris sense (some folk dancing, etc.). The minimum charge is about thirty shillings.

But after all, the real attraction in Lisbon for the visitor is not the local brand of smart night-spot but the truly unusual and indigenous: the fado and the bullfight. Probably an evening out that started with the bullfight and ended in the fado house would be about as lisboeta as you could get. For the bullfight, the Campo Pequeno is the place. Tickets can be got at the bull-ring or in town at the office directly behind the Avenida Palace Hotel in the Restauradores. As to fado, the choice is wide. A lot depends on how 'fadista' you like your fado. There are some popular places where the fado is watered down to suit the foreign trade. The Folclore is one, O Faia is another. Those who want to try the real thing should go to one of the 'serious' places, for instance Taverna do Embuçado ('tavern of the one who covers his face with his cloak', is the only way I can translate this) where Celeste Rodrigues (Amália's sister) has now set up and provides, as always, the classic purity of the old tradition.

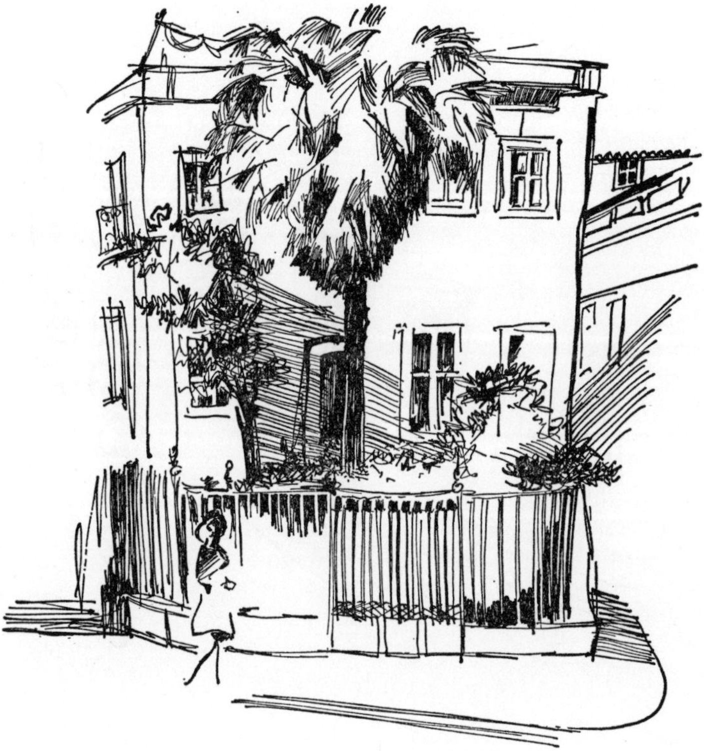

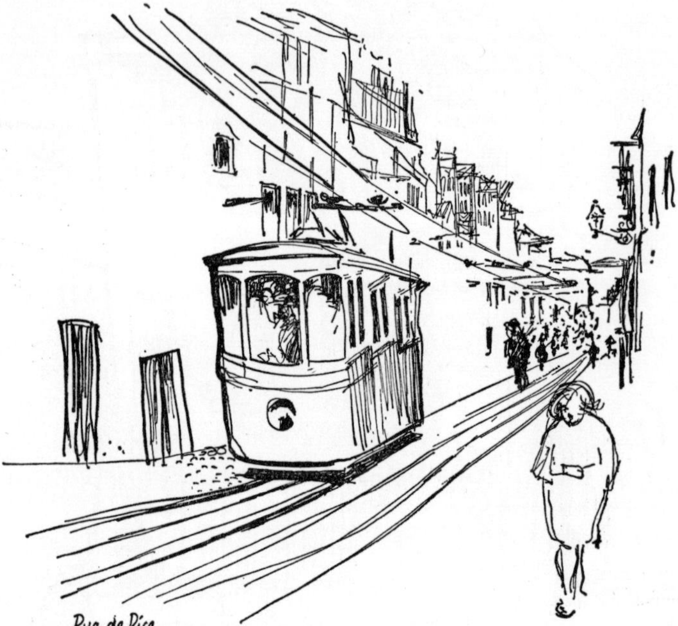

Rua da Bica

Index

Hotels and restaurants are listed under Lisbon if in the city, otherwise under individual names.

Abrantes, 198–202
Afonso Henriques, Dom, 151–2
Alfama, 15, 23–4
Alpiarca, 197–8
Alto da Santa Catarina, 70–1, 73
Amaral, Francisco Keil, 54, 97
Antoñete, 126, 128–9
Armitage, Kenneth, 12
Arrábida, 228, 233
Arronches, 217–18
Arruda, Francisco de, 178
Auden, W. H., 12

Avenida da Liberdade, 113, 191, 241, 250, 261
Avenida da República, 192–3, 261

Bairro Alto, 47–8, 98, 110–13, 144–7, 260
Beamish, Huldine, 50
Beckford, William, 36, 41, 61
Belém, 172–84
Black Horse Square. *See* Praça do Comércio
Book Fair, 261
Borba, 220–1

INDEX

Boytac, 174–6
Bridge, Ann, 218
Byron, Lord, 36–7, 41

Cabo da Roca, 36
Cabo Raso, 36
Cacilhas, 55–6
Cais do Sodré, 263
Campbell, Roy, 19, 42–3
Camões, Luis de, 103, 252
Campo de Santa Clara, 24–8
Campo Pequeno, 115–30
Cantinho de S. Pedro, 39–40, 59
Carmo (church), 45–7
Casa dos Patudos, 197–8
Cascais, 36, 62, 242
Castelo Branco, 202–7, 238
Castelo de S. Jorge, 15–18, 248
Castelo Vide, 210–12
Castro, Machado de, 32–3, 50, 225
Chamusca, 198–9
Chanterene, Nicolau, 100
Chiado. *See* Rua Garrett

Dom Diniz, 199, 203, 212

Elvas, 217–20
Estalagem dos Cavaleiros, 37
Estalagem Gado Bravo, 196
Estoril, 36, 242
Estrêla, Basilica do, 50
Estremoz, 33, 219, 222–7
Estufa Fria, 64
Ethnological Museum, 176–8

Feasts of S. António, S. Pedro, and S. João, 262
Feira da Ladra (flea market), 24–8

Feira de Arte Popular, 180–3
Feira Popular, 261
Fielding, Henry, 50
Flea market. *See* Feira da Ladra
Freitas, Lima de, 19, 22, 31–2, 78–81

Ginsberg, Allen, 58
Gonçalves, Nuno, 162–3, 165
Gonzalez, Damaso, 126–30
Graves, Robert, 216
Greig, Desmond, 23–4, 27
Guarda, 235–6
Gulbenkian, Calouste Sarkis, 187
Gulbenkian Foundation, 186–9

Henry the Navigator, 163
Hotel Alentejano, 222–4
Hotel do Mar, 233

Janelas Verdes. *See* Museum of Ancient Art
Jardim Bôtanico, 63
Jerónimos. *See* Mosterio dos Jerónimos
João IV, Dom, 155–7
João V, Dom, 56, 59, 158, 183–4
José, Joaquim, 112
Joyce, James, 95
Junot, Marshal, 22, 200, 203

Lagoa, 79
Largo do Carmo, 10–11
Léger, F., 215
Lisbon
  Fado Houses
    Adega do Mesquita, 111–13

INDEX

A Severa, 110
Guitarra de Alfama, 106–9
O Faia, 110
Parreirinha da Alfama, 134
Restaurant Folclore, 110
Solar da Mandragoa, 109–10
Taberna do Embuçado, 110, 264
Hotels and Pensões
Avenida Palace Hotel, 257, 264
Borges, 257
Bragança, 258
Estalagem do Cavalo Branco, 258
Fenix, 257
Florida, 258
Francfort-Rossio, 14–15, 257
Hotel Rex, 33–4, 257
Metropole, 258
Mundial, 257
Pensão Santa Catarina, 66–9, 75–7, 258
Ritz, 257
Tivoli, 257
York House, 258
Restaurants and Cafés
A Bicaense, 146–7
Avis, 134, 259
Bomjardim, 141
Brasileira Café, 11, 20, 93
Café Suiça, 89–90
Cervejaria da Trindade, 142–3
Coral, 79
Cortador, 138–9, 259
Estrêla da Sé, 51
Galo d'Ouro, 113
Gondola, 137, 259
Irmãos Unidos, 19, 22–3
Leão d'Ouro, 11, 140
Martinho da Arcada, 139–40
Martinho dos Arcades, 241–2
Parreirinha, 24, 134, 259
Pastelaria Marquês, 93
Porto de Abrigo, 140
Quinta, 141, 259
Sagres Cervejaria, 142
Tavares, 138, 259
X, 135
Lurçat, Jean, 216

Madre de Deus, 168–71
Máfra, 56, 59–62
Manueline, 38, 153, 172–6, 246, 250
Marceneiro, Alfredo, 114
Marvão, 209, 212–13
Melo, D. Francisco Manuel de, 103
Mesquita, Domingo, 112
Milhões, Monteiro dos, 21–2
Monsanto, 204, 249
Mosteiro dos Jerónimos, 172–4, 251–2
Muge, 197
Museu da Cidade, 184–5
Museu dos Coches, 183–4
Museum of Ancient Art, 161–7
Museum of Popular Art, Belém, 33–5, 180–1

National Theatre, 90–1
Neilson, Peter, 117–20
Neves, Cesar das, 104
Night clubs, 264
Nisa, 208–9

Palácio Laranjeiras, 29
Palácio Quintela, 21-2, 29
Pena, 37, 41-2
Pensão Lisboeta, 222
Pessoa, Fernando, 19, 31-2, 100-1, 251, 253-4, 256
Pombal, Marquês de, 21, 45, 152, 158-9
Portalegre, 213-17, 237
Praça da Figueira, 15
Praça do Comércio, 25, 45
Praia das Maçãs, 62

Quadros, António, 31-3, 245-55
Queluz, 56-9
Quental, Antero do, 99
Quieroz, Eça de, 19, 21, 69, 95-100, 131-3, 138-9
Quinta das Torres, 230-3

Régio, José, 237
Ribeira, 262
Rodrigues, Amália, 105, 112, 114
Rodrigues, Celeste, 264
Rogerio, Mestre, 81-6
Rossio (Praça Dom Pedro IV), 43-5, 89-93
Rua Áurea, 45
Rua da Bica, 71
Rua da Rosa, 48-9
Rua dos Correeiros, 45, 134, 135
Rua Dr. Luis de Almeida e Albuquerque, 69
Rua Garrett (Chiado), 20-1, 92-4

Sampaio, Alberto, 99
Santa Auta, Mestre de, 171
Santa Catarina, 73-4
Santa Luzia, 248
Santos, Manuel dos, 112
São Pedro de Sintra, 39-41
São Roque, 158, 167-8
Savory, H. N., 247-8
Schwarz, Samuel, 204-5
Sé Catedral, 165-6
Sebastião, Dom, 155
Sesimbra, 233-4
Setubal, 228-30
Severa, Maria, 109
Sintra, 36-43
Sitwell, Sacheverell, 218
Southey, Robert, 36-7
Sutton, Michael, 23

Tagus, Rio, 148-50
Telles, David Ribeiro, 117, 121-4, 128
Terreiro do Paço. *See* Praça do Comércio
Torre de Belém, 178-9
Troia, 228

Veiros, 227-8
Vicente, Gil, 169, 172
Vila Franca de Xira, 196
Vila Viçosa, 220-2
Vimioso, Counts of, 21, 109
Viuva Lamego, 80-2

Zenkl, Gustavo, 122, 125, 128
Zoological Gardens, 29-31

KEY TO ENDPAPER MAP

1. Praça do Comércio
2. Rossio
3. Luis de Camões
4. Chiado
5. Largo de Barão do Quintela (statue of Eça de Quieroz)
6. Bairro Alto
7. Estação do Rossio
8. Santa Catarina
9. Largo de S. Roque
10. Largo do Carmo
11. Castelo de S. Jorge
12. Alfama
13. Campo de Santa Clara
14. S. Vicente
15. Museu de Artilharia
16. Madre de Deus
17. Av. da Liberdade
18. Praça Marquês de Pombal
19. Parque Eduardo VII— Estufa Fria
20. Praça Duque de Sadlanha
21. Campo Pequeno
22. Av. da República
23. Gulbenkian Fundação
24. Praça de Espanha
25. Estrêla
26. Jardim Botanico
27. Largo do Rato
28. Rua do Seculo
29. Largo do Conde Barão
30. Museu de Arte Antiga
31. Largo de Santos
32. Cais do Sodré
33. Mouraria
34. Praça de Londres
35. Praça Pasteur
36. Sé Catedral
37. Martinho (café restaurant)
38. Brasileira (café)
39. Gondola (restaurant)
40. Irmãos Unidos (café)
41. Leão Douro (restaurant)
42. Mesquita (casa do Fado)
43. Ascensor de Santa Justa
44. Cortador (restaurant)
45. Tavares (restaurant)
46. Porta do Abrigo
47. Promater (nursing home)
48. Parreirinha (restaurant)
49. Borges Hotel
50. York House
51. Fenix
52. Tivoli
53. Ritz
54. A Quinta (restaurant)

A CIDADE DE LISBOA

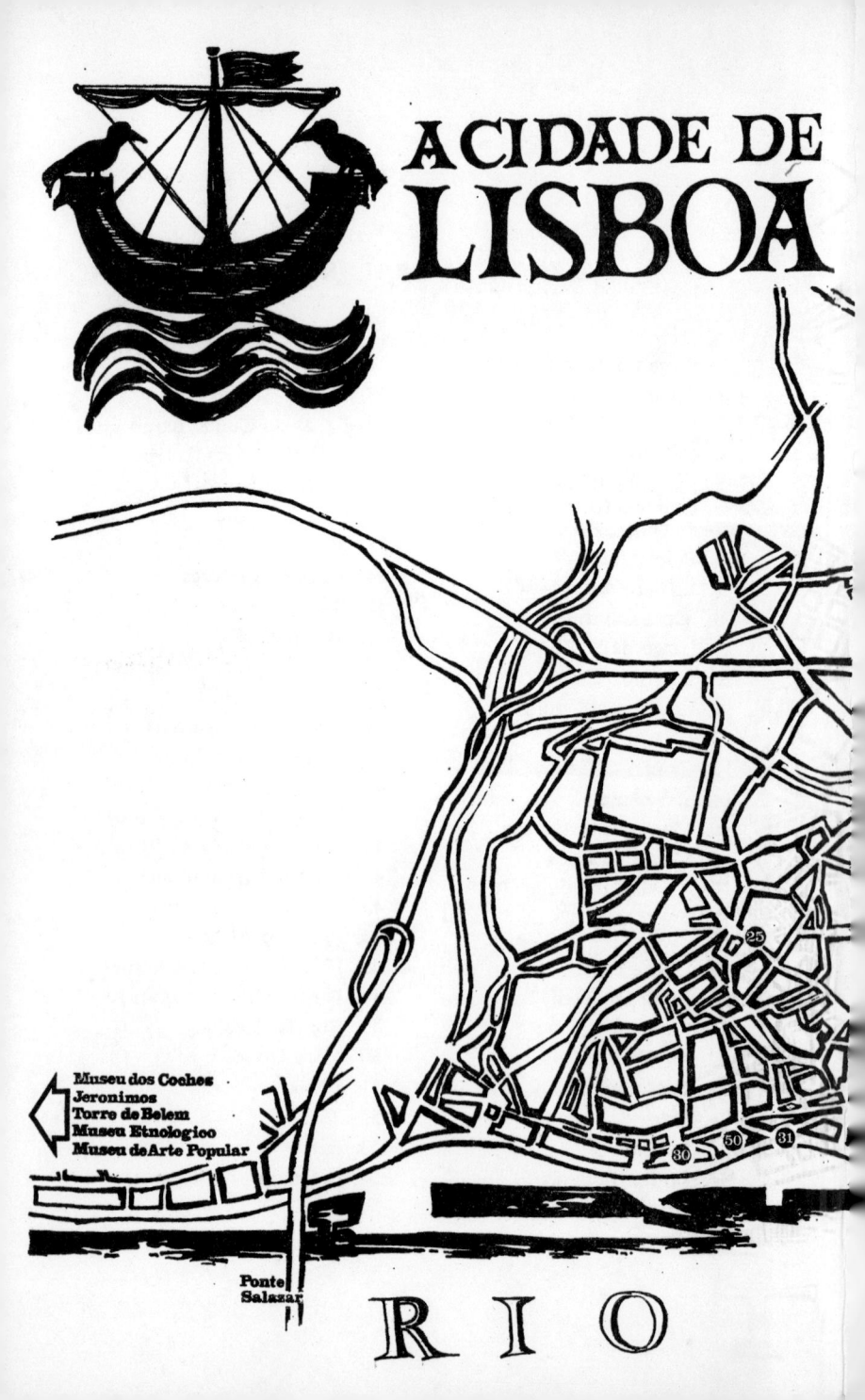

Museu dos Coches
Jeronimos
Torre de Belem
Museu Etnologico
Museu de Arte Popular

Ponte Salazar

RIO